JAN 2015

Down Syndrome Parenting 101

Down Syndrome Parenting 101

Must-Have Advice for Making Your Life Easier

Natalie Hale

Foreword by Martha Beck

Woodbine House ■ 2011

© 2011 Natalie Hale
First edition

All rights reserved. Published in the United States of American by Woodbine House, Inc.,
6510 Bells Mill Road, Bethesda, MD 20817. 800-843-7323. www.woodbinehouse.com.

Library of Congress Cataloging-in-Publication Data

Hale, Natalie.
  Down syndrome parenting 101 : must-have advice for making your life easier / by
Natalie Hale. -- 1st ed.
      p. cm.
  ISBN 978-1-60613-020-9
  1. Down syndrome--Popular works. 2. Children with mental disabilities--Care--Popular
works. I. Title.
  RJ506.D68H356 2011
  618.92'858842--dc23

                                                                                    2011032597

Manufactured in the United States of America

10 9 8 7 6   4

To Jonathan and Rebecca,
whose wisdom and presence
trained me well.

Table of Contents

Foreword by Martha Beck ix

Preface xiii

Introduction 1
    1. The Yellow Raincoat / 3
    2. Unbutton That Raincoat / 10
    3. Getting Started / 16

Essentials of Your Parent-Friendly Manual 23
    4. Other Gifts / 25
    5. Honestly, Now / 35
    6. Intuition / 40
    7. Nurturing the Parent / 46

Beginning Years 55
    8. Extraordinary Awareness / 57
    9. A Word about Doctors / 67
    10. Self-Talk / 75
    11. Read This: Literacy Is the New Norm / 80
    12. Your Personal Humor Coach / 95

Discipline Years 103
13. Born to Rule / 105
14. The Noncompliance Face-off / 113
15. If All Else Fails, Try Being Real / 127
16. How to Ruin Your Child / 136
17. Communicating Emotions / 140
18. It Takes a Crew / 146
19. When It's Not Down Syndrome / 152

School Years 167
20. The Education Battleground / 169
21. Student One / 185
22. Student Two / 190
23. Inclusion and Testing / 195
24. Watch Your Language! / 204

Wahoo! Years 211
25. The Transition Process / 213
26. Traveling Alone / 220
27. Dance Rocks / 224

The Last Word 229
28. Dance and Drum / 231
29. Epilogue / 234

Foreword
by Martha Beck

When my son Adam was diagnosed with Down syndrome, some three months before he was born, I was utterly devastated. I was only 25, had no obvious risk factors, and was a graduate student at Harvard, immersed in an environment where intellectualism came first on the cultural priority list. The fact that I already loved my son seemed a tragedy, not a blessing either to me or to many of the people in my community.

Because Adam's diagnosis was prenatal, I was unable to immediately immerse my baby in early-intervention therapies designed to make him more "normal." Helpful professionals kept describing these therapies to me, assuring me that truly wonderful innovations in working with children like Adam would help my son learn "useful skills." By this they meant skills that might enable someone to excel at Harvard: language, math, analytical reasoning.

I was, and am, deeply grateful that these committed, compassionate people—people like Natalie Hale—have been hard at work for the past few decades, devising ways to help people with Down syndrome fit into society. But at the end of the day, I knew my child was simply genetically different from those without the syndrome. The more I heard people talk about teaching my unborn baby to be "normal," the more they began to sound like animal trainers whose specialty was teaching kittens to act like puppies. The assumption seemed to be that everyone wants a puppy, and that getting a kitten by mistake was a tragedy, to be avoided if possible, grieved and mitigated if necessary. While I would have given anything to take away Adam's condition, it also occurred to me there might be things about kittens that could be appreciated on their own terms.

So from the moment he was born, part of me simply watched Adam to see what he did naturally, like a person who had previously seen only puppies and was now watching a kitten. I found him fascinating—not *less* than a person without Down syndrome, but simply *other*.

I wanted my son to have highly developed life skills, of course, but I also suspected he had skills that I didn't, and this fascinated me. Often, I found that my attitude upset other parents and many experts. They seemed to take it as a given that children with Down syndrome must be made as "normal" as possible, and that their success should be measured by how close they come to "normalcy."

Natalie Hale is one of the few people I've met who seems as impressed with the gifts of Down syndrome as I am. This is true both of her approach to mothering her radically awesome son Jonathan, and of the way she teaches her many lucky students. In a dog-eat-dog world, she's one of very few experts who can not only train your "kitten" child to act a bit more like a "puppy," but help you rejoice in the perfection of your child as he or she already is.

Natalie's top-notch intellect isn't fixated on itself; it sees the person before her as a unique and amazing being, not a "deviation from normalcy." She's willing to learn the language of these remarkable people with Down syndrome, the way their minds often work (though each individual is, of course, unique, there are similarities). This helps her know what they mean and how they tick. More important by far, Natalie's methods allow children to feel seen, heard, and appreciated.

Natalie is excellent at teaching "different" children, but I think her book's most important contribution is her gentle and enthusiastic way of teaching the rest of us. She knows that we parents are every bit as fallible as our children; that we can be unhinged by fear, stubbornness, and judgment—our own profound intellectual disabilities—and blame it on Down syndrome.

She knows how to help us unhook ourselves from our negative patterns and offer us better life skills. It turns out that once we've done that, teaching our kids is much, much easier.

Not only is Natalie an exceptional parent and educator, she is a wonderful writer. Many of the books I read when Adam was small seemed oblivious to my limitations, let alone his. I remember bursting into tears while trying to follow the directions in one well-meaning book, whose author adamantly insisted that mothers must use sign language to create a stream of language while changing their baby's diapers. I still can't imagine how that author changed diapers (with her elbows?), but I never caught on. That book, like many that were equally well-intended, left me feeling exhausted and inadequate.

Natalie's work is completely different. Just when other authors seem to get rigid or pedantic, Natalie will break up an academic explanation to tell a story about a real child, to point out her own errors with self-deprecating humor, or to simply observe that the most important thing about parenting is not forcing a child to be a certain way, but finding a way to appreciate the way the child is. She never fails to remind us that our real work, as the poet Mary Oliver says, is "mostly standing still and learning to be astonished."

If you have just embarked on the journey of raising a child with Down syndrome, there is much astonishment ahead of you. As I've watched my son grow, I've been continually amazed and humbled by his strengths, his gifts, his intelligence.

I'll give you a brief example: At twenty-three, Adam still has only basic expressive language, and can't deal comfortably with situations that a "normal" person would find fairly simple, such as taking a bus by himself. But recently, after hearing a song he liked on the radio, he searched for and located the song on the Internet, purchased it, and figured out how to program it as the ringback tone on his cell phone. (I've tried to do the same; I'm completely lost.) When you call Adam's phone, you hear the song's chorus: "Be true—true to yourself—and you'll be magic. Be kind. Believe in others' help, and you'll make magic."

This message is so important to Adam that he went to considerable trouble to make sure everyone who calls him will hear it. Each time I dial his number, I'm reminded all over again that I'm one of the few people in the world who gets to live with someone who's absolutely true to himself, absolutely kind, and absolutely magic. Adam's presence has transformed my life in countless ways, all of them positive.

I know Natalie sees people with Down syndrome this way, too. Her book will seduce you into her world, where puppies are beautiful and perfect, and kittens are too. The more Natalie's wisdom thaws any frozen places in your heart, the more you and your child will enjoy life. And *that*, rather than getting into Harvard, is what makes our existence worthwhile.

I've often said that having a child with Down syndrome is an experience I wouldn't wish for my worst enemy—but I would wish it for my best friend. It is a connection to a different and beautiful way of being human, fraught with difficulties, but worth every moment. Read this book, train your kitten, love your child, and care gently for your own body and soul. Be true. Be kind. Believe in others' help. And you really will do magic.

Preface

When I read books that recount detailed descriptions of past conversations, I figure the author is just doing what a writer does: inventing the dialogue. Poetic license, don't you know.

But in the case of this book, what you'll read is what there was, because I kept a journal from the time my son was a toddler. Whenever he did or said something that I wanted to remember, I wrote it down. There were some months, even years, when time was so crunched that the best I could do was scribble a few sentences—on napkins, anything—and stuff it into his bulging blue book. (I kept a red one for his sister.) And if I hadn't stolen those minutes to scribble fleeting treasures, the book you're holding wouldn't be here today.

So my first tip to you is this: keep a journal of some kind, any kind. Let it be your Joy journal, your Amazement journal, your She Drives Me Nuts journal (that phase will pass), whatever suits your soul. The form doesn't matter; but the content may one day mean the world to you.

It is interesting to note that anthropologist Margaret Meade's mother made it a habit to study, to observe her child as she was growing up; she filled notebooks with her observations of Margaret. Why? She wanted to understand her daughter. And of course the study of human nature became Margaret's life work. I guarantee that keeping some kind of quick journal about your child/teen/adult will bring you deeper understanding, and occasionally put you in a state of awe.

The chapters in this book are deliberately short, because frankly, my dear, you don't have time to read. I have this on my own authority as well as the backup nod of every parent I know who has a child with Down syndrome. Brevity in this case is merciful, and I have tried to scatter as much mercy as possible throughout these pages.

Above all, know that you are one of the most extraordinary parents on the globe (*true*—and you are not allowed to dispute that), and know that I was mindfully aware of that fact when I wrote this book.

Natalie Hale
Los Gatos, California
September 2011

Introduction

The Yellow Raincoat

"Who seeks shall find."
—Sophocles

The Overview

Pat, pat, pat. Jonathan tapped gently on my shoulder as I cooked dinner. "How's it goin', Boop?" he whispered. Then, turning to his dad, Kelly, *whack!* on the back. He boomed, "How's it goin', Dude?"

I almost missed the sensitivity. He could have whispered to his dad and boomed at me, whacked me and patted his dad. He didn't. He changed his energy just as automatically as he turned physically from me to Kelly.

We got grilled on our mental states throughout the day. "How'd you sleep? How was your day? How's your dinner?" He expected a positive answer: "Fine, great, two thumbs up." If our response was less than ideal on his positive-thinker's scale, he repeated the question until we got the answer right.

Twenty-six now, Jonathan was eighteen at the time of this visual snippet, and I'll be direct: as far as Down syndrome goes, he's average. This book didn't grow from life with a super-achiever: Jonathan is somewhere in the middle of that wide spectrum we call Down syndrome.

Look around you at the general population. What you see there is what you'll see in Down syndrome: from brazen to shy, hilarious to serious, handsome to plain, social to solitary. Social? Some of our kids can work a room like a politician; others, like Jonathan, prefer the solitude of his kingdom (his room), where music and dance reign supreme. The full spectrum is what you'll see and what you'll get in Down syndrome.

The Yellow Raincoat Theory

If you're holding an infant with Down syndrome in your arms right now, the sky's the limit. If you have a child or preteen, you already have a good preview of future possibilities. If you have an adult with Down syndrome, you certainly know about the Yellow Raincoat. The what?

I believe in the Yellow Raincoat Theory. It's my belief based on observation, understanding, and experience.

Years ago on rainy days (think early "Dick and Jane" books), many children trundled off to school in shiny yellow raincoats. Remember those old illustrations?

Now picture your child with Down syndrome wearing one of those impenetrable yellow raincoats. In fact, the raincoat *is* Down syndrome. It covers the child; it keeps everything hidden, unknown. At first, you notice that all the raincoats look alike; after all, most were genetically manufactured in a single factory, located at Chromosome No. 21. And the "care instructions" attached to the garments all indicate: *See medical protocol on reverse. Oh, and good luck.*

So Dick and Jane stand before you in their yellow raincoats. In the overwhelming emotional complexity of those first months, you might not notice that the raincoat has buttons. When you do, flashes of possibilities might flit briefly across your mind. Buttons. Yes…there are buttons! Maybe, just maybe, you can help Down syndrome to hang a little looser around your child.

I'm here to tell you, *"Yes, you can."* And you will. It's your job to unbutton that raincoat, roll up the sleeves, and give that child within some breathing room. In the process, you will yourself experience a welcome zephyr of relief, if not awe.

Medically speaking, it is of course widely accepted that Down syndrome is all-pervasive in the individual who happens to have this diagnosis. While this is true in the chromosomal makeup of anyone with Trisomy 21, and partially true for those with mosaic Down syndrome, I posit that, *in truth,* this is not the case at all.

The Yellow Raincoat Theory postulates that Down syndrome does not completely cover our children, and that it never can. It is incapable of cloaking forever those brilliant flashes, those thrilling qualities hiding in our children; and so they remain untouched, unaffected, and completely outside the grasp of Down syndrome.

Awesome.

Further, this theory proposes that these children are perfect, unique, and immensely gifted in ways parents themselves can only dream of being. It's as if the raincoat signals the start of a lifelong game of hide-and-seek: *Here I am. Do you recognize me? Can you find me?* And the child laughs and runs off. The game is on.

Unbuttoning The Raincoat

The first button, the most obvious and easiest to unbutton, is personality. Like any child, this child before you has an exquisitely unique personality, preferences, and characteristics. Unlike a typically developing child, that personality, those preferences and characteristics, are quite likely to be disarmingly larger-than-life. Hilarious, exasperating, heart-melting, infuriating, and invariably moving in a way that is jaw-dropping.

Gradually we begin to get the hang of working with those buttons. We learn to see past the obvious, to sense what lies underneath that raincoat. Working with one button at a time, we learn to observe, to perceive, to develop our own awareness and vision beyond the obvious, beyond that raincoat. We begin to understand.

"Look Your Eyes"

Has the Yellow Raincoat Theory been researched? No.

Is it true? You bet. Ask the parents of a teen or adult with Down syndrome; ask an experienced teacher of these children, and you'll get the same answer. Experience proves the theory.

Borrowing from a younger Jonathan's arsenal of short but effective in-your-face phrases, this one used to dryly point out something obvious,

"Look your eyes. I point to it." Look at these facts:

Jonathan cannot chew (unusual even for someone with Down syndrome) nor do anything well that involves using a brush (hairbrush, toothbrush). These skills involve his fine motor control, which for him is unusually poor. His speech is often unclear. He has difficulty understanding abstract "wh" questions: why, where, what, when. Yellow Raincoat.

Yet he can tell you the names of the actors who do voiceovers for Disney and Pixar movies; knows the names of the lighting and sound designers of his favorite movies; knows how to find and download movie sound effects (or anything else) from the Internet, and has been thoroughly knowledgeable about the details of orchestral instruments (and their working parts) since he was a child.

And electronics? At age five, he instantly figured out how to work the remote control for our first-ever CD player, while I was still trying to figure which way to point the silly thing.

Jonathan is not an anomaly; you will hear similar stories from other parents of children, teens, and adults with Down syndrome. And just in case some well-intentioned and respectably trained specialist offers you the phrase "splinter skills" to explain these abilities, remember my politically correct response to this: "Naaaah."

We are not talking about a child who somehow manages to have a few odd abilities splintering off from an otherwise inferior tree trunk. *We are talking about being able to glimpse the true child hidden within the syndrome.*

In the process of learning to unbutton that Yellow Raincoat, the truth begins to dawn: *you're* the student, and your child is the teacher. And I will argue that on some significant level, it is conscious teaching: your child is aware that you are learning certain things you need to learn.

On Being a Good Student

When Jonathan was three, we lived in a small community where I daily took him out in the stroller. After a while, I noticed a curious phenomenon: depending on whom I stopped to chat with, Jonathan presented two entirely different pictures.

With certain folks, Jon was bright, alert, and smilingly responsive. With others, he slumped listlessly, thrust his tongue out, and drooled. *What's the deal?* I couldn't make sense of it until I thought about it on a deeper level. Then I got it: he was responding to the energy of the other person, to what they were projecting toward him, and he gave each person exactly what they expected. Their minds, their consciousness, were like an open book to him.

When we strolled past college students who didn't know beans about Down syndrome and thought he was adorable, Jon put on his bright face, and they were charmed. But when we talked to some others, like one retired nurse who had unfortunately been trained in the "old days and old ways" and looked at him with undisguised pity, he slumped and drooled.

Learning to unbutton that yellow raincoat, I began to observe Jonathan more, to understand more, and soon realized that as far as getting a vibrational shakedown on people was concerned, Jonathan's assessment of them was smack on the money. I could pick true friends by this child's radar. And so I did.

Amy, the mother of seven-year-old Ava, talks about her daughter similarly:

> "I remember when Ava was born that she received a lot of attention. Not just attention from medical and therapeutic professionals, but from complete strangers. Anywhere we went, people would stop and talk to her, to us. I brushed it off as innate joy and curiosity toward a newborn child.
>
> "But it kept, and still keeps, coming. From the time of her birth, Ava has attracted people everywhere we go. And she "knows" who the "good" people are. I call it 'Avadar.' She can read strangers like no one else I've ever encountered in my life. She will hug or take the hand of someone and know full well before she does that they will reciprocate her actions and hug her back. Or hold her hand, even if only for a moment.
>
> "One of our most startling moments was in the grocery store. An elderly man was walking toward us in the pasta aisle. She saw him and actually growled at him. Now, that's not the kind of behavior you want your child to show toward strangers, but I absolutely took her word for it, and we turned around and walked the other way. I don't know how she does it, she just knows. I've learned to trust her instincts."

Transformations

For a while after moving to California, I taught reading to students with Down syndrome in my home, which was an upstairs apartment. During that time, I had a downstairs neighbor who, in my daughter Becca's words, was a "sour cookie." Definitely a cookie, but sour. This neighbor—I'll call her Rita—objected to the noises my students with Down syndrome occasionally made, which transferred through her ceiling. Rita had lived a long time and was weary of many things.

I tried unsuccessfully to pacify her and keep my students quiet, but things only got worse, and the situation hit the red alert button one day when she grabbed me and yelled about the noise. I began to refer to her as "my crabby neighbor" when I asked students not to make noises on the floor for her sake. My attitude was definitely in a downward spiral.

My student Robert had just arrived for his lesson one day when he inadvertently made a loud thump on the floor. Robert was a strapping fifteen-year-old, and about the nicest redheaded teen you can imagine, raised to treat others kindly. At that age, making noise on the floor is easy to do, but I became somewhat unhinged. "Oh, Robert, please don't make noise!" Wanting to avoid another grab-and-yell session with Rita, I said, "Let's go downstairs and apologize." Which we did.

Of course, Robert had absolutely nothing to apologize for, and I had to do considerable damage control with him later, telling him he was not at fault, and apologizing for asking *him* to apologize to The Crab.

Weeks passed, and Easter neared. Robert showed up for his lesson one day holding two flowering plants. "One is for you," he said, "And one is for Rita."

Together we delivered the chosen plant to Rita. She opened her door, astonished to see Robert holding out a lovely plant. "Happy Easter," he said. "This is for you." Rita was delighted and responded in kind, "Happy Easter!"

Then with typical Down Syndrome Direct Delivery, he looked right at her and said, "Don't be mad at me." She murmured that of course she was not mad at him. Without breaking eye contact with her for a second, he pointed one arm toward me as I stood nearby. "And don't be mad at *her*."

And that is how Rita began her transformation. Two other highly intuitive young students, both eight-year-old girls with Down syndrome, picked up on the unspoken assignment. Little Makenna happened to see

Rita outside one day, and threw both arms around her in a warm embrace. You could literally see Rita begin to melt. Cassie, another little redhead, impulsively grabbed her hand one day. Ditto on the melting effect.

And that is how I began *my* transformation. Gradually my reference to "my crabby neighbor" became "my neighbor," and eventually "Miss Rita," when talking to my students about her. For her part, Rita began saving old magazines "for the children," as she said, because she knew I used magazine pictures to make personal books for them.

I was in awe.

So to repeat Jonathan's directive, "Look your eyes. I point to it." That is indeed what your child will do, however subtly: point you toward understanding and awareness.

Straight to the Store

A jazz musician I know once said, in reference to Jonathan, "Kids like Jonathan go straight to the store."

By that, he meant that our kids easily cut through the foolishness of life. They are not required to sift through the chaff as the rest of us are; they are not easily deluded as to what is real and what is unreal, what is tinsel and what is heart's gold. They are far more likely to sense and go straight for the truth.

Hopefully, they will miss much of the muddling through that most of us are required to endure in our search for verities. And in that, there is a blessing for them and a tutorial for us. It is not an exaggeration to say that, hidden in this little package we call Down syndrome, there is a life manual waiting for us, a manual that has nothing whatever to do with a syndrome and everything in the universe to do with truth.

Fortunately, the manual is interactive, customized, is a fairly easy read, and has a fascinating plot. But you already know that. Or if you don't, you will.

2

Unbutton That Raincoat

"Flaming enthusiasm, backed up by horse sense and persistence,
is the quality that most frequently makes for success."
—Dale Carnegie

Personality

Back to the Yellow Raincoat. Let's take hold of that first button and send it flying.

The first button reveals personality. Personality is, thank God, one of the few things totally—and I mean totally—untouched by Down syndrome. Not only is it untouched, but it seems to be mysteriously enhanced, larger-than-life, and often makes the rest of us seem pale by comparison.

Those of us who have already lived through years with our kids love to reminisce about our favorite hilarious moments, gifts given us by these larger-than-life personalities. For example, Melanie is a young adult with Down syndrome. Her one-liners—always disarming—are legendary among her friends. I know a couple of those friends who regularly take a "Funny Stories about Melanie" break when they're having a bad day at the office. How many friends do *you* have who, to cheer themselves up when they're down, tell stories about the funny things you've said or done, and done knowingly? I don't have any, either.

Observing parents over the years, I think the moment a parent first observes their child's core personality is the tipping point. It is at that point that a parent realizes, "I'm dealing with a powerful personality here, and I'd better be on my toes. This is going to be some entertaining ride!" By tipping point, I mean that the parent begins to breathe a little easier, to realize that there is bigger stuff at work here, and to relax their "Responsible Stiff Upper Lip" reflex. Parents begin to understand that they are not totally in charge; their child's personality will loom large, will entertain, will melt hearts, and will constantly surprise them. Not to mention instruct them.

As Jonathan frequently directs me, "Just relax."

Core Interests

So let's move on to the next button on that Yellow Raincoat. This could be anything, but I'm betting it will be the key entry point to the powerhouse of your child's motivation: his heart's interests. Some are significant and obvious; some are significant but subtle and will need your focused attention, because you don't want to lose awareness of them. You'll find an interest, nourish it, and help it to grow. Then you'll look for another.

Specific interests can lead to specific knowledge and skills, and that leads to self-confidence. More than a few eyes popped when Jonathan was nine and listening to a woodwind quintet rehearsing outdoors before a music festival. When they paused for a minute, he approached and enthusiastically chatted about the various parts that comprised the bass clarinet, the bassoon, etc. The quintet was astonished.

Jonathan knew these facts because, of course, he owned books on such things. And he owned books on such things because, of course, I fed his interests. And how did Jonathan feel about the musicians' open astonishment at his knowledge? Imagine. Our children know when others genuinely admire them. It goes right to their self-esteem and bolsters it. It becomes a platform that builds, lifelong.

Letting Dreams Live

I looked for those special interests and nourished them. It didn't matter to me what Jonathan did with those interests in the end; what mattered was that he was fascinated by something, and that fascination—

whatever it was—would feed his growth in many ways. You will do the same, and it will give you much joy.

When Jonathan was a toddler, he became fascinated by "body books," children's books on anatomy. I bought him more. We read them together. He pored over them until they were worn. As his reading skills developed, I bought him more and more, and the books became more advanced. By the time he was nine or ten, he would talk about how he liked to read about the "digestive system" or the "skeletal system." He asked for—and got—a child's microscope. I let him know that I admired his interest and his knowledge. That felt good to us both.

When he was ten, he told me that when he grew up, he wanted "to be a doctor, to help the children." Did that make me a little sad? Yes.

But was Jonathan sad? I don't think so. He had his children's anatomy books, and spending time with them made him happy. And he had many other interests. But that button stayed unbuttoned, open to expansion; no one closed it and told him he couldn't be a doctor and therefore shouldn't be dreaming and learning.

Your child's interests will be every bit as varied as they are in children who develop typically. They will be very individualistic and even painstakingly specific.

Once I was greeting parents after giving a Down syndrome workshop on teaching reading. One mom, knowing I had produced early reading books, asked, "Do you have any reading books on Woolly Mammoths or Birds of Prey?" Her wistful look was only half-joking. Those were *the* hot topics for her preteen son. She was looking to feed him, and I'm sure that in the end, she found a way to succeed. She understood: whatever floats his boat would help unbutton the Raincoat.

Crusading for Writing

If you're lucky, you may see an interest grow out of something that was once a deficiency, now healed. Jonathan was a very late bloomer with handwriting. Fine motor skills have always been a struggle for him (except, of course, when it comes to the operation of any remote control; then his fine motor is fabulous).

When he was 15 and finally ready to go to high school, I experienced an *Oh, no!* moment, antithesis of the *Aha!* moment. I panicked when I realized that, after ten unsuccessful years of handwriting lessons in school and endless encouragement at home, Jonathan was about to enter a venue where handwriting was indispensable. He couldn't even write his name legibly, much less anything else.

My search for handwriting rescue led me to the totally angelic Jan Olsen, founder of Handwriting Without Tears. She gave me sage advice, I bought her books, and six weeks of after-school homeschooling later, Jonathan could print uppercase perfectly legibly. To this day, Jan shows Jon's before-and-after samples to her audiences. Personally, I am inclined to worship at her feet. But I digress....

Over the next two years, Jonathan learned to love writing and became prolific at it, if not perfect. Prolific is often inspired, while perfect can be obsessive and obstructive, so I'm more than content with prolific in this case. As with his language, he can write clearly when he *wants* to.

As his writing evolved, he derived his own version of artistic satisfaction from filling up reams of paper with what he called his "drawings." He covered the paper with colorful printing of his favorite words...Broadway show titles, CD titles, favorite movie characters and actors, and anything he loves that has a name, which of course is everything. His designs involved not just words but colors, with certain colors used for certain words. He created elaborate "drawings" of words.

And this from a child who formerly resisted gripping anything that could write! To support his new habit, I was willing to go to the ends of the earth—or to StuffMart, whichever was closer.

StuffMart it was, because Jonathan became a Marker Collector, and often needed replacements. At any time, he might have eight or nine sets on his desk, each set restricted to a specific mug so that they didn't get mixed up. (This is very important.)

One day, after using up two of his favorite colors, he came to me asking for replacements. No problem, I said. You've got money from your paychecks and birthday money. I'll get you another set. Yes problem, he said. He only wanted two markers: *plum* and *raspberry*. They had to be plum and raspberry. Nothing else would do.

Five stores later, I was marker-less and he was disappointed. Why would I spend my never-enough-time running around to stores, opening marker boxes snooping for plum and raspberry? Because it was an interest that had already blown open a door that had been closed to him. *He wanted to write.*

My shopping crusade took me eventually to StuffMart, and *Lo*! There they were, dangling tantalizingly from a rod. Boxes with plum and raspberry tucked inside. I was overjoyed.

So was it worth it?

It is Jonathan's habit to reminisce about things he's grateful for. So weeks later, he suddenly said out of the blue, "Plum and raspberry markers… thanks, Mom." And gave me the sweetest smile. So who wouldn't go to six stores looking for plum and raspberry?

Nourish Your Vision

And if you get tired along the way and need reviving and inspiration, here's a visualization exercise for you: imagine your child, this same little person, without Down syndrome. Visualize this again and again. Realize as deeply as you can that this little person inside is the *real* person; she's only wearing a bright Yellow Raincoat which doesn't fit her very well. It doesn't fit anyone terribly well. But it's what we've got to work with, so we work with it.

Over the years, I have sometimes dreamt of Jonathan, and, curiously, in my dreams he has never had Down syndrome. Serendipitously, I dreamt of him one night recently. He had no disability. He was taller, and slender just as he is now. In my dream, he was weary from enduring some difficult experience, and we walked slowly together and talked. He talked with all the maturity of his twenty-six years, explaining some of the aspects of the difficulty he had just survived. To me, this *is* Jonathan. His "is-ness," his essence, is not bound by nor does it have any permanent ties to his physical body or condition. This is the Jonathan he sometimes allows me to glimpse in everyday life.

I believe that this is true for all of us, Down syndrome or not. We're all hidden underneath some sort of raincoat, some diverting barrier that keeps others from seeing us as we truly are in our core brilliance. Some of us manage to unbutton our own raincoats enough so that we become a powerful light for others; some don't manage that as well; and some don't even try.

You are far ahead in this: if you can learn to see past the Raincoat to your extraordinary child who has Down syndrome, then you are well on your way to unbuttoning your own, if you haven't already. But I'm guessing you have: a brown belt in Raincoat-loosening is pretty much a prerequisite for taking on this Down syndrome parenting assignment.

Speaking of dreams, I know of a number of adults with Down syndrome who have made wildly improbable real-life dreams come true. Writers, speakers, athletes, musicians, dancers, swimmers who break records, artists (who actually have a need for a bank account because they earn money through their art—a feat for any artist), others who are married and living on their own...the sky is truly the limit. And I can guarantee you that their parents virtually ripped those buttons off, one by one, determined and certain that underneath that raincoat was a magnificent human being. And they were right.

3

Getting Started

"Babies are such a nice way to start people."
—Don Herold

In the Beginning

It's so easy to fall in love with babies, and that experience of bonding and nurturing, though colored by Down syndrome, is no different with our babies. What *is* different are the choices we make in those first weeks and months. There is no absolute right or wrong. I have seen families that made very different choices, and yet those decisions turned out to be right for each family.

Nursing

The first decision to be made by the mom is "to nurse or not to nurse." There are valid pros and cons to both options: nutrition, bonding, and convenience for the former, and at the least, bonding (all family members can feed the baby) and convenience (a working mother can return to work) for the latter. Perhaps humorist and author Irena Chalmers presents the best case for breastfeeding: "There are three reasons for breastfeeding: the milk is always at the right temperature, it comes in attractive containers, and the cat can't get it."

Is nursing possible with our babies? Absolutely. I nursed Jonathan, and have friends who also nursed their babies with Down syndrome. Some babies latch on quickly and are good to go; and some mom-and-baby couples have to really work at it. Low muscle tone may compromise the baby's ability to suck effectively...or not! There may be no problem. Or the nursing efforts may be interrupted by medical necessity, as when a baby has a congenital heart condition that requires separation. But if there is no obstruction and the mother prefers to nurse her baby, it's a go.

Jonathan and I were in the "had to really work at it" category, and it took six weeks of effort before the sailing was smooth; after that, it was a piece of cake, and he nursed enthusiastically until I became pregnant with his sister.

Kathy and Dan were seasoned parents of three kids before Shawn came along, and Kathy was determined to nurse Shawn just as she had her other children. At first, nursing didn't work out because of medical interference: Shawn was whisked away constantly because of a blood condition. A misinformed nurse tried to discourage Kathy with the erroneous comment, "You know, 50 percent of these kids can't nurse." Kathy retorted, "Doesn't that mean that 50 percent of these kids *can*? *Hello*?"

Kathy had to pump her milk, put it in bottle, and the whole family fed Shawn for two long months. She was ready to give up, but her husband, Dan, urged her, "Don't you give up! Keep trying!" The very next week, Shawn latched on and from then on, nursing was effortless. Kathy nursed him until he was two years old.

My friend Martha had no problems whatever nursing her son Blair. But because of a blood incompatibility, Blair had to live in the hospital for a few days after his birth. Martha was determined to nurse him, regardless of the fact that there was no privacy, and so she nursed him in the hospital's parent lounge. The lounge was, of course, equipped with the ubiquitous TV even 33 years ago—and Neil Diamond happened to be performing on the tube one of those nights. Diamond was one of Martha's and her husband's favorite singers, and, amidst continuing tears and laughter of adjustment to the Down syndrome diagnosis, Martha and her husband, Kevin, sang lustily along with the TV, Blair happily nursing all the while.

That is, until a nurse came out of an adjoining room and asked them to keep it down. They were, after all, disturbing the peace.

Many years later, as an adult, Blair confided to his incredulous parents that he remembered listening to Neil Diamond when he was very small, lying in Martha's arms, with his dad nearby. To this day, Blair's music preferences run to Mozart, Beethoven, Chopin…and Neil Diamond.

And we are under the delusion that infants aren't aware! Some are. Some remember a great deal. One night when he was 8, Jonathan tossed and turned all night, moaning. I got out of bed several times to try to help him, but couldn't find anything that might be hurting him. In the morning, I asked him about the night and if something had hurt. He said, "It was a mistake. I dream I baby. I being born." I believe that he did remember the journey, which indeed was difficult, with forceps clenching his head. As survivors of trauma sometimes have nightmares of reliving their trauma, I believe Jonathan was remembering his not-so-fun birth experience. Better to remember Neil Diamond than to remember being born!

Now What?

What happens next is an individual decision. I went with Early Intervention, and Jonathan and I were in "school" by the time he was six weeks old.

What's That?

Early Intervention: A support system for children (birth to age 3) with developmental disabilities or delays and their families. Typically includes a system of coordinated services such as physical, occupational, and/or speech-language therapy, and the services of an infant education specialist to support the child's growth and development, as well as supports for the family such as social work services or referrals to needed resources. Federally mandated in the U.S. through the Individuals with Disabilities Education Act.

Jonathan's training, therapy, and intervention started then and never stopped until he finished high school. Most parents choose to enroll their baby in Early Intervention; it's considered absolutely best practice. Occupational therapy, physical therapy, speech therapy—we pack in all we can in those first few critical years of development, and continue as long as we need to.

Parents new to the world of Down syndrome have much to learn, and that was certainly true for me. I had no clue what my baby really needed in addition to the obvious needs of love, nurturing, and the best of care. Those first three years in Early Intervention were the beginning of my education. The experience of getting those services also goes a long way in reducing feelings of isolation that might crop up. The new parent is in a specialized school, being given essential tools and knowledge. Training right out of the starting gate is invaluable. Some examples: early use of sign language to help your baby/toddler learn to communicate before speech kicks in; learning how to strengthen your baby's low muscle tone; providing the mental stimulation so critical in the first years...the list goes on. And the chance to network with other Early Intervention parents is a bonus, and usually leads to an ongoing stream of information.

To find out how to get into your local Early Intervention system, here are some options:

- Contact your local Arc (www.thearc.org).
- Ask your pediatrician or hospital for contact information.
- Contact your local Down syndrome organization. (Google it if they haven't already contacted you.)
- You can also find your state Early Intervention agency by going to www.nichcy.org, clicking on "Babies and Toddlers," and then "Services in Your State for Infants and Toddlers."

Sometimes families decide against enrolling their baby in Early Intervention, and it works out anyway, because of the specifics of their situation. Shawn was Kathy and Dan's fourth child. When he was born and they learned about the Down syndrome diagnosis, Kathy says they were overloaded with information, pamphlets, and appointments. She says, "I needed processing time instead. I just wanted to take my baby home and love him and take care of him." Knowing that Kathy homeschooled her other children, their pediatrician gave them a cautionary okay to begin Shawn's training on their own.

Shawn is 11 now and shines as one of my best reading students; he's well-rounded and involved in many activities. But he had an unusual home situation: his three older siblings were all homeschooled, and so Shawn had a whole crew of hands-on physical therapists and teachers who lived with him, taught him, and continually interacted with him. Kathy says, "When Shawn was born, we quickly moved from 'Why us?' to 'Why *not* us?' We have three other kids who love him and play with him. We were a good match: he's good for us, and we're good for him." When those siblings eventually left home, Kathy expanded Shawn's social, athletic, and academic activities outside the home to round out the picture.

As I mentioned in the definition of Early Intervention, your right to getting those services for your child is federally mandated. The role of Early Intervention specialists is to help you set up resources that will support the goals you have for your child. On top of that, parents have a plethora of networking opportunities to turn to for guidance. Local Down syndrome support groups, online support groups, national organizations....today the Down syndrome information highway is long, and limited only by your time and energy.

Along with tapping into networking, reading resources can shore up your education fortress.

- *Fine Motor Skills for Children with Down Syndrome*, by Maryanne Bruni (Woodbine House, 2006)
- *Gross Motor Skills in Children with Down Syndrome*, by Pat Winders (Woodbine House, 1997)
- *Early Communication Skills for Children with Down Syndrome*, by Libby Kumin (Woodbine House, 2003)

All available at www.woodbinehouse.com

Choosing Your Vision

I made a perhaps unusual decision 24 hours after Jonathan's birth, when I first learned of the nonnegotiable fact that he had Down syndrome.

I made a conscious, deliberate choice that was in line with my spiritual beliefs: I decided to see my baby as perfect, and to encourage family and friends to do the same.

This is not as crazy as it sounds, and it was not denial. At that point, I had twelve years of intense yogic training behind me, training that included the practice of respecting others as the perfect beings I believe they really are, and not as they appear to be with the naked eye: to that external eye, humans are more or less flawed, and certainly less than perfect. But that appearance does not affect the reality that they are, in fact, perfect souls. That was my belief, and it was not at all difficult to apply that same thinking to my newborn son.

But how to prime our family and friends? How to set them up so they could join us in this vision of Jonathan? I knew that both my husband and I were too emotionally fragile to do that ourselves in those first hours and days. So I called a girlfriend. "Claudia, I need your help. We've just found out that Jonathan has Down syndrome. I want you to call all our friends and tell them three things. Tell them that Jonathan has been born and he's beautiful; that he has Down syndrome; and lastly, that we're fine with that and want them to rejoice with us. We welcome their congratulations and well wishes." Then I gave her our list of friends and let it go. I had done all I could.

I knew my limitations. I could not endure all those conversations, and I trusted Claudia to do a beautiful job with her assignment-of-the-heart—and she did. My hospital room soon filled with fragrant flowers and cheerful cards of congratulations. I realize that this is not the typical scenario for the new mom of a baby with Down syndrome; but to my joy, this is in fact what happened.

Create Your Own Vision

So what is your vision of your child? You can set this up any way you like.

Like the rest of life, you create your child-raising reality by your long chain of choices and your chosen attitude. The realization that we essentially create our own reality has now come into mainstream thinking. Stories abound of individuals overcoming unimaginable obstacles by first creating and nurturing the "reality" of their success in their minds, and later witnessing those very events taking place. "Thoughts become things," as author Mike Dooley insists. And he's right.

In my case, I knew I needed to build a protective shield around my own positive concept of Jonathan until my mind was strong enough to withstand opposing opinions of my son. I did not become strong overnight. For several years, I purposely avoided anyone who had a negative view of my son and the disability he involuntarily owned. I had to get strong for the journey ahead, and I knew that wasn't going to happen if I continually lost focus dodging negative "Oh, what a disaster!" bullets. When several years passed and I felt emotionally and spiritually strong enough, I knew I was ready. I felt that nothing could topple my attitude, my inner vision of my child; that vision was set.

We all deserve the privacy and space in which to hone our own indomitable attitude, and we have the right to set up whatever protection we need in order to let that fragile seed grow into its own strength. So gather your forces, choose your friends, your support groups, and your online and reading resources consciously, and chart a unique course of your own design.

Twenty-six years ago, I didn't have the Internet, blogs, chat groups, and online networks. I had a telephone, for heaven's sake. And I walked seven miles every morning through snow and sleet just to get to the grocery store, with only dry bread crumbs for breakfast ...naw, I'm not *that* old. But I rejoice for young moms today. I belong to the Silicon Valley Down Syndrome Network on Yahoo, and I am still astonished when I read a post from a mom at 8:00 a.m. asking, "Can anyone recommend a developmental pediatrician in the Burlingame area?" and see that by 11 a.m. she's got seven emails full of advice, with more on the way. The "High-speed Help Highway" is phenomenal. Go for it!

Essentials of Your Parent-Friendly Manual

4

Other Gifts

*"Tell me whom you love,
and I will tell you who you are."*
—Arsène Houssaye

There are probably endless variations on the extraordinary gifts possessed by our children with Down syndrome. They are unusually compassionate; when it's important, are aware of the unexpressed feelings and needs of others; typically feel a deep awareness of the living presence of family members who have passed on; seem to be able to momentarily step from behind their "cognitive delay" screen and display a remarkable intelligence, which for loved ones watching is profoundly moving. Each parent could write stories that would touch our souls and make us wonder about the real nature of our children. Following are a few of those stories.

On the Playground

Amy, the mother of a seven-year-old girl with Down syndrome, tells a playground story about her daughter Ava. "Sometimes people—total strangers—approach me and say things like, 'You know you have an angel there, don't you?' I never believed them at first; there was too much going on in my own head for the first year or so to think about angelic intervention. But I never forgot what they said, and I believe it now.

"When another child is crying in Ava's presence, she always, *always,* comforts them. This comes from a child who is effectively nonverbal at seven and is still learning the definition of the word 'gentle.'

"On the playground one day, a little girl fell off the play structure. She was hurt, crying, and her mother wasn't around. Ava and I went over to try to comfort the little girl, but Ava did all of the work. Ava gave the girl a hug, signed 'cry' and 'sad' to me while pointing at the girl, and then proceeded to caress the girl's head in a gesture so loving and tender that the child calmed down. I was blown away. Ava stayed with the girl until her worried mother returned.

"The mother thanked me, but I could only respond, 'I didn't do a thing. You can thank my daughter.' The mother was astonished as well. She and I are now friends and we often talk about the 'playground incident' and our daughters.

"Thanks to Ava, the little girl recovered quickly, and her mother's perspective on children with intellectual disabilities did a complete 180-degree turnaround. This whole scene took place in about two minutes. Talk about angelic intervention!"

On the Street

Bill O'Dea tells this story about his son Eric, now 24. "Eric was around six years old, and we were walking back home with our dog after finishing errands. We came across a man in a wheelchair waiting for the wheelchair lift in a van to lower. This man's arms and legs were not fully developed, making him look quite different.

"As we approached him, he asked us what type of dog we had, what the dog's name was, and if he could pet her. We told him a Bullmastiff, her name is Tara, and yes he may pet her because she's very friendly.

"Tara walked over to the man and laid her head down on his lap. After several minutes of petting her, with Tara's head on his lap the whole time, he thanked us. I then told Tara to come; she lifted her head off his lap and walked back to me.

"As if he had been waiting in a line behind the dog, Eric walked up to the man, opening his arms wide to signal giving a hug. This action took the man completely by surprise, and with just a second of hesitation, he returned the open-armed gesture. Eric gave him a hug, and the man hugged Eric back.

"That hug lasted only a few seconds, but afterwards the man started to cry. He was so filled with emotion he couldn't control his tears. He seemed embarrassed and tried to apologize. Eric noticed the man crying and moved to try to hug him again. With tears in his eyes, the man held up his hand, signaling that it was not necessary. Seeing this, I told Eric it was time to say goodbye, which he did. We continued on our way, the man continued on his, and we never saw him again.

"As we walked the rest of the way home, I thought about what Eric had done. When most people would have either stared at him or looked away, Eric did neither. Not many would have thought of hugging him, especially a child; but Eric saw right through the man's disability to the person inside, filtering out the visual differences, the wheelchair, and the underdeveloped limbs. He saw only the person, which was exactly how our dog Tara saw this person. There was no prejudging based on appearances; just simple compassion and acceptance of others.

"Eric did not just go around giving everybody hugs—especially strangers—and certainly not at age six; we had worked with Eric about only shaking hands when he meets people, and to hug only those he knows well, such as relatives. Observing Eric over all the years since then, I think he somehow knew that the man needed a hug, and that's why he reached out to him that day."

On the Stage

Brandon has been active in theater since he was six, and his mom, Teresa, says "he's happy in any role as long as he has a costume to wear and gets his hair done. It's all about the costume." By the time Brandon reached middle school, he had put in his time, and Bart Schneider, the director, thought he was ready to take on a larger role.

Brandon's dad, Tim, tells the story: "So he played the part of Tommy in the production of *The Music Man*. Since Tommy's role was pretty high profile, Bart decided to add a shadow role for Brandon just in case he forgot a line or was confused about when to come on and off the stage. It was a brilliant call on his part, which is typical of Bart and one of the reasons he was recognized as the 'Teacher of the Year' for the district.

"Brandon's shadow partner was a typically developing student named Patrick, a straight A student. This was to be Patrick's first theater experience, and he knew Brandon really well, so it was a natural fit. The two worked extremely hard and both knew the role inside and out.

"All went well until the second performance, just after intermission. Brandon missed his entrance. Or at least that's the way it looked. Tim and Teresa looked at each other. 'He just missed his entrance! What happened to Brandon?' They saw Bart dash backstage to troubleshoot.

"Meanwhile, on stage, Patrick stepped in and delivered 'Tommy's' lines. Bart found Brandon backstage. 'Hey, Bud, you're supposed to be on stage right now! Did you forget?'

"'Oh, that. I know I was supposed to be out there, but Patrick worked real hard on this play, and he hasn't had any lines to say yet. I just wanted him to have a chance, like I have already.'

"Bart was incredulous. 'So now that Patrick has had your lines, does that mean that you'll do the rest of your lines, lead the dance, and do all of the other scenes from now on?'

"'Yes, sure I'll do that.'

"By now, Bart had tears in his eyes. He high-fived Brandon and said, 'Rock on, Brandon! I am so proud of you.'

"Later, Teresa asked Brandon how he felt after Patrick delivered his lines. She says, 'Brandon put both hands on his chest, leaned toward me, and said, 'I was so happy for him! He finally got his chance.'"

In the Park

Then there is eight-year-old Cassie. A pretty redhead, Cassie has the uncanny ability to reach out and connect deeply with people, total strangers, who most need it.

Last summer she went to a birthday party in the park. She knew only the birthday girl, a child who also had Down syndrome. There were other children there who also had Down syndrome, and everyone was playing together and having all the usual fun of a birthday party.

Except for one boy, who remained apart from the other children. He had both Down syndrome and autism, and to his mother's grief, he had never in his life connected with another child. It was enormously painful for her to watch the other children with Down syndrome playing together, knowing her son couldn't.

Cassie's mother, Lynda, continues the story. "Cassie didn't care if the boy couldn't speak to her. She didn't care if he ran in circles. She was happy to be in his presence. Cassie looked straight into his eyes and somehow communicated with him.

"She took his hand, and he didn't back away. They walked all around the park holding hands. His mother wept tears of joy. He had never shown any interest in any other child, *ever*. And there he was, holding Cassie's hand.

"They separated for awhile, each doing their own thing. Soon *he* sought *her* out and reached for her hand.

"Witnessing this, I felt that something so divinely guided and magical was happening. To this mom, and this boy, this was a true miracle."

At the Stoplight

Then there was the day when Lynda and Cassie were waiting at a long red light. Cassie was uncharacteristically quiet, a fact Lynda didn't notice for some time, lost in her own thoughts.

"Finally, the truck sitting next to us caught my attention because of its loud knocking engine. I looked over and saw a big, hairy, rough-looking man. His arms were covered with tattoos, and I fully expected to see a snapping Rottweiler foaming at the mouth next to him.

"Instead, I saw this burly-faced man waving at Cassie, with a joyous smile and *tears* running down his cheeks. He and Cassie had obviously been having an interaction for some time."

How Can She Know That?

Jennifer tells a story about her daughter. Makenna is eight. The highlight of her week is her hour with Dell, the gentle horse she rides at her hippotherapy session. She's on top of the world when she's on Dell; all the students love this therapy, where disabilities become invisible and inconsequential as they ride those beautiful animals.

One day, as the family van zipped along on the way to riding class, Makenna announced, "Mommy, no Dell today. I ride Reba instead. Dell has tummy ache. Call the doctor; she help Dell's tummy."

What's That?

Hippotherapy: The movement of a horse is used as a treatment strategy in physical, occupation, and speech-language therapy sessions. This therapy can improve muscle tone, balance, motor development, posture, etc.

See: www.americanhippotherapyassociation.org.

Jennifer and Makenna arrived at the riding stable to find the vet on site, in the midst of pulling a tube out of Dell's stomach. Dell had suffered a colic attack and most definitely had a "tummy ache." Makenna did indeed ride Reba that day, and her mom had another stunned moment of recognition that her daughter somehow knows things she couldn't possibly know.

Makenna always knows when someone needs a hug–or when they don't. If they don't need one, they don't get one, by golly. But one day she arrived for her reading session with me during a time when I was under more stress than usual. I'm a determined teacher, so I typically don't get any hugs from Makenna, who is even more determined *not* to be taught, thank you very much.

That day was different: without a word, she understood that I needed hugs. She attached herself to my body with wave after wave of hugs.

After some minutes of that, while still in her arms, I wondered consciously, "Who *is* this soul? She is not the iron-willed little eight-year-old she seems to be. She is much, much older and wiser. Who *is* this, really?" I don't have an answer to that question, but as she held me, I clearly felt her energy: not a child, but a fully mature being, and a profoundly aware one.

Just to keep things real, let's swing the pendulum back the other way for a moment, to the flip side of Makenna's eight-year-old personality. I'll recount a scene from one of her school days. She had been noncompliant that day, refusing to do her work, and her second grade teacher was totally frazzled. At one point, Makenna made a dash for the teacher's desk, plopped in the teacher's chair, swung her feet up on the table, and locked her arms behind her head. In her finest master-to-slave tone, she announced, "I need a cocktail!"

Her teacher sighed wearily. "No, Makenna, *I* need a cocktail."

At the Grocery

Our children have an uncanny ability to draw people into their energy sphere. But they are highly developed discriminators: only *certain* people qualify. And you can bet money that whomever they select will indeed respond.

Mary is mom to Matthew, age nine. A few years ago when Matthew was six or seven, Mary had taken him as usual to their neighborhood grocery story in Cincinnati. Matthew had enjoyed the ride in the "kiddie cart" attached to the grocery cart, and Mary pushed him into the parking lot. As they arrived at the car and Mary reached down to get Matthew out of the kiddie cart, he objected.

"No. I not get out." He turned toward a tall, thin man who happened to be passing by. "Pawpaw will get me out."

Mary says there was nothing special about the older man's appearance; simply dressed in jeans and a plaid shirt, he was on his way into the store. But Matthew had already done his "energy assessment," and knew this was a special man, a good man. The elderly gent said, "You need some help, young man?"

Mary was embarrassed. "I'm sorry," she said. "I don't know why he's calling you Pawpaw."

"It's not a problem," said the man. "I have nothing else to do. The only thing I'm doing is watching the Reds game tonight." He reached down and lifted Matthew out of the little car.

"Matthew, tell the gentleman 'thank you' for helping you," prompted Mary.

"No. Pawpaw is putting me in the car."

Mary turned to the man, even more embarrassed. "I'm really sorry...."

"No, I want to do this," said the man. He put Matthew in his car seat and fastened the seatbelt for him. Then he turned to Mary. His eyes were piercing, almost steely, as he lasered them on her. "You have a special young man there. *You take care of him.*"

Beyond surprised, and feeling very much like the student before the teacher, Mary responded, "Yes, sir!"

In the Apple Store

Amy tells this story about her daughter Ava, who was six at the time.

"One of my children's favorite places to go when there's nothing else to do (a rare event) is to the Apple Store. On a recent trip to our local store, Ava was checking out the iPods which, of course, she can operate like a pro. She successfully found her all-time favorite song on one. But before playing the song, she hand-picked employees and customers to join her in listening.

"She literally walked around the store, went up only to people that she found 'suitable' to join her in her quest, grabbed their hands, and brought them to the iPod on display. After corralling a half dozen people, she started playing the song 'September' by Earth Wind and Fire.

"With a big smile, she had everyone hold hands in a circle, started the song, and then motioned everyone to dance. At first, everyone other than Ava seemed a little confused. I can only imagine what they were thinking: 'What's going on?'

"But after watching the smile on her face and her totally cool dance moves, her captive audience loosened up and everyone danced. In the Apple Store. To the whole song. Played at full volume. And they loved it! Ava gave everyone a high-five at the end of the song, and a big 'Thank You!' in sign language."

At Home

A moving variation on Ava's impromptu dance party is one that I have heard from several parents, whose stories follow. It is a "join-hands-in-love" experience, which shows a remarkable commonality in our children's desire to draw others out of their nonstop busy lives into a circle of love.

Many years ago, I remember Jerome Hines telling me a story about his son. Hines was an iconic figure at the Metropolitan Opera for many years; he was a "basso profundo," and I don't think that needs translating! When I knew him, he had a grown son with Down syndrome who was effectively nonverbal, using only single words for the most part.

Jerome told me about his son's custom of going to different parts of their home, taking family members by the hand, and drawing them all to the kitchen. The first time this happened, no one knew what was going on or why the boy was doing this. When everyone was assembled in one room, his son gestured for everyone to hold hands, which they did. Then he just beamed at them. "Love," he said. Was everyone moved? Even humbled? It was a circle of love, and the current was palpable. It was his gift to them, and his reminder to them of what really mattered.

Blair, now 33, started a similar ritual in his family when he was growing up. His mom, Martha, explains. "When Blair was growing up, we used to have regular family gatherings, big gatherings. On my husband's side of the family alone, there were thirty or forty people. One year we were at his parent's house for a Christmas celebration. Blair was young, about ten. The movie *The Lion King* had just come out, and of course Blair loved it. There were three generations gathered around the dinner table that night, and Blair wanted to do a toast. He stood up, looked around, raised his glass, thanked his grandparents for hosting everyone, and said beaming as only our children can, 'This is to the circle of life.'

"That same Christmas, he started the custom of gathering everyone together to hold hands and sing one of his favorite childhood songs, "Johnny Appleseed"; it's a custom we still do at holiday gatherings. The song didn't mean much to anyone that first time, but it does now. It's a tradition."

The Red Balloon

Finally, I confess a story of my own less-than-ideal behavior and Jonathan's compassion toward me in spite of that.

Jonathan was four and his sister, Becca, was two at the time. It had been a long and stressful day at the end of a long and stressful month, and I was fried. Just before returning home, I had stopped and gotten helium balloons for both children. Jonathan adored helium balloons, especially red ones, and he loved watching them float up to the sky. (I learned to tie them to his wrist.)

As we arrived home, Jonathan was clutching his red helium balloon. Just as we got in the door, one or both of the children did something naughty—I don't remember what—and I completely lost it. It was the very, very last straw for the day. I slammed the door (which never quite closed the same again) and yelled at both kids.

Immediately contrite but still stressed, I got it together enough to gather them in the family room with me. I sat down with them on the floor. "I'm sorry," I began. "It's not your fault. I shouldn't have yelled at you. Mama is not upset with you. Mama is upset about something else, but not with you." I talked to them until I felt sure they understood they were not at fault, and that I was sorry I had yelled.

Jonathan got to his feet, still clutching his red balloon, toddled over and, without saying a word, he held it out to me. He understood. I was not only forgiven; he was giving me his best treasure to comfort me. I accepted his gift because I knew it was important to receive his kindness and generosity (I returned it to him later). Such a silent, sweet, and selfless gesture put a beautiful closure on a difficult moment and taught me much about the gift of forgiveness.

No Judgment

If we're lucky enough to experience them, these loving moments reduce us to a heart-opening humility that nothing else quite can. In that single moment, we remember that we're all here as equals, soul-to-soul, and that we're all just trying to do our best on this planet. And that this extraordinary being standing in front of us understands that.

My sense is that our children with Down syndrome do not judge others. I believe they see each human being as he really is, in their hearts, unvarnished and unveiled. With disarming accuracy, they sense the other person's character and heart, and that is what they respond to, no matter what a person's appearance might be. I only wish that I and the rest of humanity might rise to that same standard. It would change the world.

5

Honestly, Now

"If I were two-faced, would I be wearing this one?"
—Abraham Lincoln

Honesty Like We Never Knew

Before Jonathan was born, I thought I was an honest woman. A good citizen, the kind of person who'd return the money if a cashier mistakenly gave her too much change. In fact, I had no idea how deep honesty could run. Not until after Jonathan was born.

With his entrance into my life, all polish and veneer was stripped off of any superficiality I still carried with me. This child opened my eyes to a reality I didn't know existed; and once that vision was opened, I found there was no turning back to blindness. My son's very existence wouldn't permit it.

I later learned that I was not alone in experiencing this. Our children help strip away any veneer that might have covered our attitudes, perspectives, and general understanding of life. Other parents may be able to plod through various pretenses and posturing; happily, we can no longer do that, if we ever did.

For me, Jonathan's birth caused a paradigm shift equal to a cosmic quake off the planetary charts. I believe it is the same for most of us. This shift of vision is our private tsunami, our individual hurricane, our intensely personal life-changing earthquake. Standing in the aftermath, after the initial storm has passed, we view the changed landscape with a new vision. So many things that we just didn't get before, we now understand. We begin to realize that these children are way ahead of us: they already understand things that we don't, and are here to teach us, even as we teach them.

I thought I was honest; but as time passed, I realized that much of my behavior had been subtly dishonest in that it was out of sync with my inmost core. I had laughed when I wanted to cry, was superficially friendly with people whose values and behavior repelled me, and wasted precious time on useless pursuits. Now I loved and lived with a child who had no veneer.

I believe that our children with Down syndrome have neither the heart nor the capability for dishonesty or pretense. They easily cut through the red tape of life and go directly to truth, and I am convinced that we cannot be parents of a child like this without belonging to the same visionary club as do our children. Our understanding is forever expanded, forever altered. There is no way back to unawareness—fortunately.

A Head Start in Honesty Training

Jonathan's very existence began working on my honesty, gently poking me through my conscience, even before he was born.

I yearned for children for twelve years before giving up all hope entirely and focusing on a career. Twelve years into the marriage, I embarked on a months-long sabbatical journey in Europe with my husband. A week before returning to the USA, I found myself alone in a London hotel room with a few hours and nothing to do.

I idly flicked on the room's TV and found a movie to watch. American-made, this film was about a newly divorced mother and her young son; the boy had Down syndrome. The movie followed their struggles for acceptance, their joys, and their eventual success in creating a rich life and a loving new family.

The sight of anyone with cognitive disabilites had always been uncomfortable for me; I never knew how to respond, what to do, how to react. No one in my world of experience had a developmental disability, and I was absolutely clueless as to how to handle the simplest of encounters, much less actually live with a child with a disability. As the movie progressed, I became increasingly uncomfortable with the subject matter. But for some reason, I did not move to switch channels.

I stared at the TV and the mother's struggles, and the longer the movie went on, the lower my heart sank and the more uncomfortable I became. Finally, my thoughts erupted: "I could *never* do that!" I remember this thought as being very strong, very determined. It was out of the question for me.

At that very moment, Jonathan as an embryo had already been nestled in my womb for ten days. I had no idea.

He was on his way to rescue me from my off-centered truth. Soon I would no longer be clueless; his very arrival was going to make me an honest woman, dissolve my discomfort, and light up my life.

Scattered throughout this book are many stories of our little Truth Mongers in action. This chapter is simply a pause to drive home the obvious, to shine a spotlight on that verity: our children will bring us back to our own truth, just in case we happen to stray.

Which brings me to the following stories.

You Stand Corrected

Or sit corrected. Or recline, or whatever, but you will indeed be brought into line by your child's inner polygraph core. My friend Dan, father to ten-year-old Emily, experienced this pinch recently.

"When Emily was born with Down syndrome, I asked myself, 'What did I do wrong to deserve this?' Now, ten years later, I ask myself, 'What did I do *right* to deserve this?' She has taught me powerful lessons. Once, when she was within earshot, I made a remark about an acquaintance that I realized too late was unkind. As soon as the words left my mouth, Emily turned and held my gaze with an awareness and a mature look of reprimand that cut right to my core. I was stunned and humbled."

Bringing Us in Line

These corrections to our honesty radio dials can be moving, even embarrassing; they can also be disarmingly funny.

Sometimes our kids bring us back to where we need to be mentally. Being naturally distracted because we're constantly multitasking, unwittingly modeling the epitome of ADD, we get off track. Not to worry. We can trust our children to help us refocus. Since the dishonesty filter was never installed on their character computers, what they see is what they say.

One evening, I was distracted while Jonathan was trying to tell me something. "Aw, come on!" he said. "Try to be focused, now!" I was caught off guard. "You're trying to get *me* to be focused?"

"Yes. It's my job!"

Our children's inner solidarity with their own truth gives them an air of confidence and utter relaxation that can sometimes be both maddening and hilarious. When Jonathan was younger and I was teaching him to wipe his nose, he had the gross habit of taking his bare hand and wiping his nose upward. No matter how many times I trained him otherwise, he was persisting in this ridiculous habit. Losing my patience with this, one day I yelled, "Jonathan, do *I* wipe my nose like this?" and I imitated his nose wipe.

"Nope," he said. "Just me."

He's still keeping me focused. One night recently, Jonathan was talking excitedly on the phone with me. He had discovered new websites where he could download pictures from some of his favorite Disney movies. To him that was a gold mine.

His housemate had been gone for a few days, visiting relatives. As I listened to Jonathan talk about his exciting new websites, I could hear background noise that sounded like the roommate was arriving back home. I interrupted him to ask, "Jonathan, did your roommate just come back?"

An exasperated sigh. "Mom, just focus on the websites."

Yes, *sir*!

One evening my friend Eve was chatting with me after a ballroom dance class for teens and adults with Down syndrome. We were admittedly having an extended chick chat when her daughter Lauren intervened. Dance is a cardio workout disguised as total fun, and Lauren had worked up a terrific sweat. But the temperature outside had dropped into the single digits, so she had her winter coat on, ready to leave. She waited patiently for a few minutes and then said dryly, "I'm *melting* here. Wrap it up, Mom."

Oddly enough, when a parent hears these types of comments from someone with Down syndrome, there is no tinge of "smart mouth kid." Why? Because whatever was said was the truth, and delivered without the slightest trace of ill will.

Her Just Desserts

On rare occasions, these corrections are remarkably subtle. For example, my student and friend Blair, now 33, has a laser-like ability to assess the hearts of other humans—and when necessary, to teach them. Blair's high school principal never could get her students' names right. She habitually addressed them by the wrong name, and of course this did not sit well with the students, who rightly felt devalued. Blair observed this; apparently it rankled his sense of respect for others, and he decided to do something about it. So, let's say the principal's name was Mary. One day she greeted him with, "Hi, how are you?" Blair answered deliberately, "I'm fine, *Alice*; how are you?" The story became famous in the school.

Truth Is Cool

My daughter Rebecca's friends, most in their mid-twenties, think Jonathan totally rocks. Why? Because he's funny, he's real, and he likes them. They in turn love his unique expressions, his humor, his insight, the affectionate nicknames he invents for those dear to him (which is all the good people in the world), and, of course, because he calls things as he sees them.

Because we typical humans are socially hidebound by politically correct behavior, and don't feel we have the freedom to say what we see, we feel an almost covert admiration for those who simply open their mouths and speak the truth.

I suggest that most humans on the planet need to have at least one soul with Down syndrome revolving in the sphere of their life. This will ensure a regular encounter with truth, humor, and humility.

6

Intuition

"Intuition is a spiritual faculty and does not explain,
but simply points the way."
—Florence Scovel Shinn

Your Secret Weapon

Seatbacks in an upright position, please. Put down those remotes and turn off every piece of electronic connecting equipment you've got. Cell phone, TV, iPad, iPhone, iPod, radio, computer, laptop, game player, Blackberry…and by the time this book is printed, there will be even more options for hyperconnection (and distraction). What I want to talk to you about is your own flawless, cost-free wi-fi: one that connects you to insights, understanding, and sound decisions.

I'm talking about your intuition. It's the most powerful tool you have in your parenting toolbox.

It's your secret weapon. Use it in any given situation, and that situation becomes clearer. It's free, always available, profoundly experienced, and is never wrong. All humans have intuition, and it is more or less developed in all of us. But I suggest that parents of children with Down syndrome receive an extra measure; if not at their own birth, at their child's birth. Why? Let's just consider it an act of cosmic kindness.

So what is intuition? Yogis describe it as a perfect balance between divine wisdom and divine love. A flawless connector between both of those essential qualities: wisdom and love, reason and feeling, the higher mind and the heart center. It is like a fine, translucent wire connecting one to the other in a pure stream of energy. That is intuition.

Where'd I Put It?

Our big problem is that we haven't used it in so long, we can't remember where we put it. Or if we do manage to find it in our toolbox, we don't trust it. Maybe it's too small, or rusty from misuse, and anyway we can't figure out how to turn it on. Here's a fact about intuition: use it or lose it. This is absolutely true. Learning to become still and listen to that "still, small voice" within is not encouraged in our society. We're trained to believe that more stuff is better, louder is cooler, and way over-the-top is awesome.

As our social environment urges us to become endlessly distracted and accumulative, we listen to our internal cell phone calls less and less. Like any person would do when ignored, intuition stops trying to call us. When we ignore our intuition's voice for long enough, it eventually stops talking to us. Why should it bother? We're not listening anyway.

When we were children, it spoke to us loudly and clearly; but as we grow up, we learn to ignore its voice and turn away to other seemingly more reliable sources of information and confirmation.

Fortunately for us, our intuition never stops trying to get through to us. That's especially helpful for us as parents of children with Down syndrome, because the waters we will sail are uncharted and we need all the guidance we can get.

This chapter is an undisguised plea for you to not only listen to the voice of your intuition, but to honor and follow it. Pay heed to it. Your child with Down syndrome is already tuned in to this channel, and you can piggyback onto your little guide and learn as you go.

How many times have you heard yourself say, "I had this nagging feeling that I shouldn't have gone to X, or done X; I should have listened, because now look what's happened! I *knew* I shouldn't have made that choice! I *knew* it!" That nagging feeling was your intuition talking to you, the voice of your inner knowledge, your core, which is wise and knowing.

I encourage you to turn a renewed, respectful ear to that voice, whether it concerns medical matters, the choice of a doctor or dentist, or an educational issue of placement type or venue.

When you get into a situation where you need to make an informed decision, do line up your ducks of research, get busy networking, etc., but place your intuition in charge of the final decision. Whatever you decide has to *feel* right inside. This doesn't mean that we will always know definitively if we're making the right decision about an issue; we may not. But it does mean that if we hear The Nagger talking to us somewhere in the back of our consciousness, we need to stop and listen. Don't let the train keep thundering on. Stop the train and check the cargo, the brakes, the destination, the fuel. Something's not right if you keep getting a tap on the shoulder from your intuition.

Nowhere is this more important than when dealing with the many professionals you will encounter along the way. As newbie parents of children with Down syndrome, we are overwhelmed and often intimidated by the professionals we must rely on for treatment and advice. This is a given, and a perfectly natural response to the situation.

But what I suggest we do is strive for balance and agreement between our respect for the professionals and our respect for our intuition. Intuition trumps trusting professional advice when The Nagger keeps tapping on our shoulder. Here's an example.

What Happens When You Listen

When Jonathan was twenty months old, his sister, Rebecca, was born. Since long before his actual birth, I had been attuned to Jonathan (that's yogi-speak for being aware of his consciousness, striving to be in gentle inner communication with him). We were strongly connected, to the point that, throughout his early childhood, after tucking him in bed and going into my own bedroom, I could feel in my own consciousness the moment he fell deeply asleep. There was no sound, no movement, before this *wooosh,* this drop into deep sleep, but I distinctly felt it in my own consciousness.

Of course, I wanted to have that same attunement with Rebecca. I had no idea it would prove to be so important.

I had the Rh Factor in pregnancy, so both of my newborn children had mild jaundice and needed to stay in the hospital under bilirubin lights for several days. Since Rebecca was otherwise well, she was placed in a ward with half a dozen babies, with nothing but a hard chair for the mother to sit in. No reclining "chair bed." So I couldn't actually sleep by her side. I stayed with her all other hours, pumped breast milk for the nurses to give her overnight, and left in the late evening. I returned early every morning.

This routine limped along for three days. The fourth morning, I woke up at home and *knew* something was wrong with Rebecca. I knew she was in trouble. I called the nurse's station.

"Oh, no, she's just fine," said the nurse.

"Are you *sure?*"

"Yes," the nurse assured me. "She wouldn't take a bottle from us, so she hasn't eaten all night. But she's fine."

I pressed her, "Are you *sure?*"

"Yes, she's fine."

I tried to believe the nurse and relax, tried to stay with Jonathan and his dad a few more minutes, before taking off for the hospital. But I couldn't. "*Go! Go!!*" The internal message was intense. I hopped in the car and drove as fast as I could.

The closer I got to the hospital, the more urgent the message was. "*Hurry! Hurry! Get there!*" I parked at the hospital lot, jumped out of the car, and *ran* two blocks to the building. Keep in mind I had given birth four days before, and was—ah—well over thirty at the time. The fleeting thought came to me, "What are you *doing*? What if you start bleeding right here on the street?"

I left that in God's hands as I raced into the building and jumped in the elevator. As the elevator door opened onto Rebecca's floor, I could already hear her screaming. I tore into the ward, threw open the acrylic isolette that kept her captive, and cradled her. She had a dent in her head three inches long and what looked like a half inch deep, though her young malleable skin was not broken, only bruised. Probably from hunger, she had been crying and pushing forward with her little legs; but each push jammed her head against the corner of an acrylic box jutting into the isolette. From the look of things, she had been screaming and hitting the edge of the box for only God knows how long.

I was *beyond* furious at the nursing staff. I was enraged. I wanted to scream at them, "I endured natural childbirth just so her little head wouldn't be subjected to forceps, and look what you've done to her! Look what you've done!" I felt like they deserved whatever wrath I could throw their way, and more.

But my yogic training kicked in. I knew that flooding my body and milk with all of the nasty chemicals that anger releases would only harm my hungry baby, so I kept calm and focused on her until she had nursed her fill. All the while she nursed, I gently massaged her cranium, praying that the injury would somehow vanish and that her skin and her soft little cranial bones would recover.

Now that twenty-four years have passed, I can be a little kinder in my thoughts and cut the nursing staff some slack. After all, maybe most four-day-old infants just stay put in their isolettes. Did they think she was incapable of scooting forward toward the stupid obstruction in the isolette? O ye of little faith! Not this one. She had traveled a good ten inches by the time I found her. Couldn't the staff intuit that this baby would grow up to be a phenomenal dancer? What were they *thinking*?

But twenty-four years ago, I was not inclined to kinder thoughts. After Rebecca finished nursing and had fallen asleep, I talked to the staff and "let 'em have it" in as controlled a manner as possible. Then I yanked her out of the hospital and took her home. End of bilirubin treatment, thanks. That same night, a dear friend who was a physical therapist specializing in cranio-sacral therapy actually came to our home and checked Rebecca's cranium for injury. He gave her the okay, and her little head recovered completely.

But what if I hadn't listened?

How To Listen

If you get that feeling in your gut, if The Nagger is tapping at your consciousness, what should you do? How do you know if it's intuition or indigestion?

We can access intuition only in stillness. There is no alternative. If our minds are racing chaotically (who, *us*?) and we are bombarded with stimuli, sounds, activity—in other words, if we are living a typical day— then we need to create a quiet place in our lives for a regular check-in with BFF Intuition.

That means finding quiet in your day, if only for five minutes. Five or ten minutes off by yourself in a quiet place. If you have the habit of meditating, then you're already doing this. If not, you can start by sitting still with your spine erect, closing your eyes and relaxing. As you let your closed eyes relax, you'll notice that they will tend to turn upward to a little above the point between the eyebrows. You may have noticed that when a baby is sleeping deeply, you can see that the eyeballs have turned upward and are in a very relaxed state. That's what you're going for.

Watch your breath as it flows in and out, in and out, in and out… and as often as your mind wanders (trust me, it will), just bring it back to watching the breath.

This is a basic beginning meditation practice. After you've watched your breath for a few minutes and are feeling more relaxed and calm, keep focusing on that just-above point between the eyebrows and inwardly ask the question that's on your mind. Then turn your focus to your heart area and feel the response there, in what yogis call the heart center. Sometimes we feel a warmth there if our intuition says "it's a go," and a coldness if it's not the best idea to proceed. This takes practice, and you will get quite good at it as you learn to go deeper into stillness and listen to that "still, small voice."

If you want to learn the real deal about stillness, it's best to learn from a source with a good reputation. The very best starting place I can recommend is the all-faith-embracing Self-Realization Fellowship site, referenced in the "Tool Box." When you land on the home page, right smack in the middle of it you'll see "How to Meditate." Click on that and you'll be off and running. I mean sitting.

A great place to jumpstart your meditation experiment: www.yogananda-srf.org.

Practice, Practice

You will have countless opportunities to practice listening to your intuition, day after day. Practice makes reliable. Practice makes confident. Practice makes secure. And as I've mentioned and will repeat on occasion throughout this book, your child with Down syndrome already has a black belt in intuition. "Watch and learn." This is one practice assignment that is nothing but enjoyable, so enjoy!

7

Nurturing the Parent

"If Momma ain't happy, ain't nobody happy."
—Southern Wisdom

Self-Care Is Essential

Let's see; how many metaphors should I deliver to get my point across?

If you continually withdraw dinero from your checking account without bothering to deposit more, expecting that you won't get slammed with overdraft megacharges…

If you addictively use your cell phone without recharging it, while following your outdated GPS into the remote mountains of Montana in mid-winter…

If you are a newbie swimmer and dive into notoriously shark-infested waters next to a beach sign that says, "Warning! Dangerous Undertow!" and expect to be home in time for margaritas…

Or how about my favorite barebones adage: "If Momma ain't happy, ain't nobody happy." And we can add, "If Daddy ain't happy, ain't Momma happy," and vice versa.

There. I've said my piece. Mom and Dad need to take care of themselves first. And be it known that I am eminently qualified to speak on this topic of taking good care of yourself, on accounta I didn't do it. Not for years. When Jonathan was five, I remember three-year-old Rebecca coming to me one day with two little wooden play figures. One was a sofa and the other was a woman. She took the little woman and laid it prone on the sofa. "Look, Mama," she said. "This is what *you* should do."

Then she gave me that sweet little tiny-toothed smile that only a three-year-old can give. Truly, out of the mouths of babes. It took some years for me to catch on, but once I began taking care of myself, I saw the light and was hooked. There *is* a God, and She wants you to lie down on that sofa.

The Parent As Savior

After Jonathan was born, for many months—if not years—I was on a one-woman mission to save him from Down syndrome. I didn't know that was Mission Impossible. I believed that if I only worked hard enough, took him to enough therapies, researched and applied all imaginable alternative therapies, and prayed like crazy, I could save my child from Down syndrome. I could erase it from his life.

I was new to this whole scene, and didn't know that I could only unbutton that Yellow Raincoat and roll up the sleeves; in my core, I was somehow convinced that I could rip that Raincoat off my child completely, and I worked daily to do just that. All I wanted was for my baby to be well, to be okay.

Some well-meaning but misinformed soul had told me, just after Jonathan was born, that I needed to stimulate him around the clock, including throughout the night; that I was to wake him every two hours to nurse and stimulate him. You know—get those neurons synapsing with each other, rapping their brain jive talk.

I struggled valiantly to do this. After two weeks, I mentioned this every-two-hour routine to Jonathan's pediatrician. "You're going to kill yourself," Dr. Weiss replied calmly. "You can't keep up that crazy schedule. Let your baby and *yourself* sleep through the night." Those were wise words from a young doctor, himself challenged with advanced hemophilia. He died only a few years later, and I will forever be grateful for his attitude toward both my baby and myself. He was one of those early angels who appeared alongside my parenting pathway and pointed the way to wisdom.

Dr. Weiss was accepting and nurturing, and in spite of Jonathan's initially poor weight gain, was totally supportive of my determination to breastfeed my baby, "low muscle tone" (affecting his suck power) or no. I'll never forget sitting in his office after Jonathan's first (and thin) well-baby checkup, watching him scribble just one word on his prescription pad. He handed me the paper. It said, "Breast-feed." I could have kissed him.

There were no lectures, no "failure to thrive" condemnations, no "head for the hills and get formula for this kid!" threats. This man had faith in us both somehow, and indeed, once Jonathan caught on to nursing efficiently, he porked up extremely well.

But the concept of "saving" my baby hounded me through the early years. I have seen other parents do the same thing; I have also seen other parents model a delightfully healthy approach to this same stressor, and their example is worth admiring and following.

Keeping Yourself Happy

Turn the attention spotlight on yourself. Do a daily balance check: how are *you* doing? Are you balancing the care of your child with the care of yourself and your marriage? This is not a sprint; this is a marathon. Take care that you don't blow all your energy in the first ten meters, thinking that's what is required of you. Check on yourself, your spirit, and your needs regularly.

Your child's special needs will still be there tomorrow; will you be up to it if you fry all your adrenalin today? If you don't already know what floats your boat, think about it until you do. Then make sure you fit that into your life in some way. What makes you feel nurtured, cared for, fulfilled, and happy?

For the past forty years, I've used daily meditation, Kriya Yoga, and Hatha Yoga as my way of measuring up to the task of life itself. Without meditation, I know for certain that I would not be the happy camper I am today, wouldn't have dealt successfully with the countless curve balls that life throws us all, and maybe wouldn't even be smiling and standing upright. It not only floats my boat, but gives me access to my core creativity.

Having easy access to that creative core has filled my life with dance, illustration, singing, and writing...all joys that I love to express.

We are all creative creatures. Expressing that creativity nourishes the soul, the emotions, and the mind....I don't think there's a part of us that it doesn't touch and heal. So it is wisdom to attend to your own creative expression. You can create a loving home, a well-run corporation, an exquisite painting, a hilarious tweet, an inspiring song, or a jazzy new bit of software that others only wish they'd thought of. There are as many expressions of creativity as there are humans on the globe. Look for yours and *do it*.

Romancing the Parents

One of the healthiest habits I admire is a weekly date night for parents. Parents Ellen and Dave go on a date every Wednesday night and have a regular sitter. Jeremy, 10, is, like, totally used to it, Dude. His parents have done this since he was born.

Jeff and Shannon's standing date is Thursday night, also with a regular sitter. Their situation is bit trickier, since eight-year-old Zoe has the dual diagnosis of Down syndrome and autism, but Shannon explains, "We have a very large social network, including many friends with whom we do lots of activities and take lots of trips. We are fortunate enough to afford a part-time nanny and babysitters. Without the marriage, there is no family; I never feel guilty about leaving the kids. We pay attention to our marriage. We take trips twice a year without the kids. The kids need to know that Mommy and Daddy love each other, and that they'll come back after a trip. I have a picture book about how Mommy always comes back, and I read it regularly to Zoe. She gets it."

Sean and Amy go out weekly, sometimes more. When their regular sitter isn't available, they—and other couples—use respite care, which in their daughter's case is a benefit of MediCal, and used sparingly. They go on trips without the kids, thanks to two sets of Grandmas and Grandpas. Like Shannon and Jeff, they put the marriage first.

What's That?

Respite Care: Respite care is a service in which temporary care is provided to children with disabilities, giving caregivers and families a break. Respite care can occur in both out-of-home and in-home settings. It may be provided free, or on a sliding scale, depending on the family's income.

Get an Attitude

Really. Whenever possible, get an attitude. An upbeat attitude. Easier said than done, but sometimes it really can be done. I watched in amazement as my friends Rob and Tina struggled through the year from hell. Their daughter Alessandra, 7, was diagnosed with brain tumors—rare in Down syndrome, but it can happen. Watching them move through the year was inspiring because of the extraordinary way they handled the entire experience: endless research; networking with their friends, who are spread around the globe; long hospital stays with many complications; chemotherapy; radiation; and a younger son in the midst of it all.

How did they handle this? As much as possible, Rob and Tina made it an adventure. The family circled the wagons and pulled in tighter. When Alessandra's immune system permitted it, they played tourist. They popped a wool cap on Alessandra's bald little head and crashed around in bumper cars and every other imaginable kid-friendly tourist attraction in the cities where they stayed for treatments. For security, Rob sported a new underarm attachment that bore an uncanny resemblance to a giant dispenser of antibacterial wipes. Which, of course, it was. Wherever they went, folks probably thought Rob was on the janitorial payroll.

Living for a long stretch in a Ronald McDonald House, Rob and Tina became family and "house parents" to other more needy families and expanded their friendship circle, which is utterly typical of them.

At this writing, Alessandra's doing well, and Rob and Tina are living checkup to checkup and are grateful for every moment. It's never easy. But having an attitude helps.

Lower Your Stress

Brian and Jenn are parents to Hailey, who has both Down syndrome and autism. They go out only once a month—to dinner, concerts, movies—but have developed other ways to lower their stress level, as a couple and as a family. Jenn says, "It may be unrealistic for some families, but it's always been a priority for us: we have always insisted on living in the town where Brian works. His worksite is just five minutes away from our home. This cuts down on stress enormously; we have more family time, much more time together. For example, if it's needed, Brian can use his lunchtime to go to a doctor's appointment with Hailey. It's a huge convenience."

Jenn found other ways to lower her stay-at-home stress: "Facebook made a huge difference for me. I love to write, especially with humor (one day she posted the day's winning score on her page: "Autism = 3, Hailey = 0"), and through Facebook I have lots of communication with supportive friends, other moms who also choose to be at home." She adds this advice, "I always tell people who are struggling to find solutions, 'Leave no stone unturned; keep pressing forward. *But take breaks.*' In those breaks, you can find the strength to keep looking."

Amy and Sean agree and echo those same thoughts. "Sometimes we feel guilt in not pursuing every little angle; yet we have to live our lives without constantly researching, digging, and working with our children. So ask yourself, how much energy do you really have? What about your other children? Your relationship with your husband? Friends and extended family? For us, striking that balance is paramount."

Teresa, mother to ninth grader Brandon, says, "I believe if parents took care of themselves first, raising their children with Down syndrome would be much easier. I was fortunate to have a great role model because my mom showed me how to do it. She woke up at least a couple hours earlier than we five kids; she exercised, gardened, read her Bible, and had breakfast started before we even finished our last dream. She was always in a good mood and everyone around her was drawn to her."

"I observed that all those years, but didn't take heed until Brandon was in kindergarten. It was always about him: learning the alphabet, numbers, potty training, and everything else that goes into raising a child with special needs.

"But one day I looked in the mirror and was shocked. I looked like a frumpy old fat mom. I took the big step and walked into Weight Watchers, and things changed.

"I believe it's the single most important thing for parents not to feel guilty about doing something for themselves. Whether it's going to Starbucks, sitting at a park, or walking on the beach, make it a priority."

You Are the Model

Consider what you are modeling for your other children. Trust me, they're watching. They are efficiently absorbing life lessons. Will they grow up thinking that "love" means to deplete themselves? That it means to give to others endlessly with no thought for their own well-being, not to mention their stress levels and immune systems? Or as adults, will they believe that caring for themselves first enables them to give others the best care possible?

If you're reading this and sensing an undercurrent of passion, you get the Intuition Award of the Week. I'm passionate about this because I made that mistake and years later had to do some damage control with my daughter, Rebecca. Now we talk comfortably about the temptation to overdo, overachieve, and lose balance, but it's an ongoing effort to resist that temptation. Balance is key for both of us now, and I recommend that focus to everyone.

Which brings me to another topic. Have you noticed that some of your other children are exceptionally high achievers, particularly if you have only two children? Anecdotal stories abound regarding the disproportionately high percentage of children with Down syndrome who have only one sibling, and that sibling is unusually bright and accomplished. If true, it defies probability and is a mystery. Or is it? Genetics and inborn intelligence and gifts aside, is there another contributing factor?

The Not-So-Typical Sibling

I know a half dozen families with this situation, and experienced it myself. When Jonathan was four, he was attending an inclusive preschool in the neighborhood. I say inclusive, but Jonathan was the only child with special needs included in the school; all the other children were typical. The owner and lead teacher had her PhD in education, and had many years of experience. It was a well-run preschool.

I decided to enroll two-and-a-half-year-old Rebecca there as well for a couple of mornings a week. After a few weeks, the teacher pulled me aside. "You don't know this yet," she said, "because you don't have older children, so I'm going to tell you: you don't have one child with special needs and one typical child. Rebecca is way beyond her peers. She is extremely bright."

So I was forewarned. But not forearmed; I wasn't experienced enough. By first grade, Rebecca was reading at a fifth-grade level and profoundly bored. A sweet, compliant child, one school morning she woke up and absolutely blew me away. Still sitting in bed, she *screamed*, "If I have to see my teacher one more time, I'll *kill* her!" She refused to go to school. This was so out of character for her that I kept her home and went to bat for her at school, to no avail. The first grade teacher was inexperienced and the large class heavily weighted to the middle part of the bell curve. That was her only focus; she didn't have the means to attend to either of the extreme ends of that curve.

That was only the beginning. Although she always got straight A's, Rebecca hated school. By the time she started high school, I had already moved her to four different schools, looking in vain for something that would meet her needs and keep her happy. In the end, finding the right educational placement for her was much more of a nightmare than finding Jonathan's! Who could have anticipated that?

She begged me to homeschool her, which I finally did in her sophomore year. We were both rescued in her junior year of high school when she was accepted at the University of Cincinnati full time. End of search: she finally loved school and is still there, finishing a master's degree.

Everyone Can Relax

If you find yourself in a similar situation, I have one important bit of advice: while trying to provide an educational setting stimulating and challenging enough to meet the needs of your not-so-typical child, work at the same time to *relax* her. Teach her that she does not have to shine brightly enough for two stars; she does not have to make up for any deficits her sibling with Down syndrome may exhibit. She will likely never verbalize it, but siblings see clearly the struggles we go through and naturally want to "make it all better."

One way of "making it all better" is for siblings to be magnificent. To achieve so spectacularly that maybe their parents won't be so burdened by the struggles associated with Down syndrome. I think you know I'm speaking the truth: these thoughts are floating, lurking nebulously in siblings' minds, and it's up to you to lovingly address them.

There. You've been tipped off. Now go for it; make sure your other children can just be themselves, without the unspoken but intense pressure hidden in the situation. This is a message you'll want to deliver to them, in many different ways, over and over as they grow and mature. They do not have to "save" the family.

And it's a message you can repeat to yourself, also over and over. The message flows both ways. *You* can relax. You can't do in one hour what you can in twenty-four, no matter how many efficiency techniques you apply. You can't do in one month what you can do in a year, no matter how many books on Down syndrome you read. Everything grows, develops, at its own pace.

All major religions teach some version of "love your neighbor as you love yourself." This presupposes that you love (nurture, cherish) yourself first. So do definitely smell the roses along the way. And the jasmine vines, lilacs, roses, gardenias....

Beginning Years

8

Extraordinary Awareness

"Yes, I will send you a child. But not yet."
—From a dream

It's Beyond Us

At some point, parents of little humans with Down syndrome reach a humbling realization: our children can see, sense, do, and know things that we can't. One day in the future, someone will research this subject; in the meantime, I can offer plenty of anecdotal evidence.

Anyone who's read Martha Beck's landmark book, *Expecting Adam,* is already primed for this chapter. If we can mentally step into this arguably paranormal aspect of our children's consciousness for a moment, we will gain a respect and an understanding that will deepen our relationship with them, and on that basis alone, this chapter is important.

While Martha was pregnant with her son Adam, who has Down syndrome, she had many extraordinary spiritual experiences and insights. I found her book pivotal in understanding the potential depth of the experience of Down syndrome. In this chapter, we will time-wind with Jonathan through moments both astonishing and mystifying. In the next chapter, you will meet more children in extraordinary vignettes.

The Child Waiting

My experience with Jonathan started twelve years before his birth.

I married in my mid-twenties, and wanted to have a child right away. Nothing happened. Six months into my marriage, I had a serious conversation with God about the situation. I begged, I pleaded. Finally I hit on the best possible argument. "You know how selfish I am," I began, "and [here came the clincher] *You* know that the best possible cure for selfishness is motherhood." There. I had God in a corner. I knew I was speaking absolute truth, and so of course I was going to get a response.

And She did respond. I believe we can relate to God as Father, Mother, Friend, or in any close way we like. For this particular problem, I was calling on God as the Mother. So I prayed ferociously before falling asleep that night, and slept still waiting for Her answer. As I began to wake in the morning— in that in-between state of consciousness where scientists and mystics and ordinary people often get their best inspirations—I heard Her response clearly within my core: "Yes. I will send you a child. But," She added, "not yet."

As I heard those words in my semi-consciousness, eyes still closed, I saw a vision, like a cameo which faded into nothing at its edge. A little boy gazed at me. He looked to be about 18 months old, with blonde hair and blue eyes. His gaze was solemn and penetrating, which at the time I didn't understand. But I instantly recognized him, as if he were an old friend from long ago. I knew this child! And this was my baby, coming at last! I was thrilled.

My heart had been set on having a girl first, but I was not about to argue with God on this point. I was just so happy to be promised a baby. And what did She say? "But not yet...." No problem. I could wait. Six more months, maybe? A year? I could hang on for that long.

Twelve years passed.

And the vision of the child returned to me six more times as the years dragged on. He always came to me when I was somewhere between the waking and dreaming state. Always the same child, the same age, the same solemn gaze. The scenes were different, but the child was always the same.

At one point, I became so involved in a career that I began to forget about my dream of having children. After all, nothing was materializing. I began to think maybe those experiences, those dreams, didn't mean anything after all. Then the child came to me again in a dream, and this time I could see him only faintly, as if the very life force was draining from him because my attention was elsewhere; I had forgotten him. In the dream, I strapped him to my back and carried him with me everywhere, so that as I moved through a career, I could keep that dream alive—that dream of having him, of having children.

In yet another dream with the child, I was sitting with him on my lap, not far from an upstairs window, and he eagerly reached out for it; I understood that he thought he could fly, and wanted to fly out into the sky. In the dream, for some reason, I used all the languages in which I knew this single word to gently scold him: "No! Nein, nein! Non non! Nyet!" Later, as a small child in *real* life, Jonathan really did think he could fly, and that resulted in a stitched-up chin that he sports to this day. Thankfully, he tried flying off a short run of stairs and not out of a window!

In spite of my repeated dream-visions of this little boy, twelve years of no materialization is a very long time indeed, and in the end, I gave up all hope. Then one evening I was sitting in meditation and felt a strange energy current in my womb. A kind of vortex of gentle electric power. My mental antennae signaled *alert,* and the next day I headed for the drug store and bought an early pregnancy test. And so it was. The blonde, blue-eyed child was already nestled within me, and, after twelve years, I had only nine months more to wait.

What's That Noise?

During the nine months I carried Jonathan—the name meaning "Gift of God"—I had unusual experiences with music.

I had first performed as a singer when I was seven, and had gone on eventually to earn an undergraduate degree and master's degree in music. So I considered myself not only experienced in classical music, but deeply appreciative of its nuances and complexity.

Imagine, then, how I felt when I realized early in my pregnancy that I could hear music—any music at all—and understand intuitively the intent and thoughts of the composer; and that what I understood most often ran contrary to my training. I could hear if it was saturated with self-centered egocentricity, insistent pomposity, pure compassion, self-serving frivolity, profound inspiration, or colossal boredom. And on and on. I felt the composer's intent, his thoughts, and his emotions as they were infused into the music he wrote.

Of all the classical music repertoire that I knew, I now found that only perhaps 25 percent of it was worth listening to at all. The other 75 percent was spawned out of thoughts that were not worthy of being attended to. Imagine! It was a shocker. For example, I might be listening to an early Baroque concerto that had long been held high as a laudable example of the best of that period. The unbidden thought would come to my mind: "They expect me to listen to that *drivel*?" And I would turn the radio off. Unlistenable. Conversely, I might be listening to Mozart's Haffner Symphony and the joyous realization would explode in my mind—again, unbidden: "Genius! Pure genius!"

Years later, I confided this to Martha Beck as we sat at dinner following a Down syndrome conference in Shreveport, Louisiana. I remember vividly where we were, not only because of my sparkling visit with Martha, but because *alligator* was offered on the menu. (The off-menu alligators were still swimming in the lobby pond.) All in all, an unforgettable dinner. But I digress. I concluded my music-interpreting story with a somewhat careless, "And of course, after Jonathan was born, I lost that ability to hear so deeply." Martha looked at me attentively and asked, "*Did* you lose it?"

Her question startled me into introspection. "No…" I answered slowly. "No, I didn't. While I carried Jonathan, it came unbidden; now it's not as keen, but it's still there. If I stop and listen to what the music is actually saying, I do understand the composer's emotions and thoughts."

Martha smiled. She had already intuited that answer.

Early Puzzles

That musical experience was, of course, internal—perhaps a sharing of Jonathan's consciousness within me, an inner attunement which many mothers can experience when they relax meditatively and attune themselves to the child they are expecting.

I got my first external hint of Jonathan's extraordinary abilities when he was two years old. I had just tucked him and his baby sister into their carseats, placing Jonathan directly behind my high-backed driver's seat. As I reached for the ignition, I paused for a moment and silently prayed for our safety. When I finished my mental prayer and opened my eyes, Jonathan piped up from the back seat, "Amen!" I was stunned. How could he know what I was doing? Or know when I was *finished* doing what I was doing? He couldn't see either me or my face, and I had made no sound.

I learned early on that I had to watch my thoughts, because he could pick up on them if he wanted to. One day when he was seven, I cheerfully fixed his lunch. I had heavier things on my mind, but years as a performer left me with the skill of acting convincingly. Or so I thought. I smilingly served Jonathan his lunch in the dining room. "Now say your own grace, Buddy," I said, "while Mama's cooking in the kitchen." I returned to the kitchen and continued fixing lunch for the rest of the family, and heard Jonathan praying aloud. "Dear God, please help Mama to feel better. And bless the whole world, and all the poor people. Amen."

My jaw dropped open. I had shown nothing but the most upbeat attitude that day, though inwardly I was struggling with a discouraging situation. How did he *know*?

He's on Vacation

When Jonathan was four, we took him to see his absolute favorite children's musician in concert: Raffi. "'Affi" was one of the first words he spoke, and for weeks he had talked excitedly about going. The whole family was revved up for the performance, and we had great seats. As the concert began, two-year-old Rebecca was dancing in front of her seat and having a grand time. But the one who loved Raffi's music the most was sitting on his dad's lap in what seemed to be a semi-comatose condition. Jonathan's body was limp, his eyes open but dull, staring without seeming to see anything. He didn't move, didn't talk. He stayed in that condition for the entire concert, and only "came to" after it was completely over. Then he behaved normally.

His dad and I couldn't understand it. We were so disappointed; why hadn't he enjoyed the concert? We had gone because of *him*, and he didn't even seem to be conscious of the music!

At the time, I mentioned his perplexing behavior to an acquaintance of mine who knew Jonathan well and practiced alternative energy healing. "Oh," she answered gaily, "Jonathan felt that his body is so limited that he couldn't enjoy Raffi's music as completely as he wanted to; so when the concert started, he left his body energetically and enjoyed the music, free of his physical form. He had a wonderful time!"

"Aaah," I murmured. Outwardly polite, I choked inwardly. "Oh, *right*," I thought. "That's ridiculous." I mentally tagged her opinion as fanciful New Age delusion and let it go.

Not So Ridiculous After All

But many years later, I had an experience with Jonathan that changed my mind. He was sixteen, and I took him for a dreaded visit to a doctor who occasionally had to clear Jonathan's ears of wax. The procedure terrified him; no amount of soothing or handholding or reassurance could allay his fear.

This visit turned out to be particularly difficult. So that the doctor could do his work, a nurse held Jonathan's head firmly still while I grasped his hands tightly, kept my face close to his, and constantly reassured him. "It's okay, Jonathan, it's okay. It'll be all right. It's okay!"

It didn't help. He looked straight into my eyes the whole time, but screamed and struggled throughout the procedure. Afterward, we both needed to recover from the trauma. It was exhausting.

A couple of weeks later, Jonathan and I were having a quiet lunch at home. He broke a silence by saying shyly, "At Doctor Will's...I on ceiling...I look at me on table."

My eyes widened. *Surely* he didn't mean what I thought he meant.

I can guarantee that Jonathan has never read books on Near Death Experiences (NDEs) or otherworldly, voluntary out-of-body travel. At this age, he didn't watch TV—preferring well-worn Disney videos—and had no exposure to this kind of thinking. So there was nowhere he could have gotten this idea unless he had experienced it himself. Again, I was stunned.

I wanted to make sure I understood what he was saying, so I asked slowly, "Are you saying that when you were at Dr. Will's office getting your ears cleaned out, you floated up to the ceiling and looked down at your body on the table?"

His face relaxed into that relieved look he often shows when I finally understand something he's been struggling to say. "Yes."

"You were really scared, weren't you?"

"Yes," he said quietly, and fell back into silence. We finished lunch without talking while I tried to assimilate what he'd said. Jonathan does not fabricate stories; he's direct and incapable of pretense, so I believed him.

But how could he have done this while he was still conscious? He was howling the whole time. I thought you had to be medically dead to leave your body and hover above it, looking down at it as separate from yourself, as the many NDE experiences we read about describe. I didn't understand how he had done that.

Sometime later, I had an opportunity to talk with Martha Beck about this, and she confirmed that Adam, her son with Down syndrome, has done similar things, and that she believes many of our children are fully capable of doing this. After working with other children with Down syndrome who clearly can energetically leave their bodies when they choose—and have done it in front of my eyes—I now concur. I don't pretend to know *how* they do it or what they see and hear, but I suspect that more of them do this than not; we just don't know they're doing it.

It may be rather like taking a temporary vacation from their bodies. Sometimes to escape unpleasant situations, but perhaps sometimes just for fun.

Zoning Out or In the Zone?

A general guideline in this ethereal area that serves parents well is this: what you see is not always what's happening. If your child seems to go into that state of consciousness (variously described as "gone, not present, not showing up," etc.), you might ask yourself, what's *really* happening here?

We'll explore that idea more in depth in the chapter "The Non-Compliance Face-off," when we're looking at discipline and our attempts to understand why our children do what they do. When our children engage in actions that make no sense to us, it is often because they are trying to accommodate a physical or emotional need, a sensory deficiency, etc. The more we understand the "why" of it, the more effective we are in dealing with it and moving the child into a different behavior or response.

But does every unusual or puzzling behavior need to change? It depends. Right now, we're talking about our children's ability to access extraordinary states of awareness. So let's take a look, for example, at the habit of perseveration.

Perseveration is the apparently mindless repetition of certain movements, speech, ideas, etc., and is often seen in individuals with Down syndrome. On the surface, they can effectively "zone out" or take a break from their surroundings by doing this. Sometimes they can become unresponsive, unreachable. This state can seem impenetrable, and, for a parent, teacher, or therapist, wildly frustrating.

What's That?

Perseveration: Repetition of a particular response, such as a word, phrase, or gesture, even though nothing in the environment is stimulating that repetition.

So perseveration is bad, no?

It took me years to figure out what Jonathan's perseveration habit did for him. Now that I understand, the habit doesn't bother me anymore. So what's his perseveration habit? He buries his head in a book and very lightly touches the book in various spots repeatedly while he sucks on his tongue and practically stops breathing. Or does, in fact, temporarily stop breathing.

Of course, that sounds bizarre. Fortunately, at his current age, he rarely does it in public; if he does, he uses a modified version and no one seems to notice.

My first tip-off as to what he *actually* might be doing with this habit came when he was nine or ten. The family was watching a movie in which one of the characters occasionally did "self-talk" when upset. This character would go into a corner and do a therapist-patient dialogue with himself using two different voices.

Jonathan, who had refused to watch the movie (it wasn't Disney, which pretty much disqualified it for him), was two rooms away doing his suck-point-keep-head-down routine. He was out of earshot, and certainly out of the visual line of the TV.

When the movie was over, I told him it was time to wash up for dinner. He set up a howl. He didn't *want* to wash his hands. He wanted to keep reading his book. I was firm, and he objected loudly all the way to the bathroom. As soon as he closed the bathroom door, I heard the following conversation:

Crying, he said, "But I don't wanna wash my hands!"

Then, in a brusque voice, "Aw, snap out of it and wash your hands!"

Again weeping, "But I wanna read my book!"

Then gruffly, "Aw, get over it. You can't read your book now."

This self-dialogue continued for some time until he finished washing his hands and cheerfully exited the bathroom.

I was dumbfounded. Two rooms away from the TV, he somehow not only "heard" the dialogue but understood the nuances of what the man was modeling, and how to immediately apply it to his own life.

He understood and *perceived* at a significantly more advanced level than he typically could. How could he do this? I was still perplexed. And you will be, too, because your own child will repeatedly surprise you with advanced understanding as well, and I guarantee that it will always be unexpected and will always amaze, if not stun, you. I also guarantee that you will enjoy the experience.

I tried to understand how Jonathan had both heard and understood what was modeled in "the movie he didn't watch." He couldn't have actually heard what was going on in the movie, and he certainly couldn't have seen it from his position two rooms away. Does this type of perseveration in general enable him and other children with Down syndrome to be temporarily free of limitations and perceive their surroundings more acutely, from a higher overview? Do they use it to get themselves "in the zone," much like athletes do? Can they, in fact, float above their bodies and go where they like?

Yogis and other meditators call this "floating body" the astral body or the electrical/energetic body, essentially a body of light. Interestingly, physics now confirms that contrary to appearances, our bodies are not so solid after all. We are made of bundles of light and energy with lots and lots of space in between particles. But that's a topic for another book, and certainly not this one! Nevertheless, as this knowledge of physics, research, and understanding becomes more mainstream, it may explain how our children do this. I don't know how; I only know that they do it.

Waterfalls and Tunnels You Never Saw

The second tip-off as to how Jonathan used perseveration to attain a different state of perception came from a long trip he and I undertook to seek a specialized therapy we hoped could help his ADHD. It was wintertime, and the drive from Cincinnati to Virginia took us South into terrain totally different than our hometown's.

We passed frozen waterfalls cascading from fissures in rocky mountainsides. We drove through tunnel after tunnel as we passed through beautiful mountain ranges. I was thrilled and kept saying, "Oh, look, Jonathan! Look at the waterfalls and the tunnels!"

But he wouldn't look. He was nine years old and short, so without looking up, he couldn't see through the van window. His books on his lap, head tucked down, he was doing his suck-point routine. I was so frustrated. I couldn't believe it. Why wouldn't he look? Here we were, passing through amazing scenery like he had never seen in his life, and he wouldn't even lift his head!

Days later, when we arrived home, I was flabbergasted to hear him chatter to his dad enthusiastically about the frozen waterfalls and tunnels he had seen on the trip, and about how exciting it was and how beautiful.

At that point, the picture began to come into clearer focus for me.

Perhaps Jonathan uses this perseveration habit to change his energy, to push the "pause" button on his body, so that he can *really* "be here now." So that he can enjoy or perceive something without the limitations that his body and Down syndrome imposes. Perhaps he changes his state of consciousness skillfully, deliberately.

Now when I'm with him, I watch my thoughts. I realize that I don't know where his awareness really is (I don't *always* want him to read my mind), nor do I know what he's actually observing.

This skill is apparently not limited by distance. There have been other times, even when there are thousands of miles between us and we're talking on the phone, when I hear him pick up on and respond to my most silent thoughts.

If there is one major lesson our children have come to teach us, it is this: there is so much more to every human being than meets our eyes. Our children are able to perceive truths and realities that we, sitting right next to them, are blind and deaf to. So we would do well to be their students as well as their teachers. They have much to show us.

9

A Word about Doctors

"Diagnosis is not the end, but the beginning of practice."
—Martin H. Fischer, physician

The First Doctor

I have been incredibly lucky, blessed, and gifted with highly skilled doctors who have cared for Jonathan at one time or another. These doctors were not only experienced, but trusted their own intuitive core in treating my son. They have enriched my life and understanding.

My first remarkable encounter took place just hours after Jonathan squeezed his way into the world. Not knowing in advance about the diagnosis of Down syndrome, we had selected Dr. Weiss, a young neighborhood physician, to be Jon's pediatrician. Dr. Weiss shared a practice with his dad, who happened to be on hospital duty the day Jonathan was born. So it was the elder Dr. Weiss who showed up at the foot of my bed that day.

He entered my hospital room shortly after the staff broke the news of Down syndrome to me. Dr. Weiss had been around the medical block more times than he could count and was near retirement. He was a straight-shooter, and he aimed right for me.

"I have a number of young patients with Down syndrome," he began. "They're terrific." His chest puffed up a little and he smiled. "They call me 'Pop.'" Then he hit me with the real message: "Don't ever let anyone tell you what your son will or will not do. He could have the cognitive functioning of a two-year-old or a twenty-two-year-old. The sky's the limit."

Still reeling from fresh news of the diagnosis, I grasped and hung onto his every word. Determined to have a choice in the matter, I thought, "Okay, I'll take the twenty-two-year-old."

A Lid for Every Pot

So began the medical adventure of Down syndrome. I have very few horror stories, though a few are enough. But my work tutoring children with Down syndrome has brought me into close contact with many parents and their struggles or triumphs in finding a doctor who is a good fit for their child and themselves.

In some ways, times have changed since Jonathan was born, thankfully, but today I still see parents making the mistake of "settling" for a doctor who reads from a very different book than they do. My message to you is: don't settle. *Don't settle.* Did I say that already?

There is a best doctor for every family, "a lid for every pot." You just have to find the right fit. Don't give up until you do, because you'll need to rely on this doctor's help for years.

My own search took eight years. When I finally found the right doctor, my relief was palpable. I finally had a "team doctor," and I knew we would work together for Jonathan's best care. I absolutely trusted him, and nodded to his knowledge and experience when we were of different minds. This was especially important when I strayed too close to the cliff in my efforts to approach medical situations as naturally and noninvasively as possible. There were times when he had to rein me in; but I trusted him, and followed his best advice. There was mutual trust.

This is what you're going for: confidence in the doctor's knowledge, experience, and intuition; and mutual trust and respect.

"Sometimes I feel like *I'm* the doctor when I meet with my daughter's pediatrician," one young mother told me. If you find yourself thinking, as she and other parents have, "Who's the doctor here? *Me?*" you might want to weigh the strengths and weaknesses of your choice and consider putting out a new search.

Right Pot, Wrong Lid

As I mentioned in "Nurturing the Parent," the younger Dr. Weiss was a great help to me as Jonathan's pediatrician, but his hemophilia took him away after we had been with him only a few years. We switched to the elder Dr. Weiss until his retirement; then I had to search out a new pediatrician. I took the recommendation of a friend with two young typically developing children. Mistake number one! I was too new at the game to realize that I needed a doctor with special qualifications, namely a sensitive heart and knowledge of Down syndrome protocol.

My first visit to this new doctor was a shocker. As he examined my son, we heard a child crying in another examining room. "Another satisfied customer," he grumbled bitterly. Should I have gathered my child in my arms and skedaddled out the door pronto? Yes, of course. But I was new at this, too new to recognize a completely burned-out professional who was a poor fit for my son. So I stayed. After all, my girlfriend said he was a good doctor.

Then Jonathan—somehow—developed scarlet fever. I thought you had to go slumming with Charles Dickens to pick that up, but never mind. Here we were, and there he was. The doctor. He sat far across the room from me and the sick child I was cradling. The nurse started to move across the room to us, but the doctor barked, "Stay away! He has scarlet fever!" The nurse froze. I was stunned.

Somehow in the course of the visit, I managed to weakly suggest that I might want to try Homeopathic treatment as well, in an effort to help my child recover.

"If you don't do exactly as I say, you're outta here!" he said sharply. Needless to say, as soon as possible, I marched "outta there" for good.

How to Find the Right Doctor

Then I began my real search for a doctor. This time I asked other professionals I had grown to respect: physical therapists, occupational therapists, massage therapists, as well as friends whose children had similar issues and who traveled in the same open-minded medical circles as I did.

I also formulated a list of questions. I decided that, by George, I was entitled to interview the doctor and decide if *he* was worthy. I tried to turn around my mental construct and realize that the doctor would, after all, be my employee, and not the other way around. I had rights. So when I brought my children (by now there were two, and my daughter had developed chronic asthma) to a new doctor, I was on an Interview Mission.

With a list of questions on my lap, I began with, "How important to you is the mother's input into her child's condition?" Gutsy, I know, but why not start with a potential relationship deal-breaker?

His answer was sensitive; he valued the mother's input. The mother knows her child best, and he respected her insight as part of a holistic approach to healing the child. My "list" lasted for only a couple more questions, and then lay idly in my lap. There was no more need for it. I had found my doctor. We stayed with him for many years until he moved his practice to a holistic medical center that our insurance didn't support.

One more essential audition criterion when you're interviewing a doctor: pay close attention to your child's interaction with him or her, observing the energy on both sides. I watched to make sure the doctor was sensitive to Jonathan, and that Jonathan seemed to trust him. That was also a green light.

If you've found a doctor who's the right fit energetically for you and your child, but the doctor isn't up on current protocol for treatment of Down syndrome, no problem. As long as he's open to acquiring that knowledge, there are doctor-targeted videos, booklets, and books produced by various organizations and publishers.

You can get your hands on information by searching online (our Tool Box will get you started on your search) and personally deliver that cutting-edge information to your doctor. That's *your* job. You are the information interface between your child and the medical professionals who will help you for many years.

Sometimes It Goes Both Ways

On occasion, the tables might be turned and you may actually have a chance to make at least a small difference in a doctor's life.

- **Blueberry Shoes Productions:**
  www.blueberryshoes.com (producers of the DVD *Down Syndrome: The First 18 Months*)
- **Down Syndrome: Health Issues:**
  www.ds-health.com. "Health Care Guidelines for Individuals with Down Syndrome."
- **National Down Syndrome Congress (NDSC):**
  www.ndsccenter.org. (Click on "Informational Resources," then "Healthcare")
- **National Down Syndrome Society (NDSS):**
  www.ndss.org/index.php. (Click on "Healthcare," then "Information for Healthcare Professionals")
- **U.K. Down's Syndrome Medical Interest Group:**
  www.dsmig.org.uk. (Click on "Resources," then "Medical Resources.")
- **U.S. Down Syndrome Medical Interest Group:**
  www.dsmig-usa.org.
- **Woodbine House:** www.woodbinehouse.com (publishers of *The Guide to Good Health for Teens & Adults with Down Syndrome* by Drs. Brian Chicoine and Dennis McGuire).

When Jonathan was five, it was finally time to do the needed heart repair we knew was coming. I'll call the surgeon Dr. Bale. I had been warned early on by other parents who had walked the heart surgery path, "Dr. Bale has zero bedside manner, but when it comes to a doctor cutting into your child's heart, he's the one you want holding the scalpel."

So I had been warned, and didn't expect any smiles when I first met with Dr. Bale, and I wasn't disappointed. No smiles. His manner was quiet and efficient, contained. He gave good information, and I was trusting.

In 1989, heart repair of this kind was still done by open-heart surgery and involved sawing through the sternum and putting the child on a heart-lung machine. So this was no small deal, and I prayed my way through the hours of surgery. This was one of those critical times in life when the "unknown" you're dealing with is so far, so totally beyond any possible control of yours, that you have to let go. Even though I "let go" to the best of my ability and tried to focus on my belief that God would guide the surgeon's hand and the other many hands helping in the operation, the anxiety, of course, built as the hours passed.

When it was finally over and it was our turn to be the parents waiting in the doctor's consulting room, the wait in that isolated room seemed interminable.

Then the door opened, and quiet and contained Dr. Bale entered. He informed us that all had gone well, the repair was complete, and Jonathan was fine. For life.

The tension suddenly burst within me. I shot out of my chair, flew across the room, and threw my arms around him in a tight bear hug. Dr. Bale was startled, his eyes wide with surprise. Evidently this wasn't a typical response.

Then it happened. He smiled. Shyly, happily. When I met with him some weeks later for a follow-up consultation, he was already primed. When he gave me the good news that surgery results were exactly as hoped for, he was actually *grinning* before I even popped out of my chair. He knew what was coming, and he got it. Hugs were easy to give to this man, built like a teddy bear, and responsible for fixing my son's heart.

Seeing that doctor's last expectant grin embellished the already rich memory of seeing my son's heart repaired for life. I keep it tucked safely away in my mind.

Dentists

Let's get real. You know how much you and I look forward to going to the dentist. We love it, can't wait, mark the coming event with champagne glasses on our calendars. Yeah, right.

With a little imagination, we can empathetically surmise how our kids with Down syndrome feel about that very same experience. This is one introduction that has to be made slowly, carefully, and with love—the goal being lifelong cooperation with the guy/gal who's going to keep them chewing happily forever.

This is particularly challenging if the child has sensory issues. As in, "(*scream*) Don't touch my body with that thing!" issues. The great news is that there are dentists who specialize in working with our kids. My search led me to one at Cincinnati's Children's Hospital. His name was Dr. Dock, and I kid you not. Doc Dock.

Jonathan already had a gorilla-sized phobia about doctors in general (do I need to list the many encounters which led to this?). But going to the dentist was above and beyond his limits. Knowing this would be a potential mine field, I asked our trusted pediatrician for a recommendation. He knew Jonathan and he knew the medical community, and pointed us in the right direction. Once we found the gentle Dr. Dock, I heaved a huge sigh of relief. I could trust this man. He was loving, patient, and knew exactly what to do.

Jonathan refused to even come near the "big blue chair," much less recline in it, so we began our every-three-month sessions with Jonathan sitting in my lap and Dr. Dock doing what he could from that position. Of course, the standard start is to "count teeth," painless but still unacceptably invasive from Jonathan's point of view.

The most effective technique Dr. Dock used was to show Jonathan just one instrument (say, the mirror) and offer to let him hold it. That done, Dr. Dock would take the mirror instrument and stroke the back of Jonathan's hand lightly with it. A "this is how it feels" introduction. Then he would stroke it lightly along Jonathan's cheek, talking gently the whole way. The man was a saint. He did everything that way: in tiny, reassuring increments. It took time, but it worked.

Eventually, Jonathan did sit in the "big blue chair" and have his teeth cleaned by a dental assistant; but it took years. Patience and a great dentist are the key players in this game. We had an extra measure of a "perfect lid for the pot" in Dr. Dock: he was supportive of my efforts to use natural alternatives to control Jonathan's gum disease (gingivitis), which is sometimes encountered in Down syndrome.

When it comes to major work being done, as needed to happen when Jonathan was around ten, we elected to have it done under anesthesia. Then *all* the troops moved in…the guys who couldn't normally draw blood for annual thyroid tests (a moving target is hard to pierce), the folks who put tubes in the ears, and of course the dentist, who needed to remove a few extra teeth and do whatever else dentists need to do in that little mouth.

The really great news is that, for some reason, dental caries (cavities) are rare in individuals with Down syndrome. There. I've given you something to smile about today. No cavities.

Sayonara, Baby

His many early encounters with various doctors left Jonathan with a wary attitude toward the entire profession. Since new neighbors Sam and Kay were both doctors, I avoided any mention of this fact to eight-year-old Jonathan.

As a result, he enjoyed visiting them. One day, as we all sat relaxing in the sunshine, the couple gifted Jonathan and his little sister with child-sized folding chairs, cute and colorful. Jonathan was delighted and sat contentedly in the little chair next to the couple.

Somehow, through some ghastly indiscretion, someone mentioned that Sam and Kay were both *doctors*. Not missing a beat, Jonathan wordlessly got up, folded his chair, slung it over his arm, and marched home. End of visit.

But you notice he kept the chair.

10

Self-Talk

> *"If people with Down syndrome ruled the world, people engaged in self-talk would be considered thoughtful and creative. Self-talk rooms would be reserved in offices and libraries to encourage this practice."*
> —Dennis McGuire, PhD

Who's Talking Now?

What is self-talk? Talking to yourself. Our children, teens, and adults with Down syndrome use it with great effect to deal with various situations in their lives.

I think Dennis McGuire explains the real-life benefits of self-talk best. Dennis is a clinical social worker on staff at the Adult Down Syndrome Center in Park Ridge, Illinois. Dennis had this to say about self-talk in a speech entitled "What Would Happen If People with DS Ruled the World?"

Dennis explains, "People with Down syndrome have a reputation for 'talking to themselves.' When conducted in a private space, self-talk serves many adaptive purposes.

"It is a wonderful means to ponder ideas and to think out loud. It allows people to review events that occurred in the course of their day.

It allows people to solve problems by talking themselves through tasks. It allows them to plan for future situations. It is also helpful in allowing people to express feelings and frustrations, particularly if they have difficulty expressing their feelings to others."

So how about a real-life example? Here's a moment from my son's life. As a child, Jonathan had to take a dose of unsavory medicine one day, and this is what I overheard:

Jonathan: "Puh! I *hate* this medicine!"
Jonathan: "Calm yourself, Jonathan."
Jonathan: "No, I can't!"
Jonathan: "Just relax. It's fine."

Dennis continues tongue-in-cheek, "There is even evidence that athletes who do not have Down syndrome use self-talk to motivate themselves. Certainly people without Down syndrome talk to their computer (particularly when it crashes), and likewise many people talk out loud when driving in Chicago. (Of course they may also make odd gestures as well; not recommended if long life is one of your ambitions.)"

Exactly.

You can read the whole text of Dr. McGuire's speech at:
www.nads.org/pages_new/news/ruletheworld.html

And here is a fact sheet on self-talk from the National Down Syndrome Congress:
www.ndsccenter.org/resources/documents/self_talk_excerpts.php

If you want to read about self-talk and its many aspects, there is always Google for an interesting read. The one constant I have found in articles about self-talk is that it is usually harmless and can be a healthy processing tool for feelings. If you feel self-talk is becoming a problem for your child, you might want to read the book on mental wellness in adults with Down syndrome that Dr. McGuire co-authored with Dr. Brian Chicoine. You'll find tips there for helping teens and adults understand when and where it is appropriate to do self-talk, and guidelines for recognizing when there might be a problem.

■ *Mental Wellness in Adults with Down Syndrome* by Dr. Dennis McGuire and Dr. Brian Chicoine (Woodbine House, 2006).

Self-talk Is Comforting

One evening partway through his dinner, nine-year-old Jonathan brought his half-full supper plate into the kitchen.

"Seconds!" he demanded.

"Jonathan, you have plenty of food left on your plate," I said. "Finish your first serving, and then I'll give you a second helping."

"No! I want seconds *now*!"

This verbal tussle went on for some time, both of us absolutely refusing to budge from our positions. Being the taller and more intimidating of the two, I eventually won out and he trudged mournfully back to the dining room, half-full plate in hand.

Shaking his head, he murmured consolingly, "Poor Jonathan...poor little thing!"

Self-talk Is Therapeutic

In the chapter "Watch Your Language!" I will describe how Stephen, a young man processing great personal loss, used self-talk to help move through his grief. Within a short span of a couple of years, death removed Stephen's best friend, grandfather, and grandmother. Stephen had enormous difficulty dealing with his anger over these devastating losses.

In his case, he used the safety valve of profanity behind the privacy of his closed bedroom door. For obvious reasons, I'm not going to give you a sample of his self-talk, but it helped him move through the process and begin to heal.

Self-talk Is Hilarious

Fifteen-year-old Daniel is one of those rare students who has an unbridled enthusiasm for anything having to do with reading. That automatically puts him on my "preferred student" list.

But Daniel's speech is often not decodable by anyone except those closest to him. As seasoned as I am, I cannot usually understand his speech, unless he's reading aloud from a book, in which case I can.

However…

Recently, I was sitting across from Daniel during a reading session. I paused for a few minutes to create some new flashcards for him, leaving Daniel temporarily unoccupied.

Suddenly a look of surprise crossed his face. His "cell phone" was ringing (he doesn't have a cell phone). He reached into his "pocket" (he didn't have a pocket) and pulled out his "cell phone." Carefully flipping the phantom phone open, he pressed it to his ear and turned aside for some privacy.

"Hey, Baby. Wuz' up?"

"How you doin', Baby? You okay?" (polite pause.)

"Oh, fine. Good."

"Hmmmm? Oh, going out with my dad. Yeah, right."

Every single word was clearly and apparently effortlessly enunciated. It was all I could do not to double over. "Daniel," I finally interrupted with a straight face, "Tell her you have to go now. Your flashcards are ready."

To me, he responded, "Yeah, right…" then turning away to privately finish his conversation, "Okay, Baby. I gotta go. Okay?"

Apparently she said okay.

Daniel's father, Frank, recounts the day the family was driving in the car while Daniel was "talking" on a toy cell phone. Daniel stopped talking and asked his dad to "turn down the radio!" because he couldn't hear the person on the phone. Somehow it's very easy to play along with Daniel, and his dad respectfully turned the volume down while hiding his laughter.

Self-Talk Helps

Shawn's self-talk helps him to process his objections: for instance, his mom wanted to take him along to the grocery store and he didn't want to go, so he conferred with himself:

"I don't want to go. What do *you* think about going to the store?" (pause)

"You think it's okay?" (pause)

"But I don't want to go!" (pause)

"Oh, all right!"

Self-talk helps my son Jonathan "get with the program" when he doesn't really want to. One day I couldn't find a video that Jonathan had his heart set on watching. He was naturally upset with this change in plans, and went into the next room to try to work himself into crying. I'd seen this act before, and expected him to reach full-blow wailing. But instead, what I heard was:

"I'm so sad!"

"Oh, come on, it's going to be fine."

"But I'm so *sad*!"

"Just get over it."

This continued until he was perfectly fine and was able to move on.

Another day, I was having a hard time—as usual—getting a noncompliant Jonathan to go upstairs for his bath. "Jonathan," I yelled, "get your little feet on the stairs *now!*"

I heard him talking to himself.

"Oh, boy!"

"Okay, Jonathan, time to *move it!*"

And he hoofed it pronto up the stairs. I don't know what I'd do without that "self-talk helper."

Encouraging self-talk can be more effective than the most helpful adult. When Jonathan was ten, I overheard him struggling to get a difficult shoe on.

"I can't do it! It's too hard!"

"You *can* do it! You can!"

Then cheerfully, "Okay!" And he did.

I often hear my reading students tell themselves, "Good reading, Blair!"; "Good job, Makenna!"; "Awesome!" And of course they mean it with all their hearts. They are truly congratulating themselves.

What a terrific model for us to imitate. Imagine if we used self-talk to encourage ourselves: "Great job coping with your work day from hell! Wow, you *rock*. What a champ!" Imagine. We would all be heading to those "Self-Talk Rooms" in the employee's lounge, the dentist's office.... There could even be self-talk drive-through stations for people who drive in Chicago. Sign me up!

11

Read This: Literacy Is the New Norm

"Any book that helps a child to form a habit of reading,
to make reading one of his deep and continuing needs,
is good for him."
—Maya Angelou

Our Children Can Read

Help me onto my soapbox, please? Thanks ever so much.

And indulge me while I harp on my absolute favorite passion, which is teaching our kids with Down syndrome to read. Make that kids, teens, young adults, older adults, babies...have I left anyone out?

And that's the crux of it: we leave no one out. Nonverbal? Vision impaired? We can work this out. We *will* work this out.

One of my favorite quotes concerning reading and our kids is from Sue Buckley, founder of Down Syndrome Education International, which is based in the UK. She writes, "It is always too early to say that children, young people, or adults cannot learn to read....Children with Down syndrome can 'take off' with reading at any age."

From my experience teaching students ages 3 to 33, I agree. Sue adds, "Almost all children with Down syndrome are capable of reaching a level of reading achievement that will be functionally useful if we, their parents and teachers, believe that this is possible and steadily help them to progress."

Here's an important tip: "steadily" is the operative word here. I have seen too many cases where a child in the early years of elementary school is beginning to read, but somehow the ball is dropped and the child loses what reading ability he had. He becomes a teenager and still can't read. So what do I mean by "steadily?" It's pedal to the metal until reading fluency is achieved. If we stop before that point is reached, before the skill is solidly established, backsliding and loss of reading ability is inevitable.

If this has already happened to your child or teen, is it worth another try? You bet it is! In most cases, an impasse occurs because: (a) the progressing student loses the teacher who had him rocking and rolling, and the next teacher (and the next) didn't possess the tools to teach him, or (b) the child stopped progressing with the methods which at first worked well for him, and his teacher didn't know other methods to fall back on. In both cases, the unfortunate assumption typically made is: "He can't learn to read." Not fair! If you can't teach the child through the front door (the first method), you go in through the back door, the windows, the chimney… you get the picture.

The Reading Whisperer Gets Started

My passion for this work has led some of my students' parents to give me monikers such as "The Reading Whisperer" and "The Reading Guru," and I accept those affectionate gestures, but of course it's not true. What *is* true is that I believe that, as Sue Buckley said, almost all children with Down syndrome can learn to read. When there are multiple diagnoses involved, reading can get dicey, and in isolated, very challenging cases, reading may be quite limited; but I've seen too much success to immediately label anyone as unteachable when it comes to literacy. We just go for it, keep at it, and use best practice guidelines and interest-targeted materials…and a liberal serving of patience.

So how did I land on this soapbox?

Once I met a crazy man in a library. All right, he wasn't really crazy; I just thought his question was. He was the librarian, and when he saw me come in with five-year-old Jonathan who-clearly-had-Down-syndrome, he asked, "Can he read?"

This was 1990, so I hope you will pardon me for thinking what I was thinking. And what I was thinking was, "What is *this* guy thinking, anyway? The school system is going to take care of that…isn't it?"

Jonathan raced off in the direction of his favorite haunt, the children's book nook. I managed a weak, "Uh…noooo, he can't read."

His gaze nailed me. "Jonathan could read *today*. You only need to know the right methods. I can show you in five minutes, if you have the time." I didn't believe a word he said, but of course I had five minutes to donate to the remote possibility that I could teach Jonathan to read.

Greg Zarnecki, as he turned out to be, then explained patiently that he had a daughter who was globally delayed, had spent several years at a respected institution learning how to work with her, and did indeed know what he was talking about. Then he said something that would transform Jonathan's academic life.

"If Jonathan enters kindergarten already reading, the school system's expectations of him will skyrocket."

That hit me where I lived. And in the end, that's exactly what happened when Jonathan entered the school system already reading.

But back to the library. I was ready to listen. I spent much more than five minutes with Greg, learned what he wanted to teach me, and got to work with Jonathan.

I understood the method: start with sight words and very large homemade flash cards, initially done with red marker, red being visually appealing to most human brains, and especially to children's. Ask the kindergarten teacher who ordered 20 little red chairs for her classroom, only to have 10 blue and 10 red arrive. Was there a fight over the red chairs? You bet.

Next, I was directed to create simple homemade books. But what words to teach through those short books? I had a five-year-old ready to oppose me. The combination of Down syndrome, ADHD, and Oppositional Defiant Disorder is not your ideal combo for teaching. Teaching him "Run, Spot, run," was not going to cut it. I had to begin where he lived.

Spaghetti!

Homemade Books

That was it. I would begin with his favorite food, build a very short, funny book around that, maybe ten words max, teach him the words with oversized flashcards, and present him with the homemade book. So I did. Following Greg's instructions, I flashed the cards quickly and repeatedly, about one per second. In saying each word clearly to Jonathan as I flashed it, I tried to make my voice lively and interesting.

Two weeks later, after lively drilling with the oversized flashcards, Jonathan knew all the words cold. For the first time, I handed him the equally oversized book I'd made, "Spaghetti!" This five-year-old child with more challenges than most of us will ever face read it aloud, cover to cover, with no picture cues whatever until the last "reward" page. There is no way to measure the thrilled grin on his face afterward, or the depth of my astonishment.

This *worked.* Jonathan was reading! I was on fire, and made many more cards and books, all targeted to his life and interests. Jonathan learned word after word and read book after book, and his reading vocabulary exploded. The flashcards got smaller, the books got longer and more complex. My background as a graphic designer was serendipitous at this point; I gradually refined the format of these books, experimenting until I had a highly effective book design that worked. I saw that clarity, interest, and accessibility were requirements for the child; proof of reading ability was key for the teacher or parent.

For that latter reason, and to keep the child focused on the words themselves rather than pictures, I separated text pages from picture pages. In Jonathan's homemade books, the left-hand pages were always blank, and text was on the right page. When he turned the next page, he got the reward of a picture page. I *knew* he was actually reading, as did anyone watching him.

The View From Others' Eyes

Jonathan and I were intoxicated with reading, and many people were impressed, including one speech-language pathologist (SLP) whose reaction I'll never forget. Jonathan was five, and he and I were waiting for an appointment with his SLP. Meanwhile, the head SLP of the speech clinic came in and saw Jon sitting reading his homemade books aloud to me. She grabbed her tape recorder. "Do you mind if I record him? This is astonishing." Jonathan was more than happy to oblige, and as he read for the recorder, another SLP colleague came into the room and listened. The head therapist turned to her and said, "Have you *ever* seen anything like this?" Neither had. That was 1991. Today it's a very different story. Today, we expect a child of five with Down syndrome to have begun reading; but this was long ago and far away....

Guests visiting our home inevitably had to sit through several book readings until I could tactfully interrupt the little book hound and suggest that he could go play in his room now. On one such occasion, Jonathan had just finished reading for friends who were visiting us. As he scampered off to his room, homemade books tucked under his arm (they went everywhere with him), one of our guests turned to me. "I'm confused," she said. "I thought mental retardation came with Down syndrome."

She was confused? I was dumbfounded. She was saying in effect, "Jonathan reads well. Therefore he is not cognitively disabled. How can this be?"

I remembered Greg's initial comment about raised expectations, and an explosion illuminated my understanding. *This is how people will see my child now.* To describe this as an "Aha!" moment could never do it justice.

I have students who seem to be very "involved" with Down syndrome plus apraxia or plus autism or plus, plus—you name it. Yet when these children prove that "I can read!" even to a moderate degree, they gain higher respect from those who work with them, be they teachers, aides, or therapists. It's automatic. This is the way we humans are built.

The medical profession is included in this statement regarding giving higher respect. When Jonathan was six, I had a remarkable experience at Cincinnati's deservedly well-respected Children's Hospital Medical Center.

Jonathan was in for a medical test that required being still for an hour, while an attending nurse monitored various machines. I knew this ahead of time and came equipped with some of his homemade reading books. I held them so he could read them aloud as he lay on the table. We went through a number of them and then got to a new, more advanced one I'd made based on his school's visit to the zoo. Jon and I did lots of casual talking back and forth, typical for us.

After some time of silently watching us, the nurse asked, "Mom, do you homeschool?"

I was surprised at her question. "Yes."

"The doctor called me into the next room a few minutes ago and asked, 'Does he have Downs?'" I said, 'Yes, he does.' The doctor was incredulous and said, 'He is remarkably advanced. Remarkably.'"

The nurse continued, "He really is. We see a lot of kids with Down syndrome in here, and his development is remarkable. Especially things like his reading. But also the fact that he obviously understands everything we've said, and his ability to understand directions like, 'Lie on your back.' We don't see much of that in here. Remarkable. He really is."

That moment for me was an emotional payback, though I didn't feel I needed one. Reading was a rush for both Jonathan and me. And what about her comment that "he obviously understands everything we've said, and his ability to understand directions?" Many years later, research has proven that early reading helps to develop receptive language, working memory, and cognitive development in general. So it all makes sense.

Real Books, Please!

So far, Jonathan and I were cooking on all four burners. But creating the cards and books was time-consuming, and I wanted some help from the trade book industry. I went on a search for "real" books, books that we could segue into with little trouble. I wanted books with clarity, good spacing between words, text type that was simple ("sans serif" rather than "serif," which is harder to recognize), illustrations that were uncluttered and as easy to "read" as text should be.

Yeah, right. I was asking for my own personal genie. I found zero, zilch, and nada. I railed inwardly at publishers. Didn't they understand what kind of design helped a child's brain and visual pathway to connect with the book? To see, to read? What were they *thinking*, not producing books like that? In the end, I returned to creating Jonathan's books, and then moved on to modifying trade books on his favorite topics.

Modifying Books

After buying a book that I knew would fire his jets, I'd park at my computer with full-sheet labels from an office store. I condensed the text to suit his reading level, chose a simple font like Arial or Verdana, chose as large a type as would fit the page with the space available, double spaced between each word, and typed the new text. I cut that text from the label sheet and smoothed it onto the page to cover the original text.

This is the method I still use today with my students. This makes all the favorite or "hot topic" books that they love available to them as early reader books. The minute a new favorite movie hits the screen, I'm hounding stores looking for books marketed as "Early Readers" (which they're usually not) so that I can modify them for my students.

Which reminds me. Buyer Beware: When you're shopping for reading books for your child, *do not trust "Early Reader" books that say, "Step/Level 1, 2, or 3."* Reading levels in the trade book industry are not—I repeat, not—regulated, much to the frustration and confusion of parents. Trade book publishers can "grade" their books in any way they like. There is no bespectacled Quality Control Schoolmarm sitting in judgment yelling, "What, are you *crazy?* Level *one?* You publishers get back to your desks and get it right!"

I've seen trade book readers claiming to be Level 1 and they're closer to Level 4. So don't rely on the grading mark you see on the cover. Just look at the text and see if it matches your child's level: it should stretch her a bit, but not so far that she's frustrated.

The most reliable line of trade book "early readers" found in most bookstores is "Step Into Reading" by Random House: www.randomhouse.com/kids

Once you land there, do a search for "Step Into Reading." Depending on the reading level of your child, you may still have to modify the book, but you'll have a much better reading tool to start with.

A Reader Is Launched

After two and a half years of almost daily teaching, Jonathan's reading boat was launched. He was an independent reader, and continued natural development on his own. The week he turned seven, we had a multidisciplinary evaluation done at Cincinnati's Children's Hospital. Jonathan's symptoms of hyperactivity had become more than his dad and I could handle, and we knew it was time to have him evaluated and diagnosed.

While getting a firm diagnosis of ADHD was helpful, having a reading evaluation done was equally enlightening. That week of his seventh birthday, Jonathan was tested as reading at a typical seven-year-old level. The last time his reading was tested, in eighth grade, he read at approximately a seventh-grade level, with comprehension lagging behind at fourth grade level, which fits the typical picture for comprehension when special needs are involved. I was one happy mom.

And on the topic of launching a reader: do you know when a child is first nestled into that pre-reading boat? As soon after birth as is practical; that's when I recommend you start reading aloud to your child. Little readers are cultivated from birth by being read to, through exposure to the colors, images, and sounds of books being read aloud to them. The fact that they are cuddled on dad or mom's lap is a warm enhancement to this life-expanding experience.

Because of medical complications, I started reading aloud "late" (in my book) to Jonathan: he was three weeks old. We snuggled and read twice a day, and he was soon permanently hooked. I remember sitting on the porch one afternoon reading to six-month-old Jonathan; by that time, his attention could be riveted on books for as long as twenty minutes at a time. His little hands would caress the pages, and his eyes were mesmerized by the illustrations. He was so quiet and attentive, and a passing neighbor marveled: "How does a baby *that young* sit still for so long?"

Love. Love of books and being read to, of seeing a new world opened with each book, of being close to Mom or Dad. I recommend a mix of books: beautifully illustrated books; simple, easy-to-see books; funny books; serious books; books full of rhyme and rhythm. Is it ever too late to start reading aloud to your child? Of course not. You begin wherever you are. You are teaching many things when you read aloud to your child: language, grammar, concepts, ideas, experiences…the list is long and satisfying.

On to the Next Step

After Jonathan was reading fluently, reading became my passion, if it ever wasn't; I had been in love with books since I was a child. But more accurately, teaching our children with Down syndrome to read became my passion. I studied research and best practice and ardently followed the research and educational work of our enlightened sisters-across-the-pond, Down Syndrome Educational International, in Portsmouth, UK.

On the subject of educating children with Down syndrome, Down Syndrome Education International (Downs Ed for short) leads the pack. Their publications and books are packed with essential information on teaching reading, math, and writing, and their work is both research-and-practice based. One of my fantasies is to make a trip across the puddle and spend a week in their teaching center, just absorbing and loving what I see.

Here is the Down Syndrome Education International site: www.dseinternational.org
    Check out their "Down Syndrome Issues and Information Series" on education, development, adult living, and more.

You'll find tons of great information, especially the "Reading and Writing" Series. These and more are available at this site: www.down-syndrome.org/publications

For new parents, one book you will actually enjoy is the book I began this trek with, recommended to me by Greg, the "crazy librarian." The book is Glenn Doman's *How to Teach Your Baby to Read.* It just celebrated its fortieth anniversary and is going strong. I think this book (now in many languages) continues to garner praise because, quite simply, the method works. In addition to that, it's fun. Other methods and companies have spun off Doman's work, but this book is seminal and will take you far.

Another resource I recommend is Pat Oelwein's book, *Teaching Reading to Children with Down Syndrome.* By the time the book was published, Jonathan had been reading independently for several years, so I didn't need it. But I recommend it to parents, especially as a reference book. It explains how to use a sight-word reading method and includes help with teaching phonics, as well as many success stories, activities, and teaching materials (some on CD).

Years passed, and I began to speak to parent and educator groups across the country. Eventually I became a publisher and founded Special

Reads for Special Needs. Now I publish those reading books that I urgently needed and couldn't find twenty years ago, so that today's parents don't have to do what I did laboriously by hand.

Creating books for a child whose cherished interests I knew well was easy; but how to do that for a broad audience of children-teens-adults with Internet access? My solution was to build these reading books around the topic of favorite foods. Pizza, ice cream, macaroni and cheese…it worked. Once I was exhibiting at a Down Syndrome conference when a twenty-something man with Down syndrome passed by my booth with his mother. He saw my "I Want Pizza!" book and said to his mother, "I want that book!" She said, "But Stephen, you already *know* how to read. You don't need that book!" Stephen answered, "Yeah, but it's about pizza, so I want it!" I had to laugh.

- *How to Teach Your Baby to Read* by Glenn Doman: www.gentlerevolution.com
- *Special Reads for Special Needs* books and early reading materials: www.specialreads.com
- *Teaching Reading to Children with Down Syndrome* by Patricia Logan Oelwein: www.woodbinehouse.com

Reading "Phonetically"

Should you worry that if your child learns to read first by sight, that is, by "logographic reading," that she will have difficulty learning to read phonetically later? Will she have trouble decoding or sounding out words? Not at all.

Logographic reading is the natural first step not only for our children, but all children. I realize that this flies in the face of many school systems' curricula, which force teachers to teach "alphabetic reading" (learning to read by phonics) first, but it's the most natural beginning.

Some of our children with Down syndrome learn to read phonetically with no trouble whatever. Many others have difficulty, partly because of cognitive delays, and partly due to compromised hearing and recurring ear problems (requiring tubes, for example) which interfere with aural clarity. This can make learning phonics difficult and frustrating, because they can't actually discern the difference between subtle sounds.

What if your child can't or won't learn phonetically? Is alphabetic training and reading essential to get from logographic reading to orthographic (automatic) reading? As it turns out, the answer is no.

I particularly enjoyed reading a passage on that topic in Sue Buckley's books in the "Reading and Writing Series" (from Down Syndrome Education International) that I referenced earlier. She writes that some students with Down syndrome who are not able to learn alphabetically simply bypass that stage until it develops naturally with continued reading support, usually by the time the child's reading level reaches approximately a third-grade level.

I say I enjoyed reading that, because that's exactly what happened to Jonathan. I knew my son, his personality, and his hearing ability well, and I knew better than to try to teach him phonemic awareness. It would have so frustrated him that I would have lost my little reader. So I didn't. And sure enough, by the time he read fluently, decoding had naturally kicked in.

> ### *Reading Progression:*
> 1. Logographic reading (sight words): The child learns each word by recognizing its shape/characteristics (its logo) but does not yet understand that if b-a-t spells "bat," then m-a-t must spell "mat."
> 2. Alphabetic reading (phonetic decoding): The child understands what sounds each letter can make and can blend the sounds together to sound out new words. It should be noted that nondecodable words such as "know" and "thought" have to be learned logographically rather than alphabetically.
> 3. Orthographic reading (skilled automatic reading)

Phonics or Whole Language?

There is enough fodder in this quote from Wikipedia to start a gang war:

"Two contrasting beliefs for teaching beginning reading exist. Proponents of phonics argue that this relationship needs to be taught explicity and learned in order to automatically facilitate rapid word recognition.... Proponents of whole language approaches argue that reading should be taught holistically, and that children naturally intuit the relationship between letters and sounds…that any phonics instruction given should be embedded within a holistic approach, that is to say, through mini-lessons in the context of authentic reading and writing tasks."

I say "Do whatever works," while you keep in mind the guidelines I've given that point the way to effectively teach our children with Down syndrome.

I used the whole language approach with Jonathan, and it worked for that particular child, as it has for others. Now let's look at tiny Hailey, just four years old and starting to read. She's one of my reading students and, oddly enough, got a huge headstart in her reading life because she's a picky eater. Her mother, Bae, explains what happened when Hailey was about eighteen months old: "My husband and I had such a hard time getting Hailey to eat anything that even the smallest meal took a long, long time. Hailey didn't want to sit that long, so we handed her my iPhone to keep her occupied. We downloaded lots of pre-kindergarten educational apps and showed her the basics of how to use them. It worked for all of us: we got her to eat, and she learned all of the alphabet sounds—and much more—before she was two."

I've seen Hailey on her iPad (she's graduated to larger electronics), and if I ever need instruction on how to navigate my way through the many learning apps she now has, I should hire Hailey. Not everyone can fit an iPad into their budget, but it's a great item to save for. The explosion of education apps (and special education apps) is impressive: everyone wants to hop on the iPad bandwagon, and our kids can benefit hugely…from learning reading and math, to using it as a communication device when language is difficult.

Start Early and Keep Going Till You Hit Paydirt

Two bits of pithy reading advice I most love to pass on to parents are these:

First, start early.

Second, make a conscious choice: you can either keep the "pedal to the metal" for a few years until you reach success; or you can do the fitful by-starts-and-stops method for twenty years, with little success and a great deal of frustration for all, never quite reaching the goal. This latter situation is what I see far too often.

Here's a story of parents who followed both bits of advice: reading study started at age three, and has continued nonstop for nearly three years. Little Ava is one smart cookie; now seven, she's a good reader. Her mom, Amy, describes the moment the light got turned on.

"My husband, Sean, came excitedly out of three-year-old Ava's room one day after they had been reading together. "You'll never believe what Ava just did! She was on my lap enjoying the books we were reading. As I was reaching for another one, she glanced down at her little stool (which said "AVA"), then up at me and, plain as day, she signed 'A-V-A.' The bigger thing, though, was that she then pointed at herself. She signed 'Ava' and made the connection that it was her name. That 'Ava' was her.

"This was probably the biggest 'BINGO!' moment we'd had since she was born. She just read to us?! She's barely walking on her own, yet she's reading?

"We wanted to make sure. We pulled out another book, one that had one word (with no picture) on the first page, followed by another page with the same word coupled with a simple illustration. She had to identify the word first by itself. Well, right as rain, she signed at least 12 of the 15 words that were in the book. We kept going. And going and going and going….

"I didn't know how to proceed, and scoured the Internet for resources on teaching Ava. Special Reads for Special Needs was one of the resources I found. At the time, I had no idea that Natalie lived just a mile from my home. Once I discovered that, Ava began reading lessons and has been a regular student ever since.

"Ava's now seven with severely limited speech due to her Childhood Apraxia of Speech (CAS). But she reads like a champ! She entered kindergarten reading dozens and dozens of words. Because Ava is essentially nonverbal to the world around her, we are dedicated to constantly improving her reading—and now writing—abilities. The way we see it: if she can read and write, she's golden in this world. And she will continue to stun those around her."

The story continues: though by age six, Ava had excellent teachers in her Special Day Class, they underestimated her reading ability. In essence, they didn't know she could read past a few words. This easily happens when our children with Down syndrome are nonverbal. So Amy and Sean brought me in to meet with the staff. I gave them an abridged version of my "Reading Made Easy for Learners with Down Syndrome" presentation, and explained both how Ava could best learn and how she could be tested.

The receptive staff readily embraced the approach and set to work creating materials to teach Ava a new batch of a school-related words. Within a couple of weeks, Ava had learned them all, and the teachers were both thrilled and somewhat dismayed. Thrilled, obviously; why dismayed? Because the materials they'd created were now obsolete, relegated to a shelf somewhere, and they had to make more! It was a nice problem to have, and one they did not complain about.

The Orthographic Reader

And what about Jonathan? Today, he is 26, and he tells me he doesn't read books anymore. "Just computer and magazines, Mom, not books. Computer." That's his story, and he's sticking to it. I am secretly delighted. What he reads is his choice, and his spelling is excellent, which equips him well to fill one of his current job descriptions: Google Hound (focus: Disney and music of all kinds—from rock to opera).

Targeting the life interests of any learner is the fastest way to success; motivation is built in. That's why I applaud Maya Angelou's comment at the start of this chapter: *"Any book that helps a child to form a habit of reading, to make reading one of his deep and continuing needs, is good for him."*

I remember when Jonathan was in his early teens and our whole family went to see *The Lion King on Broadway,* which had finally come to Cincinnati. The show was terrific, of course, and as a special treat, I'd bought Jonathan the pricey program book to enjoy. Intermission came, and the rest of the family headed to the lobby to chow down on whatever we could stand in line for. "Jonathan, do you want to come with us?" I asked. His head was buried in the program book, and he refused. "No, I'll just stay here." "Okay," I said.

On the drive home after the show, the rest of the family was talking about how great the cast was. Blockheads that we were, we didn't memorize the actors' names, so had to refer to them by character name: "Wasn't the Mufasa terrific? And Scar was awesome, too...." At that point, Jonathan joined the conversation: "Yeah, Scar was played by Patrick Page. He also played the role of Lumiere on Broadway, in *Beauty and The Beast.*" Silence. His dad, sister, and I were stunned. While we had been guzzling our pop, Jonathan had been *studying the program.*

I now live in California, quite a distance from Jonathan's apartment near his dad's home in Cincinnati. We love Skyping to stay in touch between visits, but I don't often get a chance to see him actually read—other than watching him scan his computer files when he's *supposed* to be looking at the Skype window and paying attention to me, his Skyping mom.

But last year, on our annual trip to Disneyland, we stopped into a Disney mega-store (an "if we ain't got it, you don't want it" store) to shop for a CD or DVD Jonathan might like. Having amassed a sizeable CD/DVD collection by this time, Jonathan is a discerning shopper.

What happened next was a gift to me, a moment I fortunately didn't miss.

He selected a potential purchase and flipped it over to read the fine print. At that point, I completely lost his attention. My pestering mom questions ("Do you like that one, Jonathan? Is that the one you want?") didn't even register in his consciousness.

I watched his eyes. With intense attention, he was searching, scanning every bit of fine print on the jacket's back cover, and was so focused that he couldn't hear me. At that moment, I realized that his reading was automatic: for him, the *process* of reading had long ago become unconscious. All he cared about was the information in that fine print, and was sucking in every bit of it: *Who are the artists? What are the titles? Which movies or shows are the tracks from? How many tracks are there? How long are the tracks?*

His progression from logographic reader to alphabetic reader to orthographic reader was complete, and had been for a long time. That moment was a gift to me, a reminder of what a seasoned reader he is and of what an indispensable gift reading is to his life. A reminder of how effortless it is for him to absorb information in print.

He was reading like I do.

12

Your Personal Humor Coach

"Humor is the affectionate communication of insight."
—Leo Rosten

You Qualified

Did you ever wonder why you were given the distinction of being selected your child's parent? Of course you did. The answer (and I have this on high authority) is that your extraordinary sense of humor qualified you. It so qualified you that you were given a Personal Humor Coach. Your very own Fun Monger, your Hilarious Reality Checker, your On-Site Lighten Up Manager. I have one of my very own, and he's given me some of the best laughs of my life.

For many years, in my reading presentations to parent and educator groups, I often remarked that "Children with Down syndrome have a heightened sense of the ridiculous." I believed what I preached, because I'd experienced that truth for years with Jonathan, and knew that he wasn't the only one; I sensed that it was common to those with Down syndrome. So when I created my series of early reading books for our children, I always used humor, often ridiculous. I knew *they* would understand.

Imagine how stunned I was *years later* when I stumbled across a quote from Dr. Langdon Down, identifier of the syndrome, who said that in his opinion, "Individuals with Down syndrome have a lively sense of the ridiculous."

"Individuals with Down syndrome have a lively sense of the ridiculous."

"Children with Down syndrome have a heightened sense of the ridiculous."

Na-na-na-na, na-na-na-na (for those of you who remember the theme from "The Twilight Zone.") How did *that* happen? I have no idea; I'd never read any of Dr. Down's writings. But there it was. Perhaps the explanation is that truth is truth, and I happened to pick up on it.

Beethoven's Joke

A violinist friend of mine once told me a fascinating story. She belonged to a professional orchestra that occasionally did benefit concerts. Once, they were performing at a benefit for adults with mental disabilities, most of whom had Down syndrome. During the concert, those adults sat up front in the seats of honor.

On the concert program was a movement from Beethoven's Symphony Number 8, which contained a hidden musical joke. The orchestra had performed this piece many times, and never had a moment's reaction from any audience. Ho-hum. But on this occasion, as the orchestra played the passage containing what classical connoisseurs consider a musical joke, that special section of the audience erupted with laughter.

The musicians were absolutely stunned. *How* could these individuals get that sophisticated musical joke, when it went right over the heads of their ordinary audiences? My violinist friend never forgot that experience.

I can't answer that question except to quote both myself and Dr. Down: they totally get "ridiculosity" and think it's absolutely hilarious. They enjoy living there and viewing the world from that perspective whenever possible. And they can do it with a sophistication that is disarming because it is so totally unexpected.

Training the Parents

In Disney's movie *Toy Story 1,* there is a scene in which the hero, Woody, tries to calm the anxious toys who are dashing about in a frenzy of worry over their latest disaster. Woody tells the toys, "Save your batteries!"

For months afterward, whenever I switched into "Mom Manager Mode" and barked orders at Jonathan—*collect the trash! clean up your room!*—he would instruct dryly, "Aw, Mom, save your batteries."

At age twenty, he would drive me crazy in the car punching the radio buttons in one-second sound bites, looking for music he approved of. *Punch–punch–punch.* The problem was, he could do this forever without ever making a choice.

When I couldn't stand it anymore, I said, "Jonathan! You're driving me crazy. Pick a station—I don't care which station—just pick one!"

Without missing a beat, *punch–punch–punch*–he said dryly, "Just relax and watch the traffic."

Another phrase he frequently threw my way when I objected to his behavior was, "Just ignore it." As if he were the counselor and I the patient.

Which brings me to the truth of the matter: *he* is so often the teacher. Over and over again. The truth is that I *should* have been watching the traffic instead of scolding him. The truth is that I could have saved my batteries by being more relaxed instead of barking orders at him.

At the start of this chapter, I quoted Leo Rosten, "Humor is the affectionate communication of insight." And that is exactly what our children so frequently do for us: give us their insight, affectionately clothed in humor.

So maybe I should "just ignore it" more. Unless, of course, he overdoes the parental instruction. He went through a phase of saying, "Don't worry about it!" whenever a parental unit issued instructions which didn't appeal to him. One night, his dad told him, "You say that too much, Jonathan; too much 'Don't worry about it!'" His sister Becca and I were also in the room at the time, and in response to his dad's comment, Jonathan looked each of the three of us in the eye and pointed to each one in turn: "Don't worry about it!…Don't worry about it!…Don't worry about it!"

Pulling the Wool Over

My friend Martha took her then-eighteen-year-old son Blair to a government office to apply for Supplemental Security Income (SSI). Somehow Blair totally understood that he was being screened to make sure he qualified for SSI support: he needed to "prove" that he was disabled enough to qualify for a monthly government support check. Blair is sharp and extremely social, so this would be a piece of cake, and Martha knew he would of course cooperate. He sat across the table from the woman whose job it was to interview him, ready to answer the typical battery of simple questions. Martha sat beside him.

"What's your name?" the interviewer asked.

"Uhhh…."

"How old are you?"

"Uhhh…."

"Do you know your address?"

"Uhhh…."

Martha was dumbfounded: "He was just about comatose by the time the interview ended. I couldn't understand it." Needless to say, Blair failed competency with flying colors and qualified for SSI. As soon as they'd left the interviewer's office, he elbowed his mom. "*So,*" he said, eyes twinkling. "How'd I do?" and started laughing. His mom's jaw dropped. She whispered, "You *stinker!*"

Occasionally, if Martha scolds him for something he has or hasn't done, he'll say in the most condescending tone he can muster, "Mom, you have to realize that I have Down syndrome." Martha retorts, "Don't even *try* to pull that card on me, Blair." He laughs.

The Movie Star

Brandon has been involved in theater since he was six, and loves the experience. He also has a girlfriend, and he loves that experience, too. Recently his mother, Teresa, told me that she'd just gotten a call from the vice principal of Brandon's school. Trying not to laugh, the VP said, "Hi, Teresa. I had a little talk today with Brandon, to discuss not displaying affection on campus because it goes against the student code."

"Do you know what he told me? He said that rule doesn't apply to him because he's a movie star. I told him, 'You may be a movie star, but at school it breaks the code of conduct.' I pulled out the handbook and had him read that section; after reading it, he hung his head. Then he brightened up and asked, 'What about *after* school? What if we're off campus?' Without waiting for my answer, he put his finger up as if to say 'hold that thought' but said instead, 'Let me think about it and I'll get back to you'—as if his agent will let my lawyer know his answer!"

The vice principal laughed and added, "The next time I get in trouble with my boss, the Superintendent, I'm going to use Brandon's line: 'That rule doesn't apply to me because I'm a movie star.'"

Not at the Table

Jonathan was raised not only with an appreciation of classical music, but with a deep love of orchestral instruments. I once succeeded in training him to stay in his seat on the school bus by promising him a really cool laminated picture of one orchestral instrument each time he arrived home still in his bus seat. It worked. And by grade school, he knew not only the instruments of the orchestra, but the individual parts: the mouthpiece, bell, and reed of the oboe, for example. He loved listening to classical music and identifying the instruments he heard playing: "That's the flute…now the cello…."

One evening at the dinner table, Jonathan passed gas quite loudly. His dad and I had trained him to say, "Excuse me," of course. But that night, he didn't. He cocked his head as if in deep thought and said, "Sounds like a bass clarinet."

When the family had partially recovered from being doubled over, I countered, "How about a double bassoon, Buddy?"

"Nope," he said. "Bass clarinet." Well, he knows his instruments, so I'm not about to argue with that.

The Negotiator

Ben is ten. At his first Cub Scout Leadership camp, his leader warned Ben to "behave today." Ben agreed to this and did behave, but in the evening, he began to act up.

"Ben," protested the leader, "You said you'd behave today!"

Matter-of-factly, Ben illuminated the leader: "It's night time now."

And we sometimes think they don't know *exactly* what they're doing?! One evening as his mom was cooking dinner, Ben asked her, "Can you help me play Legos after dinner?"

"Maybe," said his mom.

"*Don't* say 'maybe'!"

"Okay," said his mom, "'*NO*' then."

"Okay, then you can say 'maybe'."

Peter Pan and Santa Claus

When Jonathan was seven, it was the height of my "time out discipline" application, which of course he disliked enormously. One day as I put him in time out, he said, "*No* time out! You put me time out, I get lost...fly up in sky like Peter Pan. Come back in four weeks." (Maybe in four weeks I'd have forgotten his transgressions and would welcome him back warmly.)

One Christmastime, trying many ploys to get Jonathan to be obedient, I said, "Santa Claus won't bring you any presents unless you're good." To which he replied, "No problem. God's friends will bring me *lots* of presents."

Talk about friends in high places.

Wrong Drum

One morning when Jonathan was nine, I was helping him make up his bed. Sharing the space in his bedroom was a full drum set, which he played for hours each day. As I leaned across the bed to straighten the sheet, Jonathan whacked me on the bottom with both hands. "Are you *spanking* me?" I was surprised. "No," he said, "no spanking. It's a *drum.*" We laughed and talked about the incident for a while, and then he chuckled and said, "Right place, wrong thing."

Good Idea

Shawn, ten, is one of my reading students. He was keen on a couple of reading books I had that were part of a series of four; but I had purchased only two. Shawn could see by the back cover that there were several more in the series, and kept asking me to get them. He was persistent, so one day, to put off the question yet again, I said, "Well, I don't know, Shawn. I'll have to see if I can buy them."

To which he offered thoughtfully, "Check with your parents."

I should be flattered that he thinks I'm young enough to still get allowance from my parents…or that I'm young enough to still *have* parents!

Bugs Bunny

Some of us remember learning our first classical music at the revered feet of Bugs Bunny cartoons. There's the famous *Barber of Seville* overture where Bugs gives Porky Pig a head shave; Bugs again as the dying opera diva in *Die Walkure,* etc. Jonathan grew up knowing and loving those classic cartoons. His dad, Kelly, now retired, was a professor of opera then, and one evening I brought both kids along to one of the opera concerts their dad was conducting.

I didn't mention to Jonathan, then nine, that Rossini's *Barber of Seville* overture was on the program. It didn't occur to me. But as his dad lifted the conductor's baton and gave the downbeat, with the very first musical phrase, Jonathan cried out, "Oh, Bugs Bunny! Oh, my *goodness*!"

That was pretty much the top of the audience's entertainment for the evening, as Jonathan's outcry came—of course—at a rare moment of silent pause in the musical phrase.

From the time Jonathan could use language effectively, he has disarmed me and doubled me over with his unexpected one-liners. I know many parents who can say the same thing. It's an unexpected and fun part of the Down syndrome ride, so fasten your seatbelts and prep your funnybone. You're in for it!

Discipline Years

13

Born to Rule

"No! Not a month! My birthday's coming in a week,
and you don't have a choice!"
—Jonathan Hale, 10

It's My Mission

Toddler: "No!"
School age: "I don't wanna!"
Teens: "In your dreams, Mom."

The expression varies with age and development, but the message is the same: *I am not going to do what you want me to do because I don't want to do it and that's the end of the subject so get out of my life.*

Children with Down syndrome, it is my belief, enter this world with the firm determination that *they will be in charge.* As Jonathan flatly countered when I tried to redirect his questionable choices, "It's my mission." What can you say in the face of such dedication, such vision?

Not so fast, Dude.

Since my son came packaged with not only Down syndrome but with ODD and ADHD as well, I have had the privilege of amassing vast experience in the field of noncompliance.

What's That?

ODD (Oppositional Defiant Disorder): A behavior disorder characterized by pervasive resistance to direction or authority; not to be confused with stubbornness!

ADHD (Attention Deficit Hyperactivity Disorder): A developmental disorder that causes difficulties focusing and sustaining attention, hyperactivity, or both, with symptoms starting before the age of seven.

The first word Jonathan spoke as a twenty-month-old was "NO!" It was his very first utterance. Clear and unmistakable. Should I have been alerted that this might possibly portend dire warnings for future interactions? Should I have intuitively understood the multilayered nuances of this word and shielded myself for the grueling battles ahead?

Naw.

I was utterly charmed because my child was *talking*.

Flop and Drop = Grab and Drag

I see so many parents struggle with the exact scenario I faced for years. As long as the child is small enough for the parent to simply "grab and drag" the self-determined one on to the next scheduled event of the day, things can rock along somewhat steadily for *years*.

This is called denial. This is called avoidance. It is also called survival.

So here's what we're dealing with: From the moment of diagnosis, this child was dragged where he didn't want to be dragged, made to do what he didn't want to do, made to move his body in ways it sure as heck didn't feel like moving, made to attend, to repeat, and to comply, ad infinitum.

What he of course wants to do at this point is gain control. Like you and me, he wants to run his life, make choices that suit him, feel comfortable in his surroundings, and call the shots in life. Well, guess what? At some point, he will figure out that he can't. This is not good news, and flies squarely in the face of The Mission with which he entered this whole scene. Imagine.

So now our little visionary moves on to Plan B. This plan is commonly known as "flop and drop," and there is not an experienced parent reading this who doesn't know what I'm talking about.

Having the amazing ability to temporarily double their body weight, our children simply flop heavily onto the floor. Thirty pounds of weight morphs into sixty pounds instantly like the flick of a light switch. Mom or Dad then has to bench-press these weights from the floor to their chests and waddle away awkwardly because there are now two extraneous legs dangling perilously between their own. "Flop and drop" requires "grab and drag." Trust me. I've seen this.

Hold that picture in your mind for the moment, and let's move on to the parent's dilemma. "Flop and drop" notwithstanding, the parent *must* continue to run the household and family from event to event, from appointment to appointment, also ad infinitum. There are no options here; the parent must meet these scheduling deadlines, many of which are necessitated by the *very* fact that this child has the diagnosis of Down syndrome. How crazy-making a conundrum is that?

Two Goals

Let's hit the drawing board with this one. We need a selection of solutions that accomplish two things:

1. Enable the child to feel more empowered, yet
2. Place the parent firmly in charge.

In the next chapter, we'll look at a smorgasbord of options for making sure we attain Goal #2, placing the parent firmly in charge. But first, let's get a deeper understanding of factors that inform this situation; if we can do that, we can begin to shift a few paradigms.

Giving the Child Empowerment

To begin with, offering your child control in areas that are negotiable is *primo*. What does that mean? It means go out of your way to think of small areas in which your child can make an empowering choice. In the course of a day, conjure up and put in place as many of these as you can. For each child this varies widely, depending on what floats his or her boat.

"Honey, do you want to wear your blue jeans today? Or do you want your black leather pants with the chains instead? You choose."

"What do you want to drink with your breakfast? Milk or bourbon?"

"What do you want to do first right now? Go slumming or clean your room?"

Okay, I'm stretching the point, but you get where I'm going with this. We have to create these opportunities for choices; think it through, and you'll find small negotiable islands during the day that will work for both you *and* your child.

It's most effective to make these options a visual choice whenever possible. Our children with Down syndrome are usually strong visual learners, and seeing a visual cue can make all the difference for them. Giving them the abstract choice between blue jeans and black pants is one thing; laying out both on the bed is a different story.

Not only does that give the child a strong visual cue; even more importantly, it moves the focus off the parent and onto the choices. This is critical. Of necessity, we boss our children around all day and evening. By making a choice visual, we put the focus on the choice, not the demanding overseer.

The Respect Factor

Hand in hand with this gift of power and choice that we give to the child are the inherent gifts of respect, sincerity, and even admiration for the child's choices. What do I mean by that?

I mean that we're not patronizing him, pretending, and patting him on the head for pseudo-choices. We're giving him real choices, to prepare him for the lifelong job of making good choices. So we attend as he makes those decisions; we respect them, and even express a sincere admiration for those decisions when it's merited.

Get Out the Microscope

Let's take a closer look into the heart of the matter. Why does noncompliance seem to be common in individuals with Down syndrome? Well, why not?

From the time my son was six weeks old, he was in school. His body and mind were pushed this way and that way: "*Do this! Do that!* Do it *my* way. Yeah, it hurts, but it's for your own good. Learn this *now*." He cried. I cried.

Who in his right mind would not want to resist? For our children with Down syndrome, these experiences typically come early and heavy. I confess: I still have trouble forgiving one of Jonathan's first therapists in the world of acronyms: PT, OT, and SLP for starters. I was new to this game of Therapy-Go-Round, and sat meekly by as the expert did her work.

As my two-year-old sat struggling unsuccessfully to fit wooden puzzle pieces into their proper slots (he has poor fine motor, remember?), the therapist sniffed disapprovingly. "He should be able to do this by now." Oh, give me a break. Who spit in *her* coffee?

A few months later, the heavens themselves opened and we found a new physical therapist. Donna Lilley was a Zen-like guide who saw what others couldn't, and didn't move to action until she had first observed and absorbed.

What's That?

PT (Physical Therapist): A healthcare professional who diagnoses and treats individuals of all ages, from newborns to the elderly, who have medical or health-related conditions which limit their ability to move and perform functional activities. Typically, PTs focus on improving gross motor skills, such as walking, sitting, jumping.

OT (Occupational Therapist): A specialist who helps individuals participate in needed activities through the therapeutic use of everyday activities; the work of an OT includes helping children with disabilities to participate fully in school and social situations. Typically, OTs focus on improving fine motor skills, such as using a fork or scissors, writing, or tying shoes.

SLP (Speech-Language Pathologist) or speech therapist is a specialist who evaluates and treats communication disorders and may also help with feeding skills.

It was from Donna that I learned that there was always a good reason for Jonathan's variant actions. Or the actions of any child with a disability. She dangles keys in front of her face? He sits with a book and repeatedly touches a certain spot on the page? She runs adoringly after humming vacuum cleaners? Well, *why*?

The wisest of parents, therapists, and educators understand that when children exhibit behaviors outside the norm of their diagnosis, it is because they are acting instinctively to accommodate a need of some kind, to compensate for an imbalance or discomfort in their bodies. In addition to pursuing the normal intervention strategies for your child, ask yourself thoughtfully, "What is it *doing* for him?" I learned from this outstanding physical therapist that, whatever the objectionable or strange behavior, it serves the child in some way; otherwise, the child wouldn't be driven to do it automatically.

That is not to say we won't intervene. Of course we will.

But we will also try to understand *why*—first, last, and all along the way. Understanding why the child does what he does helps us to determine an informed plan of action to move him into a different behavior, while meeting whatever needs drove him to that action in the first place.

In Donna's case, she had not only an intuitive gift, but also the technical training to apply subtle physical adjustments to Jonathan's body. That helped give him what his body needed, and he could move more easily through the behavior. Rather than the rough "Bend this way! Move your leg this way!" approach Jonathan had first experienced, Donna's subtle, knowing touch and movement was easily accepted by both his psyche and body, and amazingly effective. To this day, I am grateful for her.

And while you're going through those "PT years" (they don't last forever), you might find those sessions a blessing in unexpected ways. That happened to our family. My daughter Rebecca suffered from colic as an infant; the only thing that made her stop crying—and actually smile—was letting her stand on my lap while I supported her under the arms. I did that from the time she was six weeks old. By the time she was three months old, I realized to my alarm that her little feet were permanently splayed outward; her little bones had been too soft to support any of her standing weight at just six weeks of age, and now her feet turned outward all the time.

I brought her in a panic to Donna, who was of course calm. "Take her out of every contraption. No walker, no swing, nothing. Put her on the floor and let her do everything herself. Don't even help her into a sitting position.

Let her body do all of the natural movements on its own. As she moves and plays, her bones will correct themselves and her feet will develop normally."

And they did. Thank you, Donna, and all extraordinary PTs who go that extra intuitive mile.

Applying Acceptance

In walking the rocky noncompliance road, I also learned acceptance. This goes a long way in dealing with noncompliance. It takes the edge off for the parent, which is a gift that cannot possibly be overvalued.

When Jonathan was eighteen months old and I was seven-months-great-with-next-child, his dad, Kelly, and I hauled him across the country to spend a week at a progressive training institute. The institute was geared toward children with autism, but worked with many disabilities. I thought they would train us to work with Jonathan. I did not expect them to work on *me* as well.

I mean, what adjustment did my attitude need, anyway? But having plunked down the big bucks to do this, I had no choice but to go with the program.

In that long and extraordinary week, I learned to accept the moment and support my child through it, always with an eye to the next moment, but always with acceptance of the *now*. To accept and move *with* my child, not to act as an outside force pushing and pulling my child from point A to point B.

At that time, Jonathan used a highly effective avoidance tactic, honed from his days of being coerced by total strangers to do nearly impossible tasks. The tactic? Don't show up.

When I sat with him on the floor to teach him anything, he simply went away mentally, totally and effectively. To him, I was as invisible as the colored blocks I was coaching him to stack.

Needing a *modus operandi* to help get him "gone," he hit upon a handy perseveration tool. He'd stick one finger in a hole—any hole, anywhere, any slight indentation in anything—and suck fiercely on his tongue. Forever.

Gone. No Jonathan. I tried to move him out of this trance-like state, with zero success.

But at the institute, I learned first to accept this behavior as being something Jonathan clearly wanted to do, and, perhaps for some reason obscure to me, *needed* to do. There I learned to good-naturedly *join* him in a nondestructive—though apparently useless—activity. Joining led eventually to moving out of that activity.

The point was that I was accepting him; the theory was that if this acceptance was coupled with my own desire to move him through it in whatever way he was willing to allow, it could do just that. And it did.

After that, whenever I was teaching Jonathan anything and he opted out for the nearest hole or indentation in anything, I dropped teaching and joined him. I learned to do this with enthusiasm and no judgment. Naturally, I did not usurp his hole; respect was part of the deal, so I had to find my own hole to poke.

A most unexpected thing happened. He snapped out of the trance in an instant.

"No! Stop!" he protested.

"But I *like* it!" I protested equally.

"No!"

Within seconds, we were back to the task at hand. This was a powerful lesson in learning to become the breeze beneath my child's wings, of moving in softly under the radar to join in his energy, lift him out of it, and move him on. He soon made the decision to always show up, and learning took off.

In the beginning, I had no idea that this accepting attitude would work; it meant a significant paradigm shift for me. I was willing to try it only because I trusted the founders of the institute, who had moved their son fully out of autism by applying methods that included this approach. In the end, I was wowed by the results, and recommend it without reservation. It can form an underlying cushion of safety for both you and your child, and at the very least is a fascinating experiment.

Ready, Get Set, Go!

Without even taking into account the powerful impact of personality—which I believe is refreshingly larger-than-life in many of our children—I hope this chapter has helped you understand more about the underlying setups which might incline our children to be not only stubborn, but noncompliant.

With this chapter solidly imbedded in your parenting DNA, let's move on to the next chapter and look at practical methods for shaping these born rulers into team members.

14

The Noncompliance Face-off

"You can learn many things from children.
How much patience you have, for instance."
—Franklin P. Jones, Humorist

Okay now, gird your loins. Loins, not lions. This was a practice in ancient Rome of drawing up and tying your tunic so you could run faster and trip less. Be prepared for battle, don't you know. Well, guess what? It's time to gird your loins.

You've been prepped with the "Born to Rule" chapter. Now let's get serious and look at various tools for reaching the compliance goal of your dreams.

From the gentle to the tough, here we go.

The Fantasy Pause

If we can get our children down off their stubbornly high horses for a moment and move them to that sweet spot of feeling listened to and supported, we can work with them much more easily.

This first approach looks like a powder puff, but I have two words for you: try it. This fantasy pause is a technique I learned from Faber and

■ *How To Talk So Kids Will Listen And Listen So Kids Will Talk* by Adele Faber and Elaine Mazlish. New York, NY: Harper Books, 1999.
Faber and Mazlish have some savvy ideas (that actually work) for parent/child communication. Available from most brick-and-mortar and online bookstores.

Mazlish's book, *How to Talk So Kids Will Listen and Listen So Kids Will Talk*. I recommend it for parenting of any kind.

Here's an example of how the fantasy pause works. Years ago, Jonathan was howling that he wanted to go see *The Little Mermaid* in the movie theater. He wanted to see it NOW. He did not want to wait until Saturday, when we planned to go. My attempts at reasoning were futile, and his crying escalated. I was studying Faber and Mazlish's book at the time, so I decided to try one of the techniques. I sat on the floor by his side and, conspirator-like, I began to fantasize.

"Wouldn't it be great," I confided, "if we could go to see *The Little Mermaid* RIGHT NOW?" He stopped crying, totally attentive. "Oh boy, we could get seats close up where we could see really great. We could get popcorn and have a blast. Wow, it would be awesome. It's too bad we can't go today. What a disappointment. It would have been so much fun."

Then I sat there with him, silently *together* mourning the loss of an immediate viewing of *The Little Mermaid*. Slowly he concurred, "Yeaaaah." With a sigh, we moved on with our day.

What happened? I listened to him. I heard him, and I let him know it. I think it surprised him at first as it dawned on him, "She gets it. She gets *me*." I sympathized with him, mourned his loss with him. I didn't demand. We sat in silent understanding for a while, then we moved on together.

The Mature Version

This approach evolves as the child matures, but continues to be effective as long as it's done sincerely. Fast-forward twenty years or so for a moment. Recently, I was chatting on the phone with Jonathan about this and that. He switched the topic to his current disappointment: the three

CDs I had burned and sent him in the mail had *not* arrived on the day that the United States Postal Service swore that they would.

So he was facing a weekend without the new music he'd been counting on enjoying. There were some in-between years when I would typically have responded, "Oh, honey, I'm so sorry the CDs didn't come Friday," and I would add something therapeutic such as, "You must be really disappointed." He characteristically responded well to that; but at this point in time, I was an adult talking to an adult, and I moved into a different position:

"*Well*," I said, "*that's* a bummer!"

To which he replied, "*Yeah*!!" As of old, we sat awhile in comfortable silence. Then I said, "Geeze. Maybe they'll get to you on Monday, huh?" And our conversation continued along those lines; he moved on with no discomfort.

The difference here, when you move into an adult-to-adult conversation, is that you're not a parent sitting across from your child. Instead, you hop on their train, sit beside them, and look at the passing scenery from their point of view: "Well, *that's* a bummer!" You're just two adults looking at an event with the same eyes, the same sincere understanding. This is both comfortable and affirming to them.

One of my favorite quotes I've kept for years—and I apologize to the author, whose name I neglected to write down at the time—is this: "What people of all ages can use in a moment of distress is not agreement or disagreement; they need someone to recognize what it is they're experiencing."

Walk the Honesty Walk

Nearly every parent, profoundly well-intended, starts out training his or her recalcitrant child with sweet-talk: "Oh, you're such a good girl; I know you'll help Mommy/Daddy get your shoes on now because we have to go pick up Sissy at school."

In your dreams.

You have just given her total control. Your child's internal computer just double-clicked on the file, "DIG HEELS IN NOW."

Granted, when first introduced with a small child, this method will probably work initially, because the child has yet to figure out who's in charge and realize that she actually has an option to sabotage the whole deal.

But once that honeymoon phase is over, you get the "DIG HEELS IN NOW" open file. At this point, wise parents try many typical next-phase approaches, searching for one that actually works. We barter, threaten, negotiate, compromise. Anything to get out the door and pick up poor Sissy, who by now thinks Mommy has forgotten her.

But as the child matures and grows heavier, we often run out of options. The "grab and drag" option is by now a wistful memory. We feel stuck. The bigger, more savvy child is now running the show.

At this point, honesty becomes absolutely your best plan of action. It works. It may take some finessing on your part as you learn how to apply it with your child, but it works. And it will be invaluable for preparing your child to live in this world as an adolescent and adult.

What do I mean by honesty? Be real. Be there. I know you'll read these very same words in other chapters, over and over again. Am I repeating myself? You bet I am.

Being real yourself also gives your child a chance to show up. Speak honestly. "Sissy is crying right now because Mommy isn't there to pick her up. She is very sad and upset. I need you to help Sissy by getting in the van *now*." If that didn't work and I had to go further, I would go straight to compassion—which our children possess dearly—and might say, "Close your eyes. Look in your heart. See Sissy crying." Then, "Will you go help Sissy by getting in the car?" Our children live from their heart center. If we don't overuse this, we can—when in dire straits—appeal directly to their hearts and compassion and get understanding cooperation.

We often expect the child to be able to read through our façade. What façade? You know—the one that looks like Dad or Mom is always feeling patient; that looks like they're never exasperated or at their wit's end with the child's behavior. Why does the child think Dad or Mom is coolly dealing with her behavior? Because the parent is striving endlessly to be patient, be a good parent, a good teacher, and to love the child unconditionally. This works until Mom or Dad has been pushed over the limit and explodes. We all lose it sometimes. Honesty, sooner rather than later, helps us avoid the explosion.

This "get real" honesty is so important that I've devoted an entire chapter to real-life examples of applying this "walk the honesty walk" idea. (See "If All Else Fails, Get Real.") It's that important. Too often, we use honesty as a last resort rather than right out of the gate. It is not only important, but multilayered: there are many uses for and applications of honesty. I believe that they all work well.

Negotiation

Along with honesty and communication, there is nothing wrong with negotiation. I long ago threw "bribery" out of my parenting vocabulary. No sirree, it ain't bribery. It's just human nature. Would you go to work for eight hours a day if you weren't getting something for it? There has to be something to look forward to at the end of any effort. As humans, we love to have something to look ahead to, to be excited about. It drives us on.

The obvious first rule of bribery is that we negotiate with "extras" that are desired but not harmful. (Heck, there goes most candy.) The second essential rule is that rewards are never, ever given (not even once) before compliance is complete.

In negotiations, follow-through is critical. Always deny what you said you'd deny if she didn't do "x." Always. Don't weaken because you're tired, it's more convenient, or you're in a hurry. The stronger you are in being consistent, the shorter the period of time you'll have to put your energy into all this. Once your child learns that you mean business, she's learned it. From then on, she knows she has to live with the consequences of her choices.

If, however, you have the strength to do it on Monday but by Friday you're so fried that you cave in, you'll be at this a lot longer. So drink your coffee, eat power foods, and prepare for battle. I think this is one of the most difficult things we as parents have to do because there are so many demands on our energy; but if you can do it, you'll work yourself out of a job much sooner.

Strong Parent of the Year Award

To inspire you and spur you on to loftier heights, I offer you this story of Ellen, mom to Jeremy, who was five at the time and has Down syndrome. I give her the Strong Parent of the Year Award. Maybe of the decade.

Ellen and Jeremy had gone to Barnes & Noble to browse the children's book section. After some time in the store, Ellen told Jeremy, "Okay, Jeremy, it's time to leave; you choose two books and we'll go check out."

He picked his two books and they got in line for the cashier. Once they were actually checking out, Jeremy began to yell, "No, no, no!" because of the way the cashier did something. Ellen was never able to learn *what* the cashier did that was so horrendously offensive to Jeremy, but on the spot, he had a total meltdown.

He kept trying to get back in line again to buy the books *his* way. Mom said, "No, Jeremy, we're done, we already paid for them." Jeremy screamed. *"No, no, no, no!"* Complete high-volume meltdown on the floor of Barnes & Noble.

Ellen put her hands under his arms, dragged him outside, and sat on a bench outside waiting for the meltdown to end. It took a full hour. Ellen is a phenomenally determined mother. She sat unperturbed for an hour. "I don't have to be anywhere right now," she told herself. "I have the time. I'm going to sit here and wait."

And so she did. Concerned passersby stopped. "Can we help? Is there anything we can do?"

"I can't imagine what that might be," responded Ellen, "but go ahead and try if you like." Ellen knew better. Jeremy's will was made of Super Glue, and he had attached himself to the concrete. She waited it out for a full hour. "What was I going to do?" Ellen said. "If I forced Jeremy into the car, he would be on the floor with no seatbelt and no car seat; that's not safe. I was willing to just sit there and publicly wait it out. I was going to go the distance no matter how long it took."

Jeremy was five then; he's ten now, and if he ever has a meltdown, its duration is two or three minutes. Ellen, Tiger Trainer and Strong Parent of the Year.

The Sandwich Method

Now that you've had your heroic dose of inspiration, we'll get to the meatier approaches to noncompliance. Once your child is past the toddler stage, the sandwich method is terrific when used repeatedly, and of course it has nothing whatever to do with sandwiches.

It is one of the most effective psychological helps I have found in working with a child who was born with the word "NO" on her lips and cradled in her very atoms.

The Sandwich Method is a system of A-Z-A, Z being the end zone of what you actually want the child to do.

A: I'll give you what you want if…

Z: You give me what I want.

A: Remember, I'll give you what you want.

Heads up: the most important thing to remember in using this formula effectively is the *speed* of delivering the second A. As with a successful comedian, timing is everything, as you'll see in the following transition example.

The sandwich method is enormously helpful in facilitating transitions, the accomplishment of which simply does not come naturally to many of our children. Getting them to stop one activity and begin another is, frankly, a bear. Let's look at a demo of this.

Katie, ten, is busy playing and is in no mood to stop and unload the dishwasher. But she's capable of doing the job, unloading the dishes is her chore for the day and, by golly, you want her to learn to work so that she can grow to be a happy, well-adjusted, contributing adult. And besides, you need help with the housework.

So you're determined. Katie, however, is just as determined to take a break from her playing only long enough to watch a Disney movie. Then she plans to resume playing in her room.

You first deliver A.

Using whatever words are tailor-made for your child, you say the equivalent of, "Hey, Katie! How's it going? You've having fun, huh?" She responds positively, of course, and maybe you chat briefly about whatever she's playing. Then, "Would you like to watch *Toy Story 10*? You *would*? Oh, that would be great!"

Bear in mind that, since Katie is innately poised to say "no" to any interruption, the whole point of delivering A is to get Katie's endorphins up and running. The serotonins are high-fiving the dopamines, the acetylcholines are dancing, and *everybody's* happy. Fabulous.

Then *quickly*, briefly, and as under-the-radar as possible, you deliver Z: "…and just before it's time for you watch the movie, I want you to unload the dishwasher."

At this point, all the neurotransmitters are doing a dying swan routine, and frowning serotonins and dopamines are giving you ferocious thumbs down. Quick! Redeliver the A: "And just the second you're finished unloading the dishes, you can watch *Toy Story!* Oh, it will be so much fun! Wahoo!" You could even do a joy dance here for effect. (Your call on this.)

At this point, the neurotransmitters begin to regain consciousness, and, with luck, give you a thumbs-up. Endorphins are on the way!

Timing is critical in this method, and only practice brings success. Underneath all of this hoopla, of course, is common sense. What we are actually doing is engaging the will of our children. When that is in place, when the inestimable force of that little will is plugged into our child's thoughts and actions, then we've hit the mother lode. Nearly anything is possible.

Au contraire, of course, if Z is presented first, all bets are off. "Time for chores!" Or exercise. Or homework. Or whatever. That little will slams the door shut, turns the dead bolt, rams the bar across the door, and muscles the nearest boulder into block position.

And we find ourselves with little recourse except to force our own will home, come hell or high water. Either that or we retreat, feeling foolish and vanquished, waiting for the storm to clear before we make another attempt at gaining compliance.

Think of your child's will as having an on/off switch. It's a "don't push my buttons" situation in the extreme. But there are skillful ways to work with this. As I said, timing is everything. Part A flips the "on" switch. Part Z of course flips the "off" switch, but if your reflexes are fast enough, you can zap in there and switch it back to A before your child has a chance to go into full noncompliance mode. Practice makes perfect with this method; work it until you can finesse it like a pro.

Pete and Repeat

What if Katie repeats her "No" despite AZA? It matters not, my friend. You become a broken record and do the whole thing all over again. Stand firm. The Katie in our example is ten now, not a toddler; you have more reasoning and bargaining leeway at this point.

You *will* get your Z even if she doesn't get her A, and *that's* an unappealing option you can offer if her objections continue. Let's say you've repeated the AZA method several times, and Katie's not budging. Offer her ZZ, and if she's older and mature enough, she'll understand that she just shot herself in the foot with her noncompliance.

In the beginning, I had to do that with Jonathan until he eventually got the message. AZA in this case was: DVD time/Recycling/DVD time. But he wasn't buying what I was selling. So I switched gears.

"No! I not do recycling!" he said, for the third time.

"Well, okay," I said cheerfully. "Let's just skip the movie. You collect the trash and do the recycling and forget about the DVD; do you want to do that?"

His startled expression betrayed the realization that he was just about to be bamboozled, and his response time was quick. "*No!*"

"Okay. Recycling time, then DVD."

And recycle he did. When I say, "stand firm," I mean that quite literally. This is "Stands With A Fist" in action. Don't give up and go anywhere. Jonathan responded because he knew from experience that I wasn't going *anywhere*. I had planted my body on sacred territory (his room) and I would grow roots there until he cooperated.

A word of encouragement: don't be tempted to measure your success by your child's verbal response to this. If she gets off her tush, you can open the champagne. You have been successful.

It often happened, as Jonathan was complying and collecting the trash, he would sometimes—if he was still mentally in transition—object *as he was actually doing the work*. "No trash! No recycling!" he grumbled. *stuff, stuff, sort, sort.* "No trash! No recycling!" *stuff, stuff.*

Of course, by the time he'd finished the chore, he was happy, grinning, and high-fiving the parental unit who stood firm. After all, he was on his way to watch a DVD. And he had *earned* it. No one can convince me that self-congratulation wasn't part of what was behind that high-five.

You Want Milk or Milk with That? The ZZ Method

Thankfully, as our children mature and survive the Sandwich Method, our job gets so much easier. We can move on to the ZZ method, going straight to the end zone: both choices give us what we need the child to do at that moment.

A child who has successfully graduated from AZA can now easily read the word "inevitable" written on the proverbial wall, and the objections should be relatively short-lived.

"Honey, it's almost homework time. Do you want to start in five minutes, or would you like to wait ten minutes?" If she says, "I don't wanna do homework," we simply repeat the mantra: "I see you're disappointed because you want to keep playing, and you're having fun. But we have to do homework. So do you want to start in five minutes, or wait ten minutes?"

Here we've combined a dip into the Fantasy Pause in that we've acknowledged and verbalized her feelings, but we swing back immediately to Z. By now, we have developed a laser-like focus and feet planted in cement, and besides, we have a reputation to uphold. We've become skilled at the broken record routine, and she already knows how this story ends.

The One-Two-Three Alert Method

New parents: you will figure out very quickly to use the One-Two-Three Alert Method. These are timed reminders to give our children a chance to adjust mentally to the fact that they are going to have to do the unmentionable: *transition* from one activity to another. Transitions are the bane of their young lives.

You'll need to start with three alerts and work your way down to just one: "15 more minutes until we leave for school!" then "10 more minutes," then "Only 5 minutes until we leave!" An add-on to this is: make it visual. Visual takes the pressure off of both parent and child, and hands-on visual is even better. For example, making large-lettered notes on three different-colored sticky notes: one says 15, the second 10, and the last, 5. When you give the alert, you can slap the note on a wall near where the child is playing. "Fifteen minutes!" I would always scram after doing this, so as not to catch any flack, and also to give Jonathan time to mentally adjust to the bad news.

Losing Privileges

To this day, I believe in offering the loss of treasured privileges as a natural consequence of noncompliance. It is a powerful motivator to incline the child eventually toward the wiser choice.

Though this takes maturity on the child's part and repetition through time to be increasingly effective, it is a just and wise approach to discipline. Why? Because that's the way healthy societies work. Individuals who transgress acceptable boundary lines of behavior are thrown in jail or otherwise punished with loss of privilege, whether that privilege is money, years of your life, or life itself.

If we're training our children to become a working, cooperating part of the social community, then loss of privilege goes with the territory.

Early on, because of Jonathan's impulsivity problems arising from ADHD, I had taken the step of having deadbolts installed on doors to rooms that needed to be off limits to ADHD's destruction. One of these deadbolts, by design, was on the door to Jonathan's large toy closet.

For a truly serious infraction, I had to laboriously follow through on my threat to take away *all* his toys and entertainment and lock them up for 24 hours. Trust me, I did not look forward to having to back up my word in this case; it took time and energy I didn't feel I had. But I did it anyway.

The only thing I did not lock up for these major infractions were the hundreds of books on his bookshelves. No way I was going to haul 400 books in and out of the closet. I have my limits.

So all Jonathan had to occupy himself for those 24 hours were his books, and absolutely nothing else.

For some amazing reason, this disciplinary action turned Jonathan into the sweetest soul imaginable. He would sit on his bed for hours reading the books. He never once complained or demanded his toys, movies, or anything at all. He simply waited patiently for the 24 hours to run their course. For an historically impatient child, this behavior was amazing if not baffling.

When I checked on him periodically in his room, he would be sitting on his bed with the sweet contentment of a little Buddha, and give me a welcoming smile.

Was he in some Zen-like way relieved to be freed from his possessions? No worries, no need for making choices, only the ease of simplicity? It remains a mystery, since I never figured it out, but it certainly made those 24 hours a peaceful experience.

As for its effectiveness, I think the lasting impression for Jonathan was that consequences were not lightly threatened, and would definitely be carried out. On that he could depend. If my memory is correct, I had to threaten and carry through on this particular gargantuan consequence only twice.

For very young children who are still trying to master basic receptive language, we can start out simply. Repetition will eventually get the idea across, and the smaller and simpler the teaching unit, the better. "Time out" is a good example of simplicity.

Time Out

Welcome to Boot Camp. "One strike, and you're out." Sooooo simple.

One infraction lands you in time out. Right here, right now. On the floor, on the sidewalk, we don't give a hoot where, just drop and sit until you're repentant. When repentance overwhelms the transgressor—or at least occurs to him—life can cheerfully continue.

I used time out for Jonathan from the time he was two or three through pre-teen years. It definitely works, though of course you have to be clever about where time out occurs. It goes without saying that you *never* put a child in time out in her own bedroom. It has to be a profoundly boring location and within your visual periphery.

Jonathan's time-out spot was a little blue chair, easy to relocate and very identifiable as The Time-Out Chair. One of the best places to put him in time out was the hallway, devoid of any and all entertainment save a picture of Grandma and Grandpa hanging way overhead.

He complied with time out at first, and all went very well with this training tool until he became older and wiser. By age six, he had figured out how to obey the letter of the law ("Stay in the chair!") and break it at the same time (go where he wanted, do what he wanted).

He would grip the seat of the chair with both hands, making sure it stuck to his bottom solidly, and tiptoe to his room carrying the chair on his tush. "Stay in the chair!" (Check. No problem; got that.) Once inside his room, he would slam the door and start banging on his drum set.

Why, you ask, did he bother to tiptoe while stuck to the chair and yet slam the door and bang on his drums, as if I wouldn't hear him? Silly question. I have no idea.

For new parents who might not know yet, general guidelines passed down to us from ancient ages suggests a two-minute time-out for a two-year old, three for a three-year-old, etc. Updating it for our kids with Down syndrome, I'd cut that time in half or less. Just enough to get the idea across.

What do you do if your child won't stay in the chair? With some children, it may not be easy at first. Remember the old days when a child's time-out chair was planted in a corner, with the child facing the corner? Brilliant. You can plant your body behind the chair and block any attempted movements. Get creative.

My aunt Miriam, caring for her particularly obstinate and smart-mouthed granddaughter, resorted to a "time-out box," a cardboard box that had once contained her washing machine.

"Where's Hillary?"

"Oh, she's in the time-out box."

Now I'm not endorsing this, but Aunt Miriam was unabashedly creative. I hasten to add that Hillary was not scarred by this experience, and grew up to be a beautiful young woman who excels at teaching. (I wonder why.)

Last tip: never, ever, ever delay a consequence when you are first teaching your child. The consequence must immediately follow whatever dastardly deed was done, in order for a child to make a clear connection. One minute later is too late. The deed is long gone from childish memory, and confusion results.

Whistle-Blower

By the time Jonathan was eight, I was also dealing with out-of-control hyperactivity and stepped up the discipline. I was using a whistle at that time, one of my countless experiments in dealing with a severe ADHD problem, which in Jonathan's case could not be treated with drugs. I had read in one of many parenting/discipline books that literally "blowing the whistle" on your kid was one way of handling a variety of situations. So we were currently in the "whistle" phase.

I'd put Jonathan in time out, and when I felt his energy had changed to one of adequate if not mournful repentance, I would blow the whistle to signal his immediate freedom.

He quickly became a veteran of this routine, due to its inordinately frequent use. One day, whistle hanging around my neck, I directed him to the blue chair and he sat for time out. Mere seconds later, he turned around to face me.

"Aw, c'mon, Mama. *Blow it!*"

The Goal

Compliance: one goal, many pathways there. We owe it to our children to help them find their way to compliance. They deserve to be cooperative, functioning, contributing members of the society in which they live. And we parents deserve to one day sit back in our Maui beach chairs, relaxing with a tropical drink, relishing the fruits of our labor—which is the knowledge that our grown children are taking their place in the community.

Ahhh…pass the drinks, will you?

15

If All Else Fails, Try Being Real

"To thine own self be true, and it must follow,
as the night the day, thou canst not then be false to any man."
—William Shakespeare, *Hamlet*

Pint-Sized Lie Detectors

Let's suppose for a minute that you—and perhaps your child's teacher—have tried every imaginable approach to a behavioral problem, and nothing's worked. What then? Behavioral specialists have been called in, methods have been tried, but the behavior remains unchanged. In the event that your child has not budged an inch, what do you do?

There are two things to look at, and both involve the fact *that your child knows the truth*. What truth? What am I talking about?

Thing One: if the person involved in trying to change the behavior dislikes your child, is impatient, etc., your child knows this and digs his trench deeper. There is absolutely no winning in this situation, and the difficulty will only escalate. If you will indulge me, our kids operate on a "love frequency"—scientifically speaking, of course; it is their nature. The vibrational radio frequency of "dislike" drives them deep into oppositional behavior.

Thing Two: if you are not being honest and respectful with your child, he knows it. Again, game over, and he wins.

How do our children with Down syndrome know so unerringly what we're really thinking and feeling, what we're unwittingly projecting toward them? Do they have a built-in Vibrational Geiger Counter? Could be. I dunno. But *they know.* There is no fooling the child, and often the problematic behavior will not change until the dense adult realizes that the only cure in this instance is to radiate love toward the child, instead of utter aggravation. You can substitute the words "compassion," "empathy," or "good will" for the L word if you like. It is the same thing.

This is not hocus-pocus. I'm talking about a concrete observation that our children make just as easily as we notice that a cloud has passed in front of the sun. It's like data to the child, it's real, and the sooner we figure that out, the sooner we adults will reach the desired outcome.

Honesty as a Last Resort

What I'm really talking about is honesty. We can't fake our feelings with our children. Pretense and muddling through by doing the same-old-same-old is useless. Albert Einstein said it well: "The definition of insanity is doing the same thing over and over again and expecting different results."

I have seen honesty and an appeal to the child's deeper intelligence work again and again, with my students with Down syndrome as well as my son. Try it. You'll like it. When I have hit an impasse with a student and all else has failed, I "go to the mattresses," to quote the Godfather. I hunker down and talk directly to the child's core intelligence. My version of mob war.

Voluntary Coma

I taught one ten-year-old boy with Down syndrome for many months; I'll call him James. James had the amazing ability to go into what looked for all the world like a self-induced coma. I'll be darned if he couldn't hold a paralyzed pose for 45 minutes until his dad came to pick him up at the end of his session, at which time he miraculously recovered both his speech and mobility. James hated learning. He wanted to play all the time.

I tried every trick in the book to entertain him while surreptitiously trying to teach him. Nothing worked for months. Slowly, slowly—with the help of a stuffed Mickey Mouse and his lovely concubine Minnie—I moved James out of the "coma" and into some semblance of cooperation.

We limped along like this for a few more months. Then one day, I asked him to repeat reading vocabulary from a high-interest "Shrek" book I'd made just for him; the task was not difficult for him.

"Shrek," I said, pointing to the word.

"Uuhh," he grunted.

"Fiona," I said.

"Uuhh."

His response to every single word was "Uuhh." I stopped. I had hit a very important wall, and it turned me honest. I stopped being a "teacher" and became real instead.

"James," I said quietly. "I am bringing everything I have to you, trying to teach you to read. I'm using all the best ways I know to teach you. Will you open your heart to me and help me teach you?"

Eye contact. He looked, really looked at me. He said nothing in response, but from that point on cooperated fully, obligingly repeating whatever word I was attempting to teach him. Within two months' time, our sessions looked like a real classroom. Mind-blowing is a good description of his transformation.

There is a magnificent soul integrity within our children, and we would be wise to seek it out, respect it, and learn to work with it. If something's not working, stop doing it. "Stop, Look, and Listen" is a good beginning; stop what you're doing, look at what's really happening, and listen to your core, your intuition. Then speak from your own truth. Your child will hear you.

No Hitting!

I teach a five-year-old I'll call Dylan. Dylan hits people at the moment: Mom, Dad, me, anyone. In addition to Down syndrome, Dylan has a problem with disruptive behavior, and its management is still a work in progress. I have developed phenomenally fast reflexes due to my line of work, and I'd taught this very bright and responsive child reading for a year, so I was alert and prepared when he came for a reading lesson recently.

His first move was to cheerfully throw me a slug. I blocked the blow, but I'd had enough by this time—this had gone on for months. I went into honesty mode.

Forget "No hitting, Dylan. Gentle hands. Quiet hands." We'd already been through that for endless repetitions and variations. We'd done every technique known to woman and man. No, it was time to speak directly to the real Dylan, who always knows what he's doing, always has a good reason for doing it (even though we can't in our wildest speculation imagine what that reason could be), and will definitely continue to do it unless intervention occurs.

By this time, I had begun to study Marshall Rosenberg's books on Non-Violent Communication (NVC), and decided it was time to try the approach with my students. At that moment, practicing it with Dylan seemed like a swell idea.

The NVC system is honest, compassionate, and empathetic. It is also incredibly difficult to do, as it is a language we are not used to speaking. Rosenberg calls it "Giraffe Language," as the giraffe has the largest heart of any land animal.

Very simply put, it has four parts:
1. Observe (without using judging or blaming language).
2. Say what you're feeling.
3. Say what you want.
4. Make a request.

So, that morning with Dylan, I first reacted quickly by pushing away from him (out of harm's way). Then I was very still and waited until I had good eye contact with him. I said quietly, "Dylan, you just hit me. You hit me. I feel hurt. Hitting hurts me. I want to teach you to read, but I can't do that if you hit me. Will you please be gentle with me so we can read together?"

The four parts of Giraffe language hidden in those few words are:
1. Observe: "You hit me." (No judgment, evaluation, or diagnosis: not "That was a bad choice!" or "You're hurting me!")
2. Say what you're feeling: "I feel hurt. Hitting hurts me."
3. Say what you want: "I want to teach you to read, but I can't do that if you hit me."
4. Make a request: "Will you please be gentle with me so we can read together?"

I find that this language does not come easily; we are not used to it, and it takes some practice. But using it gets the results we want much faster than anything else I've tried. Once I had gotten this message across (and an apology from Dylan), when he later hit me again, all I had to do was quietly take his hand and stroke it (as in signing "gentle") and I said, "Gentle hands." With no fanfare, we moved on with the lesson. I didn't need to repeat the whole shebang that day, though of course I would need to repeat it at the next lesson. He had already gotten the message, though of course he needed to try a few more hits just to see what would happen.

Rosenberg teaches—accurately—that this will, in the end, get us the long-lasting results we're looking for far better than, "Stop it! I told you, 'No hitting!'"

Part of the challenge with this approach of NVC is that you have to first be honest about what *you* are feeling; this is often neither cool nor easy. Rosenberg writes, "NVC invites vulnerability and transforms it into strength." Because it is honest yet compassionate, this way of communicating and relating to our children, partners—anyone—deepens and strengthens our relationships. I have found it remarkable.

Three terrific tools to get you started, all by Marshall B. Rosenberg:

- *Teaching Children Compassionately.*
- *Raising Children Compassionately.*
  Both are extremely short, and I suggest both because you *are* a teacher for your child.
- *Non-Violent Communication: A Language of Life.*
  I enthusiastically recommend his seminal book for a deeper understanding of how to make this approach your own.

Setting Up The Environment

For our children who have difficulty managing their own behavior, I recommend using this approach in a controlled environment, away from other people and distractions (computer, TV, etc). There is no way to control the energy generated by others in the room (either home or classroom), so this is best handled in isolation: just you and your child.

You will want to change the energy in your heart, which will change the energy in your child, and even in the room where you're doing this.

Remember what I said at the start of this chapter? That our children with Down syndrome know the truth? That they know what we're thinking and feeling?

If you change your energy and speak Giraffe, honestly and from your heart, they know it, too—big time. It's a relief to these little "Vibrational Geiger Counters," and they are ready to respond.

Besides…heeding the advice of a man who was chosen to teach NVC to Israelis and Palestinians can't be a bad lead. If he could sit with them in one of the most volatile of situations and guide them to communicate in Giraffe language, then our job looks like a piece of cake.

Mike is another student who needs the gentler language of Giraffe. Mike has autism in addition to Down syndrome, and his school has had great difficulty dealing with him. Since the essential undercurrent of NVC is empathic connection with and understanding of another person's feelings, it works with him as well. I add a generous serving of a quiet and gentle energy to our sessions, as he is easily triggered into anger. Mike is calmed by soothing music, and since I discovered that, I use it in every session. Because it makes such a difference in his mood, I wouldn't even consider *not* using calm classical music softly in the background. This is another tool you might try to see if it helps with difficult behavior.

Now when an agitated student arrives, I try to create a space for us as soon as the door is closed and we are alone. I look at him and really see him (Stop, Look, and Listen); I ask him about himself and what he's feeling—and he can see that it's not just lip service. It doesn't even matter if a child can't respond—I'm "listening" to him. I try to calm the energy between us with a genuine awareness and empathy with him. My focus is on listening to him and being aware of what's going on inside of him, not on "teaching at him." If he becomes agitated again, I stop the lesson and try to reestablish the connection.

■ Try the CD series "Brain Music for Learning." This is the best I've found:
    Short version: http://tinyurl.com/3rjwkbl
    Long version: http://specialreads.com/teach-reading-down-syndrome-categories/10/Brain-Music.html

Compassion for Mom

Amy is a mother who has not gotten training in NVC, but her natural instincts drove her to something similar one day, and it worked: it reached her daughter Ava. Ava has an unusual convergence of challenges: Down syndrome, severe apraxia (Childhood Apraxia of Speech), and significant behavioral challenges.

What's That?

CAS (Childhood Apraxia of Speech): Apraxia of speech, also known as verbal apraxia or dyspraxia, is a speech disorder in which a person has trouble saying what he or she wants to say correctly and consistently. It is not due to weakness or paralysis of the speech muscles. The severity of apraxia can range from mild to severe.

Clearly, the behavior challenges are directly related to her inability to communicate verbally, and Amy and Sean, her wise and proactive parents, are leaving no stones unturned working on solutions. In spite of that, as Amy explains, there are difficult days.

"Oh boy, are there days. Days when I'm quite certain that every ounce of patience woven in the fabric of my soul has evaporated fully and completely, never to be replenished.

"I had one of those days recently. School days are days when I can accomplish the necessary tasks-on-hand. They're also an opportunity for a little 'me time,' when I can move at my own pace and have the time and space to really think things through. This particular school day would see little of that.

"The phone rang. 'Ava has been hitting and licking and knocking over the other students and class materials. It's an unusually bad day for her, and no form of discipline is working. Can you please pick her up?'

"'Uh…sure.' There went my day. We got home and her behavior only worsened. She had a tantrum on the way to pick up her brother from his school. Seven time-outs and umpteen toys and privileges taken away with as little fanfare as I could muster, and still…Ava's negative behavior continued.

"With her, it can be difficult at times to diagnose why she is behaving in a particular way. There didn't seem to be a specific catalyst this time, and eventually I lost it. Totally lost it and I started to cry. I looked Ava square in her eyes and asked, 'Why? Why are you behaving this way? It's not okay and I feel very sad.'

"That's when Ava pulled out her magic. She heard and understood every word I said to her. She signed 'sad' and 'cry' and 'mommy.' And then she did the most unexpected thing: she held my face in her tiny hands, brushed the tears off of my cheeks, and signed 'sorry' and 'mommy' and gave me one of her very big, very long, very special hugs. She was an angel the rest of the day.

"And my patience tank was completely and fully replenished."

The Heart of Honesty

We often make the greatest breakthroughs when we drop our "parent-stands-with-stiff-upper-lip" stance and speak from the heart of our emotions straight to the soul of our child with Down syndrome. Our children hear. They get it. They respond. It really is a core-to-core, soul-to-soul communication, and it's awesome to behold when it happens. When you're standing in that moment and living it, you will feel as if your child's cognitive delays totally fall away and reveal the actual understanding and intelligence hidden under that Yellow Raincoat. Remember the Raincoat? Good.

Our children get it. They know what's really going on even if they don't show it. So my advice is: call them on it. Be honest, both about your real feelings and about how their behaviors and choices affect your heart. Put it out there.

The inner space our children live in is, I believe, rooted in truth. Though this may be true for other humans, I think that our children with Down syndrome have far easier access to this inner realm. If you live there, too, and communicate with them from that place, they will respond.

More than the eye contact, more than the intensity of the words or their delivery, is something much more important. I have experienced this working with different children in various instances, whether my voice was soft or loud; it doesn't matter as long as the approach is tailored to the nature of the child. What matters to the child, and what makes this effective, is *honesty*. We are being real with the child, speaking from our core, and that is what communicates directly to the child's deepest intelligence.

So when all else fails, drop the methods that aren't working and stop being so "adult." Stop for a moment, feel the truth between you, and use your Giraffe language. I have found that nothing works so awesomely, even magically, as this.

16

How to Ruin Your Child

*"I've seen kids ride bicycles, run, play ball, set up a camp,
swing, fight a war, swim, and race for eight hours…
yet have to be driven to the garbage can."*
—Erma Bombeck

All Play and No Work

How to ruin your child? That one's easy. I almost did it myself.

Here's how you do it: don't make them work. Don't make them carry their weight in the family, take regular responsibility for assigned chores, or in general work as hard as everyone else does. Let them watch lots of TV and DVDs, or devote hours to educatory unmentionables such as computer games.

I had a near-collision with this very Ruin, and learned the hard way.

Having been the overworked eldest of six children, I wanted my kids to have it easier, right? So I did all the work. One day when my children were 4 and 5, I woke up and smelled the burned latte. I had created two little dragons with baaaaad attitudes.

Fortunately, the cure was simple. In the nick of time, I ran across a pivotal article in *Reader's Digest*. A study had been done on happiness and its possible origins in childhood. Researchers were looking for some common childhood denominator that would help ensure a child's happiness as an adult. They compared social class, education, race, religion, and everything imaginable. The results surprised everyone.

The *only* denominator that happy adults had in common was the fact that *as children they were expected to work at family chores.* Not just asked to, but expected to. Chores and responsibilities were simply part of family life, and so they did them. They did not complain; they did not feel put upon; they did not whine. Well, not for long, anyway. It was just life: take it or take it.

The discipline and esteem they developed as children who were integral to the functioning of the family community stood them in good stead as adults. They had *happy* adult lives. Now ain't that a corker?

After reading that article, I conferred with other parents more experienced than I, and began the transformation.

It was not easy.

The Marathon

That was when I learned the profoundly felt definition of words like "consistency" and "exhaustion," and resisted the universal "it-would-be-so-much-easier-just-to-do-it-myself" option. But I was heartened by the fact that work seemed to transform my children's personalities. By golly, this was going to work!

Little by little, my children and I learned to work together. Even a child of four with Down syndrome can learn to sort the recycling, set the table, or bring Dad his newspaper. Any small thing children can do for the family carves a functional spot for them in family dynamics. They become part of the solution, interdependent in the best sense of the word. The family begins to depend on them for those chores, and that in turn makes them…*important*.

Jonathan's additional diagnoses of ADHD and Oppositional Defiant Disorder made my self-imposed assignment of training him to work more challenging.

One Saturday at breakfast, I was outlining Jonathan's chores for the day. Before delivering his personal bad news, I prefaced the disclosure by outlining everyone else's tasks first.

"Dad has to work every day at the university, right? It's his job. Becca has to wash the dishes today; that's her job. I have to cook for the family and work in my office; that's my job." After that buildup, I thought it was fairly safe to get to the meat of the conversation, so I concluded, "and today you have to collect the trash and sort the recycling. That's *your* job."

I waited. Jonathan gazed at me with unruffled calm, serenely undisturbed. Yoda couldn't have done better. "My job," he instructed me patiently, "is to *play*."

Aaaaaa-*ha*! Thank you for clarifying.

Jonathan the Worker

Today Jonathan is twenty-six, and though I suspect there lurks somewhere in his consciousness that unchanged concept of his true calling in life, he nevertheless has learned to work fast, cheerfully, and well.

By his late teens, he routinely did not only household trash collection and recycling, he was also responsible for collecting, sorting, washing, and drying the family laundry. No folding, because of his fine motor glitches; so he delivered dry laundry to his sister's room for folding, as her fine motor control is just fine, thanks.

I must add that, in learning to do his laundry task, Jonathan tested me sorely with his inventiveness. After some weeks of his initial training, I noticed a suspicious trail of white powder coming from behind the dryer. Climbing on top of the dryer, I peered down to see a mound of powdered laundry detergent spilling out from behind the machine. For every scoop of detergent Jonathan had been putting in the washer, he had dumped another one behind the dryer. Just for fun. His job was, after all, boring.

I lectured him, of course, but as I was cleaning up the mess, I thought to myself, "Well, at least he didn't put a scoop *in* the dryer along with the wet laundry."

Never, ever, *ever* think thoughts like that! God is listening, and His sense of humor is legendary.

And so, within just a few weeks, Jonathan did that very thing: he cheerfully threw a scoop of powdered detergent into the dryer along with the wet laundry. Talk about fun to clean up.

Turning back to his more laudable job performances, Jonathan learned to vacuum our carpets like a professional. He didn't start out that way: he gave the center of the room a few swipes, ran over every electrical cord in sight, and he was *done*. Right? Wrong.

Once he got over his disappointment that his job was less than acceptable, he suffered himself to be taught and learned to do it every bit as well as I could. Along with vacuuming, he regularly unloaded the dishwasher, set the table, and generally made himself useful.

To be brutally honest, consistency was not easy at first. It took several years to convince both my children and myself that, if I had anything to say about it, regular chores would forever be a part of their lives, no matter how old they grew to be or where they might live in the future.

My own conversion was renewed every time I relaxed my efforts in a weary embrace of the "it-would-be-so-much-easier-just-to-do-it-myself" approach. Whenever I put that flaccid theory into practice, in no time at all, two little dragons would rise like phoenixes from the ashes of my cowardice, and I would magically be reawakened from my delusion.

When we first start training our children to work like anyone else in the family is expected to do, it may take some time before we reach true payoff. But it's worth it. And if we can believe reliable research, our children will have an excellent shot at being truly happy adults.

The Down Syndrome Payoff

In some cultures where ancient traditions still hold sway, young people cannot take their rightful place in society until they have served their community; service to others is part of their rite of passage. Without that being accomplished, they have not earned the right to become an adult in their culture.

Perhaps the greatest value for our children with Down syndrome lies in the inestimable payoff of heightened self-esteem and the certainty that they *belong* to the family unit as one of its contributing members. They are not there just to be served; they are there to work and contribute. They are valued and relied upon. I always loved seeing that satisfied smile on Jonathan's face when he had completed his jobs. He would race off to his room to play, and I know that playtime was much sweeter for him—he had earned it, and he knew it.

17

Communicating Emotions

"Bad mood is here!"
—Jonathan Hale, 9

"Good mood is here!"
—Jonathan Hale, 9

Saint Mom

I began my parenting determined to be endlessly patient regardless of the provocation.

Oh, *right.*

This wore thin after Jonathan had repeated whatever offense for the gazillionth time, despite the most well-worded instruction I could devise, and I would finally yell at him. Maybe I even screeched (okay, I did). Instant remorse flooded my maternal heart, of course, and I resolved to do better the next time. I continued to maintain a placid, patient face in spite of the greatest odds, time after time—until I inevitably lost my temper again. Does this sound familiar?

As Jonathan matured, I continued using the same outdated M.O., until I finally thought it through. "If it don't work, *fix* it." I talked about this earlier in the chapter "If All Else Fails," and now we'll look more closely at using that same get-real honesty in communicating emotions.

Watching how blatantly, even vividly, Jonathan expressed his own emotions, I realized that *he didn't know what I was feeling* before I finally lost my temper. I was hiding it under a patient face. How was he supposed to know my frustration was mounting? ESP?

Einstein Nailed It

Remember the Einstein advice I quoted earlier? "The definition of insanity is doing the same thing over and over again and expecting different results." Thanks, Al.

We would do well to give ourselves a timeline when we're trying out a solution to a parenting problem: okay, I'll try this for a month. If I'm getting nowhere, I'll switch tracks and try something else.

The problem is, we don't remember to switch tracks. Why? The engineer is asleep at the switch because he or she is exhausted, so the train rigidly follows a track that's not working. We read somewhere that "x" is a tried and true method that works for all children at all times in all parts of the globe, so we do that very thing. Our multitasking brains and hearts are already on overload, so it's hard to stay alert for the next opportunity to switch tracks.

So stay alert. If something is not working, it's not working. If it looks like a duck, quacks like a duck, and walks like a duck, it's a duck. Try another animal.

When Labels Are Good

"Bad mood is here," Jonathan would grumble, usually in response to a thwarted desire of some kind. Now *there's* a guy who had no trouble getting in touch with his feelings.

I believe it's a fantastic gift to give our children the words to match their inner climate, whether hot, cold, or indifferent. These are helpful labels. Knowing what you're feeling, knowing the words (or signs) to express that feeling, and knowing that there is someone trustworthy to whom you can express that feeling is both reassuring and empowering.

If a child is nonverbal, an alternative communication device can be used. I recommend using the words along with a picture icon. Why?

Because you want your child to be able to read. And because the quality of "feelings" pictures are often sketchy, they are sometimes so obscure that even I can't figure out what the emotion is supposed to be. Teach the nonverbal child to read the word, and you've made her emotional identification foolproof.

I gave Jonathan those word tools from toddlerhood, and it proved tremendously useful. From the time he was a small child, he learned to express his feelings by knowing and labeling the emotion. When I saw him caught up in strong feelings, I would give him the matching words: "Are you scared?...Wow, you must feel angry...You're excited, aren't you!" Scared, angry, excited, disappointed, frustrated, tired, proud, nervous— from his toddler years, I taught Jonathan the words for a wide range of emotions so that even today he expresses those feelings easily.

This not only empowers a child with an awareness of what's bugging her or making her happy, but it helps her manage a more appropriate expression—whether by words or actions—when an emotion is strongly negative. Being able to say "I'm *angry*!" allows a child to let off steam— without throwing a chair—and also provides a conversational entry for another person to help her work through whatever's bothering her.

Acquiring more refined words for more subtle feelings will become a lifetime habit. Even in adulthood today, Jonathan continues to expand that emotional vocabulary, and will sometimes toss one of his latest acquisitions my way, especially when I request compliance. Then I hear, "I'm so *aggravated*!"

Let Me Make This Perfectly Clear

As I discovered when Jonathan was a child, knowing and verbally expressing his feelings works well for him and his emotional self-awareness. But what about his awareness of others' feelings? How was I to get that across to him? Was I not being clear enough? Correct. In fact, I wasn't being clear at all. I was being Saint Mom. How was he supposed to know?

I got an idea one day while studying Jonathan's behavior in a store. He had his heart set on purchasing a specific music CD. He had money in his wallet, and he had me as chauffeur, so he was all set. Or so he thought. But the store was all sold out of that particular CD.

"I'm so disappointed!!" he moaned. He then went into his characteristic "disappointed" body language, right there in the store: he hung his head, drooped his shoulders forward, and let his arms hang limp. This was a *serious* disappointment, so it also merited a sad shaking of the head back and forth while he stared at his chest. "I'm so *disappointed!!*" he lamented.

The Train Runs Both Ways

In watching Jonathan's emotional responses to virtually everything, it occurred to me that maybe the train runs both ways: perhaps communicating broadly *to him* through physical posturing, along with verbal and facial expression, might also be effective, just as effective as it is when he uses that approach with others.

I decided on a plan: I would (a) let my face, body, and words show clearly what I was feeling, and (b) kick up the volume several notches.

Just as a stage actor's voice, expressions, and body movements must be broader in order for an audience of a thousand to grasp the message, and yet a TV or movie actor merely has to twitch an eyebrow to convey subtleties to the up-close-and-personal view of a camera, I decided to start showing Jonathan my reactions *broadly*. I put myself on stage.

Picking my battles carefully, I chose his most unpleasant habit, one I had not been able to break despite years of working with it. It was the Ogre Behind The Door habit. Respecting his age and privacy, I always knocked at his closed teenage door before entering. But what I heard in response to my polite knock was an ogre, not Jonathan. His response ranged from an alarmed, "*Whooop!*" to, "NO! Lemme' 'lone!"

So I began Act One. I knocked on the door politely. I anticipated a loud roar followed by a "NO!" which is exactly what I got. But I timed my opening of the door so he would see me just before yelling. My open-the-door face was wreathed in a happy smile. Good humor incarnate. Then his word hit the air, "*No!*" and I let him see that it hit me, too. My mouth drooped open and my eyes feigned surprise and hurt. My body language said, "hurt and dejected." My shoulders slumped and my arms hung limply by my sides.

Instantly his entire manner changed. "I'm sorry," he murmured.

"I feel hurt when you yell at me," I explained.

"*Sorry,*" he repeated.

He got it. Even though I sometimes felt (and certainly looked) childish in deliberately acting out these facial and body responses, I was allowing him for the first time to *see* how his behavior affects another person, long before my patience with him expired. I was struck with how clearly this worked for Jonathan, and realized that capitalizing on our children's visual learning strengths can extend far beyond the perimeters of academic/life-skill learning and into emotional realms.

When Jonathan was older, I could be more direct and help him to "see" through words alone, without using the exaggerated body language. One day I was ill with the flu, and Jonathan—of course—had a "snow day" off from high school. I had to muster the energy to draw up a flexible (and very visual) written schedule for his day and then—the tough part—I had to face him, give it to him, and tell him that even though it was a snow day, he wasn't going to play *all* day.

He immediately objected. "I'm so disappointed! I play in my room all day! It's my *mission*!"

I was preoccupied with being sick, not with being patient, and I yelled stupidly, "You cooperate with me or I'll put you out in the snow!" His casual glance told me that he wasn't even mildly alarmed, and was aware that I was flirting with lunacy.

Then I calmed myself and said, "Jonathan, I don't feel well. My stomach hurts and I don't have any patience today. So I need you to be extra cooperative with me. Okay?"

His manner immediately shifted. He became not only cooperative but a bit concerned. He read the schedule and agreed to it. I had treated him like another adult, and he responded like an adult. And because he loves me and understood that I was ill, he decided to put aside his preferences and cooperate. An adult decision. Because it was perfectly clear.

It's a Guy Thing

This ability to express feelings clearly (and then be done with it) comes in handy when a guy needs to process an overdose of girl talk. While Jonathan was still in high school, his friend Bianca called him one day and talked for a full forty-five minutes. I asked him afterwards if he had a good time talking to her.

"Naw. Talking with Bianca makes me nervous."

I was surprised; I thought he had probably enjoyed the conversation; he had hung in there for forty-five minutes. "Really?" I said. "Why did it make you nervous?"

"It makes me frustrated."

"Why?" I asked.

"Because she talks silly talk about nonsense things. It drives me crazy."

That was perfectly clear. It was also a typical guy reaction to an overly chatty female—a variation on that glazed-over look in the eyes which signals savvy women everywhere to stop talking at their men. I understood exactly how he felt about the situation, because he was perfectly clear.

I have often been told by teens and young adults who have been sitters or friends to Jonathan over the years, "I wish I could say the things Jonathan says. He says exactly what's on his mind, and it's often what I'm feeling, but I don't feel like I have the freedom to say it. He just comes right out with it, and I think that's cool." As long as that expression stays within appropriate bounds, I think it's cool, too.

Summing It Up

1. Teach your child both to comprehend and use specific words to match feelings; teach her to read the word; for a nonverbal child, teach her to use a communication device so she can easily point to the feeling.
2. Model her verbal expressions for her: "Are you excited about seeing Grandma? You are excited!"
3. Listen and give support as it's needed for those feelings, especially in processing the difficult ones.
4. Model clear emotional communication yourself. My godson Peter once complained to his mom that she was being uncharacteristically impatient with him. His mom, Carolyn, replied, "Peter, here's the deal: I have a limited amount of patience. Your friend Mick has been staying with us for two months now; he's used up 90 percent of my patience, and I've only got 10 percent left over for you." If I remember correctly, Mick moved out shortly after that....
5. Experiment with using the empathetic, judgment-free Non-Violent Communication (NVC) approach to expressing feelings. Review that four-part approach in the chapter "If All Else Fails." It works.

18

It Takes a Crew

"No one can whistle a symphony.
It takes an orchestra to play it."
—H.E. Luccock

You Are Not Alone

One of the most heartening experiences you will have as a parent will be that moment of enlightenment, of relief, of joy, when you first realize in your innermost core that you are not alone. You are not alone in this assignment, this task, this privilege of raising your child with Down syndrome. It takes a crew.

Look around you and take it in. Your crew surrounds you, whether they are near or far, whether you see them weekly, yearly, or hardly ever. Don't ever forget that they are there guiding and supporting you, your child, and your family.

Some of the faces change as they meld into new faces: doctors, physical therapists, speech therapists, occupational therapists, educators, aides…there is a natural and beautiful progression through these crew members. They come to you to work themselves out of a job. They come to leave. They teach you to fish rather than feeding you a fish; when they've trained you and your child in whatever way you need, they move on.

A very few of these early crew members will be an unsuitable match for you, your temperament, or your needs. If you give yourself permission, you will learn quickly to assess that, and dismiss the member in one way or another, without regret or discomfort. This can be uncomfortable if you've hired the person yourself and if a relationship of some kind has been established, through longevity if nothing better. Parents sometimes feel guilty in ending the association. Please don't. You started this professional relationship with only one motive: getting help for your child. If it's not an effective, nurturing help, then you need to move on. You don't need to give explanations.

If you're stumped for a way to do that, something simple ought to cover it. "My husband/wife and I have decided to take a break from therapy for a while. We'll let you know if and when we decide to resume." I love that "we" factor. It shares the responsibility, and the fact that the other parent is not present and can't be argued with helps close the moment.

Some false starts are inevitable; but true crew members are your lifesavers.

You will know them when they appear and—again, if you give yourself permission—you will become skilled in recognizing them. You will collect them like gems and treasure them in the same way. You might even take a tip from author and parent Martha Beck, who likes to post photographs of her closest friends, her support team, in a place where she can relish looking at them and absorbing the truth that they are there for her in the most meaningful ways possible.

You might assemble a Crew Photo Gallery on your fridge or favorite relaxing spot in your home. If you start feeling alone in your parenting journey, just look at the faces of your crew and get it. You are not alone.

Amy, mother to Ava, talks about her crew.

"Some say it takes a village to raise a child. I prefer a crew. To me, a village has a sense of permanence, of roots. We have moved around too much to consider ourselves rooted in one particular place. That's not to say we don't have roots—we have grown roots all around the country, and in those places live people that we continue to rely on in our ongoing quest to raise Ava the way we desire.

"In our crew, sometimes referred to as The A-Team (The Ava Team), there are people who get down and dirty on the floor and play with Ava. There are people who help reinforce proper social behaviors. There are people who discipline her. There are those who teach her. And there are others whose sole job is to love, dote upon, and spoil her rotten. Each of these individuals plays a key role in shaping who Ava is, and they come in all shapes and sizes.

"Some of Ava's best crew members are children, both older and younger than she. Children have an uncanny ability to keep things real and tell it like it is. If Ava pushes a child as a way to get his/her attention, a child is much more likely to say 'Quit it! I don't like that!' An adult would take an entirely different, more scripted approach to such behaviors, but Ava learns from both.

"I love all of the different influences Ava has in her life; they make her a more whole person. They help make Down syndrome less dramatic in her life and instead reveal the person Ava truly is.

"I rely upon the crew, hugely. As Ava's mother, I have taken the approach that I am not her be-all and end-all, nor do I want to be. It's natural that I play the roles of therapist, psychologist, mediator, playmate, doctor, teacher—all those things that all parents do naturally with their children.

"But I also know that I am a better parent when I have some time away from both Ava and her brother to concentrate on just being me. I learned many years ago, when I was barely in my twenties and my own mom was going through intensive treatments for ovarian cancer, that I can't help anyone else unless I help myself first. So I'm not hesitant to ask The A-Team for help when I need it, even if it's just for the chance to take a break from the action and sit quietly and breathe.

"I'm eternally grateful for our crew. Without them, Ava certainly wouldn't be where she is today: a vivacious, full-of-life girl, who does well in new situations and places and loves to meet new people. And frankly, I wouldn't be where I am today either. I owe a great deal to The A-Team for helping me to understand that I can let go of Ava, sit on a bench at the park, and just watch her play, knowing that there are so many others 'out there' looking after her as well."

Amy's assessment and appreciation of her crew is deeply felt because she's living it, and I will add that there is a final group of crew members, whose presence can also deeply felt if you are aware of them. Various cultures and religions call them by many names. This crew is usually impossible to see, but can be tangibly felt. Most of all, they are very real.

I want to invite you to look at this final group of crew members. To do this, you may need to suspend your belief system for a moment in what Martha Beck refers to as "bracketing." Bracketing is the anthropological process of considering another culture's experiences or beliefs without either blindly accepting them or patently rejecting them.

I will use the universal terms "God and his angels," but please ascribe to this crew whichever terms fit your belief system and bring you comfort. I believe that all semantics and belief systems are valid if they help us to truly understand that in the most profound sense, we are never alone. And that we are certainly not alone in our parenting.

My spiritual path lies along the way of meditation and yoga. Very simple, very quiet. But I had an experience many years ago that, for me, opened a transforming door into a more aware form of parenting.

It was during a stressful time of trying to rein in Jonathan's horses of Attention Deficit Hyperactivity Disorder, Oppositional Defiant Disorder, and of course Down syndrome. For years I had grappled with this team of wild horses, each one of which aggravated the others.

Jonathan was 16, and I was worn out emotionally, not to mention physically. As a splurge, I treated myself one day to a massage. The massage therapist was a skilled and sensitive young woman, and the session went well. After nearly an hour, she allowed me to just relax.

As I closed my eyes and sank deeper into relaxation, my struggles with Jonathan's behaviors flooded into my mind. In the same instant, I suddenly became aware that I was not alone in the room. Eyes still closed, I clearly saw several angelic beings standing quietly in the room with me. They radiated calm and understanding. Without a word being spoken, I understood from them that they were there to assist me in raising Jonathan: that they were right there with us both, and always had been, since his birth.

I realized that my true environment—whether in that room, my home, or anywhere else—was filled with loving, angelic beings who are there specifically to help me help Jonathan. I thought, *"I have been trying to do this alone, and all the while beatific help is surrounding me."* I cried quietly.

Then I had a most unusual reaction. Remembering my years of struggle and frustration, I became angry. Inwardly I cried to them, "*Why didn't you tell me you were there? I didn't know you were there!*" It seemed colossally unfair that I hadn't known about this divine help, which apparently I'd always had access to, but of whose existence I had been clueless.

Without words, the understanding came to me that I had been moving so fast through the moments of my life that I could not possibly see or hear these divine helpers, could not possibly be aware of them. I understood that I would have to move at the speed of stillness to be aware of them, to be aware of *any* celestial help. The biblical quote, "Be still and know that I am God" is a simple directive that we can scarcely even conceive of in our high-speed, over-stimulated world. And yet it's only in that stillness that we can connect with our true intuition, which is a direct phone line to the Divine.

At that moment, it hit me that I had been trying to do this complex job of raising Jonathan alone; this limiting misconception had led to tremendous stress and a sense of powerlessness and isolation. So unnecessary!

Determined to be aware of this loving, guiding support, this higher crew, I inwardly chanted my new mantra: "I will never, never work with Jonathan alone again!"

In no time at all, of course, I had the chance to practice my newly acquired awareness. Later that same afternoon, Jonathan's dad and I had yet another difficult moment with Jonathan. It was typical of what we were dealing with on a regular basis, and I don't remember the exact details. But we stood there, this trio of struggling humans. In spite of all our hard-won parenting skills and love, nothing Kelly or I said made any difference, and we could not budge Jonathan from his defiant position. We were at a complete impasse.

Then I remembered. I stopped and became inwardly still. I deliberately "listened" for the presence and guidance of the higher crew I had seen just hours before. Amazingly, I felt them in the room with us. Then intuitively, I suddenly knew exactly what to say to Jonathan.

The words themselves were ordinary, and out of context were nothing special; the point is that they were magic *for that moment*. It was a short sentence, quietly spoken. "We'll do it together, Jonathan." In response, Jonathan turned to me and said simply, "Okay."

It was Kelly's turn to sense that something unusual was going on. "*Wow!*" he said softly. Then we all remained silent, completely at peace. It was a moment I'll never forget.

I'd like to say that I forever after remembered to be still and listen in difficult situations, but amnesia regularly set in and sabotaged me. This member of the crew is definitely human! But fortunately, the awareness has lingered and helped me many times.

Awareness and stillness are key. Stilling the body, stilling the mind and focusing it on one thought or concept—peace, relaxation, God—are the entrance tickets into the kind of awareness I am encouraging. This awareness is called by many names: the Buddhist term "mindfulness" is my favorite, because it is so clear. We become mindful. Mindful of our own being's stillness, of the stillness around us and permeating all things. That awareness naturally grows as we practice.

It is widely agreed that the most universal tool to achieve that awareness is meditation. The benefits of meditation today are touted across the globe and the Internet, and articles on the topic are scattered through even the most unlikely of magazines. I just did a quick Google on "benefits of meditation" and found over 100 benefits—everything from lowering blood pressure to strengthening the immune system to beneficial changes in brain electrical activity. Not to mention its calming, centering effects.

I'd like to suggest one more benefit: the practice of meditation makes our parenting calmer, wiser, and therefore more effective. If you doubt that, just ask your Higher Crew member for an opinion. Of course, in order to understand the answer intuitively, you'll have to sit still and meditate. *Gotcha*!

Please repeat after me: "I have a crew. I have a crew." Know it, feel it, relax into that truth. You are not alone. If you ever doubt it, look around you at your crew: teachers, aides, developmental pediatricians, physical therapists, speech therapists, occupational therapists, friends, extended family, Down syndrome networks, special education advocates, and other parents of kids with Down syndrome. Let's see…have I forgotten anyone?

Ah, yes…the loving support and hidden guidance of God and His whole angelic crew. You are not alone. Don't ever forget it.

19

When It's Not Down Syndrome

"I do not want the peace which passeth understanding;
I want the understanding which bringeth peace."
—Helen Keller

Not Plain Vanilla

When we're new to the terrain of Down syndrome, to a large degree we expect the unexpected, because we haven't walked this walk before. So how are we to know if the issues that present themselves are because of Down syndrome or some other yet-undiagnosed condition? Understanding what we're actually dealing with does bring some of the peace Helen Keller refers to, and certainly it brings the relaxation of knowing which path we have to follow.

Our focus in this chapter is on being alert to behavioral and developmental issues that fall outside of Down syndrome itself, and only secondarily to medical issues. The task of recognizing and diagnosing medical or behavioral issues falls far outside the scope of this book; I am concerned here only with passing along parenting advice for dealing with both.

Down syndrome is in fact Plain Vanilla. What if what you see in front of you looks more like Rocky Road or Chunky Monkey? Ask, "Is this just Down syndrome? What am I seeing?" These are not only good questions; they're vital ones, and the correct answers can give a struggling family the help it needs. Not answering those questions isn't an option; don't even go there. Don't ignore red flags. If you don't ask questions, you can't get answers, and if you can't get answers, you can't get the help your child needs.

Red Flags

So what constitutes a red flag? Shannon Fallick, a lawyer and mom of Zoe, who has Down syndrome and autism, says it well: "If your child is exhibiting behaviors that don't match up with those of his peers who also have Down syndrome, think about it. Have it looked into. Don't assume that you know what autism is. Just because your child is not 'Rainman' doesn't mean that he doesn't have autism."

What's That?

Autism: A developmental disorder that results in impaired social interaction and communication, along with repetitive and/or restricted behavior. Signs of autism typically begin before age 3.

Of course, this necessitates that you network with other families who have children with Down syndrome, so that you get a good feel for Plain Vanilla, or the typical range of behaviors and abilities of children with Down syndrome. Fortunately, there are parent support groups across the country; a quick Google will get you information on the group closest to you. Regardless of whether or not you have to deal with a secondary diagnosis, this group can provide invaluable support, information, and peer friendships.

National organizations can also be huge resources for information. For example, the National Down Syndrome Society has articles on the dual diagnosis of autism and Down syndrome. An Internet search will turn up many resources for you to explore, limited only by your time!

NADS = National Association for Down Syndrome:
www.nads.org

NDSC = National Down Syndrome Congress:
www.ndsccenter.org

NDSS = National Down Syndrome Society:
www.ndss.org

Search: Dual Diagnosis of Down Syndrome and Autism on
www.ndss.org or simply enter this "TinyURL": http://tinyurl.
com/4x8oxdc and it will take you right there.

Final Answer

One definitive word: the final answer on whether or not your child has additional issues lies in *you*. In consulting with parents who are dealing with additional diagnoses, whether medical or behavioral, I saw that, without exception, every parent I talked to knew that something else was going on, that something was wrong, long before a professional of any kind gave his or her input.

Not having run this race before, you do need professional, more experienced input to confirm what you already know: that there is something going on here besides Down syndrome. You need specialists to confirm, to diagnose. But you do not need them to tell you that something is amiss in the first place, because *you* already know. You are the ultimate authority because you live with the child you love; you are, in fact, the expert on your child.

Can you guess what the Numero Uno parental advice for you is, on this topic of multiple diagnoses? Every experienced parent I interviewed said, "*Trust your gut.*"

So here is a rundown on the "been there, done that" advice to you from these parents:

For All Issues

1. Trust your gut, your instincts, your intuition.
2. Don't be afraid to speak up, to ask questions.

3. Don't take "It's just Down syndrome" for an answer.
4. Do your research so you can ask more informed questions.

For Medical Issues

5. If the first medical opinion says nothing is amiss, get a second or third opinion. If appropriate to the condition, see a pediatric neurologist, gastroenterologist, ENT, or other specialist; don't assume a pediatrician or general practitioner has all the training and experience your child needs.
6. If your child is hospitalized, write down what and when your child should get for every medication dose and give it to the hospital staff. This hindsight was earned the hard way by some parents.
7. If you have one, bring a medical friend with you to doctor appointments. (No kidding.)

For Behavioral Issues

8. Get an assessment done by a qualified, respected source. (Keep reading this chapter for details on how to do that.)
9. Make sure of your legal rights when seeking additional services from the school or early intervention program, so that your child gets those services.

Medical Snapshots

Sarah

Laura is mom to Sarah, now nine years old. "We knew something was wrong before it was diagnosed. The pediatrician didn't notice what we did, and repeatedly said nothing was wrong. One day, I reached my limits with the situation and said, 'Okay, this is it! I'm not listening to what they're saying any more. I'm taking her to the ER!'" Laura sat in the ER

What's That?

Moyamoya, or Moirmoir Syndrome: a disease in which certain arteries in the brain are constricted, blocking blood flow.

with her laptop, Googling Sarah's symptoms. "Moyamoya" popped up, and the symptoms were dead on. She asked the ER doctor, "Could this be Moyamoya?" and was told, "No, it's not Moyamoya. That's more of an adult thing." She made an appointment anyway with a pediatric neurologist, who immediately assessed Moyamoya syndrome, and tests later confirmed it.

Laura continues, "My husband has a Ph.D. in molecular pharmacology and I'm a dietician, so we're professionals; we understood a great deal, and we were still frightened! I can't imagine how it is for parents without that background. Don't be afraid to say, *'Hold on a minute!* Draw me a picture. Explain this!' That's what we did."

Tuisku

Anu, who is from Finland, is mom to Tuisku. Anu knew intuitively that something was wrong with Tuisku's left side. Repeated appeals to the child's physical therapist were dismissed with, "That's typical of Down syndrome." Then, on a visit to her homeland, her brother—a Finnish medical doctor—noticed the problem and told her to contact a pediatric neurologist.

Anu tells the rest of the story: "When we got back to the U.S., I again talked to the physical therapist. She was getting frustrated now and said, 'There is nothing neurologically wrong with Tuisku! She has Down syndrome (like I didn't know) and this goes with the territory.' I was wiser by then and made an appointment with a neurologist anyway.

The neurologist took one look at Tuisku and said she had right-sided hemiplegia, but it needed to be confirmed by MRI. So at three-and-a-half, Tuisku finally had the MRI and was given an additional diagnosis of hemiplegic cerebral palsy. Anu's advice to other parents? "Get a second and third opinion! Tuisku could have started appropriate physical therapy at a much earlier age."

Amazingly, this pattern of misdiagnoses happened to Tuisku twice. She was abnormally afraid of high places. Anu said, "I talked to various OT's (occupational therapists) ad nauseam, both within the school system and privately. Nothing. I actually had a school OT *argue* with me, saying that if Tuisku didn't want to climb, then she couldn't do anything to help her. Finally I had given up and was about to give up OT altogether, when Tuisku got a new OT at school. This therapist called me one Sunday and said, 'Did you know that your child has gravitational insecurities?' Though

I didn't know the term, of course I knew exactly what she was talking about. This OT set up a station to work with Tuisku at the school stage, and helped her tremendously."

Hats off and cell phones waving for experienced, informed professionals who take a second and third look at puzzling pictures!

A Word from Rob

Rob, the father of Alessandra, seven, who has Down syndrome and rare brain tumors, says, "It's easy to fall back and say it's just Down syndrome, but it's not always. You do your child a disservice by defaulting back to the 'Down syndrome' position. It's a process of trial and error. Sometimes you feel like you're in an episode of *CSI (Crime Scene Investigation)*; you're constantly probing. It's a process of elimination, and *you* will end up being the expert. It's a rude awakening, because if your child has something unique, most of the medical personnel you'll interact with will only have seen a few cases, if any. Even going to the 'top of the top' doctors, we found they had formed very strong biases based on just one or two cases they knew about! So *trust your gut*. You need to do that in order to counterbalance these biases."

Behavioral Snapshots

Behaviors not typical of Down syndrome are easier to spot than medical problems. Why? Because our children are in school from an early age: early intervention, preschool, etc. Oftentimes, the alert angels that swoop into these situations are teachers, aides, and therapists such as speech-language pathologists (SLP). An experienced preschool teacher or SLP might intervene; this happened often to the parents I interviewed on this topic.

As new parents of a child with Down syndrome, we don't have the long experience that these educators do. So a seasoned teacher's comment, "I think something else is going on here. This is not typical behavior for Down syndrome," is a tipoff that we need to take the next step. Since (as you've now learned) parents already know intuitively when something else is going on, a teacher's prod is just what's needed for the parents to pursue an assessment.

So actually spotting the behavioral problem is not nearly as great an issue as uncovering medical problems that masquerade as Plain

Vanilla Down Syndrome. The greater issue with behavioral diagnoses is getting a knowledgeable and official diagnosis made in the first place, and secondarily getting the services legally due the child. School systems already in difficulties, financial or otherwise, may drag their red-taped feet interminably in an effort to avoid providing needed services.

Hailey

Jenn is mom to eight-year-old Hailey, who has Down syndrome and autism. Getting a correct diagnosis was not a problem, and Hailey initially thrived with three hours daily of ABA therapy in what Jenn calls "a phenomenal program" for early intervention in autism.

What's That?

ABA (Applied Behavior Analysis): a science that involves using behavioral learning theory to modify the child's behaviors. ABA-based interventions are best known for treating people with developmental disabilities, and autism spectrum disorders in particular.

But when Hailey turned six, Jenn was told, "Your child has aged out of our program for autistic children." It was the end of the road, or so Jenn thought until she met a couple who had a son with autism. The dad was a lawyer and the mom a paralegal. They shed a welcome spotlight on the truth. "Oh, *no, no, no,*" they said in response to Hailey's "aging out" story. "No, it is your legal right to have ABA provided in the home now." They advised Jenn to hire a special education advocate, which she did. At first,

What's That?

SEA (Special Education Advocate): an individual who assists parents/guardians who are going through the IEP process. An SEA is not a lawyer; his/her primary responsibility is to represent the best interests of the student in the educational process.

they fought to get home ABA through the school district, and they were able eventually to get it through their regional center. Rights vary from state to state, so do your research if this is your situation.

Testing: Buyer Beware!

Once you're fairly certain that something more than Down syndrome is going on behaviorally or developmentally, you'll want to have an assessment done to get an official diagnosis, for two obvious reasons. First, your child will then be eligible for more services, services that are clearly needed; second, you will regain both peace of mind and empowerment. In this instance, knowledge is definitely power. Knowing *what* you're dealing with enables you to seek tools for *how* to deal with it.

Knowing what you're dealing with, no matter what the diagnosis, is a relief. Trying to manage the unknown is unnerving, frustrating, and exhausting. Once my son's ADHD was diagnosed, I had a free ride on the information highway. I knew what the problem was, and was free to explore every avenue of treatment available.

Shannon, the mother of Zoe, eight, with Down syndrome and autism, says, "Now that we know what the problem is, it's easier for us to deal with this emotionally, psychologically, and practically. We know better how to interact with her, and are getting great services."

Seven-year-old Ava's mom, Amy, explains, "A diagnosis is affirming; you know for sure that you're not crazy; that your child *is* in fact exhibiting these behaviors. Information is empowering. Since we couldn't use Ritalin for Ava's hyperactivity, we went back to behavioral strategies. My husband, Sean, and I periodically have to reinstate what we call Boot Camp. We tell each other, 'We're back in Boot Camp!' For us, that signals a parental shift, a mental shift: we temporarily put our own stuff aside to get Ava back on track. This strategy makes us calmer. We come and go, in and out of Boot Camp. We know what we're dealing with."

I have seen some families struggle because the additional problems have not been formally identified, the child gets no extra services, and untrained school staff members have no idea how to deal with the child's behavior.

Which brings me to "*Caveat emptor…*buyer beware!" Beware of fuzzy testing. What do I mean by that?

Fuzzy Testing

The assessment you're looking for needs to be done by a qualified source. Beware of having your child's assessment arranged by a school district that sends you to a poorly qualified testing resource. The good news in this scenario is that the school district will pay for the testing and you won't have to. The bad news is that often the district may not want an additional diagnosis given, because that means funding additional services for the student. So you might be sent home with a "no additional diagnosis" verdict, regardless of whether or not it's true. And you will be right back where you were before, only worse off, because now you've got a "no additional diagnosis" verdict in your child's permanent records.

This is, of course, not always the case. There are school psychologists and educators who have excellent testing credentials. Some states also contract with reputable outside agencies to provide evaluation and other services for people with disabilities (for example, California does this through a network of Regional Centers).

I know several families who took many months to persuade the district that an assessment was needed, but then it was done and done well. Once that diagnosis was given, the doors to appropriate services were open to the child. One amazing school district in San Ramon, CA, had access to a local Center of Early Intervention of Autism and an ABA specialist from that center did the assessment. That qualified assessment opened doors. It probably doesn't get any better than that!

Where to Go for Testing

If you decide to pay for an assessment out of pocket or through your health insurance plan, there are several good options for assessments. One of the best is to find a developmental pediatrician. Your local Down syndrome organization can help you find that special doctor. If your child does indeed have an additional behavioral diagnosis, whether it be an autism spectrum disorder, ADHD, OCD, ODD, or any other diagnosis, moving your child's medical care to the office of a developmental pediatrician can be a huge boon. That doctor can be a helpful resource for many years.

Another option is a psychologist or psychiatrist who specializes in autism, for example. A third option, which we've already discussed, is

What's That?

ADHD (Attention Deficit Hyperactivity Disorder): A developmental disorder that causes difficulties focusing and sustaining attention, hyperactivity, or both, with symptoms starting before the age of seven.

OCD (Obsessive Compulsive Disorder): an anxiety disorder that causes obsessions (recurrent disturbing thoughts) and compulsions (the feeling of needing to do a particular behavior) that are severe enough to interfere with daily life.

ODD (Oppositional Defiant Disorder): A behavior disorder characterized by pervasive resistance to direction or authority; not to be confused with stubbornness!

that of asking the school district to refer you to a private agency that is contracted to offer free or low-cost services to students with disabilities in the school district. In that case, they may refer you to an agency such as the regional centers in California or a facility like the Cincinnati Children's Hospital Medical Center (CCHM), where my son Jonathan was assessed.

Our Triple Diagnosis Journey

"Too much noise! Too much noise for my head. I very upset!" Jonathan would often voice these complaints as a small child. I didn't understand. "Mama, please turn that music off! I don't like it. The flute is playing tricks. It gives me a tummy ache!" I still didn't understand.

Even after Jonathan was diagnosed with severe ADHD at CCHM, I still didn't really get it. The week after receiving the diagnosis, I took him and his five-year-old sister Becca to what I thought would be a fabulous treat: Cincinnati's Festival of Lights. Millions of tiny lights in the trees, a train, crowds, music…fun, right? As we pulled into the parking lot alongside the train, the music, the lights, the crowds—Jonathan began to scream, covering his ears. It took only seconds for me to realize that, for some reason, he could not tolerate the scene. I had no recourse but to turn around and leave the parking lot. At which point, of course, his sister began to scream because she realized we were *not* going to have fun after all. I drove home with two children screaming for opposite reasons.

Totally frazzled, I called one of his diagnosing pediatricians the next morning. "What was *that*?" I screeched. The doctor's explanation calmed me. "Imagine that you have a volume button for each of your senses. And that the volume is turned to 'max' on each sense, and you have no control over that; for instance, you can't turn the volume down on your hearing while your sight volume is through the roof as you're looking at the 'million lights.' When you took Jonathan to the Festival of Lights, it completely overwhelmed him. It's actually painful. I'd advise you to avoid all situations like that; even taking him to a mall can be overwhelming."

The doctor was smack on target, and to this day, I don't take Jonathan into megastores. The last time I tried was hilarious. He was grown up by then and a good sport, so I thought we'd try it. The store was a huge grocery warehouse, but completely over-the-top, with animated voiced displays hanging from the rafters and "stuff" and noise everywhere. On tiptoes, he was pushing my shopping cart *slowly*, eyes riveted straight ahead, deer-in-the-headlights style. "This is a *terrible* place!" he whispered. I laughed, but promised him on the spot that I'd never ask him to come to that store again. And of course I never did.

The Early Tip-Off

As with autism, oftentimes hyperactivity makes an early appearance. After watching one of my sisters struggle with her son's ADHD for years, I was aware of the hallmark behaviors. So when Jonathan began to exhibit those same hyperactive behaviors by age three, my sister suggested the Feingold Diet for hyperactive children, which she'd used with her son. The diet did mollify his behavior somewhat, but by age seven, it was no longer helping. The behavior had exploded into unmanageable proportions.

I first did some research. Our local Down syndrome organization had a cassette tape from a long-ago lecture on the topic of comparing Down syndrome and Down syndrome with ADHD, a "this is this" and "that is that" clarification. After listening to it, I knew I was on the right track.

I contacted a local ADD/ADHD organization and got a checklist form they recommended. Of the symptoms on the list, Jonathan had 97 percent of them. That looked rather definitive, so I turned to the CCHM for an official assessment. At the time, I didn't realize how blessed we were to live in the same city as developmental pediatrician Dr. Bonnie Patterson, who was practicing—and still is—at the CCHM. Dr. Patterson's work has focused significantly on Down syndrome for many years, and I can't imagine a more ideal doctor to have assessed Jonathan when he needed it.

Dr. Patterson and her diagnostic team were thorough, and Jonathan's assessment was multidisciplinary, taking several weeks to complete.

Her assessment made such an impact on me that I still remember sitting in her office listening to her explain it. "Jonathan has a very severe case of Attention Deficit Hyperactivity Disorder," she said. "At this point in his life, it is a greater challenge for him than Down syndrome, and is affecting him across the board. Ordinarily, we're reluctant to recommend medication. We prefer to first take a more therapeutic approach with intervention strategies...but in Jonathan's case, we think it would be beneficial to start him on medication as well."

For decades, holding up my rep as "Ms. Natural Everything," I had devoted time to studying various methods of natural healing: homeopathic medicine, cranio-sacral therapy, massage, herbs, you name it. I had been opposed to drugs in any disguise for years; I'd tough out a headache rather than take a single pill.

So it is a telling comment of my parental exhaustion when I say that my response to Dr. Patterson was, "Can we fill a Ritalin prescription for Jonathan *on the way home?*"

Well, we couldn't, and that was that. First came an appointment with a psychiatrist. Various shortcuts to Ritalin may be common today, but in 1992, things were done the old-fashioned, cautious way, and it was weeks more until I could get my hands on the drug.

Ah, Ritalin.

When Drugs Don't Work

Though Ritalin may work well for other children with Down syndrome, my experiment of allowing Ritalin to tangle with Jonathan's nervous wiring lasted exactly three days. It was three days too much. It ramped up his hyperactivity by—oh, let's say conservatively—400 percent. On the third day, I was flirting with serious Ritalin doubts, but delivered him nonetheless to his Sunday School teacher. A callous move, I realize. When I returned after the church service, the traumatized teacher looked like she was seriously ready for Valium, another drug category entirely. Her eyes were huge as she begged me never to return with my child in that condition.

So we then—with the aid of the requisite psychiatrist—moved on to the next recommended drug, then the next and the next. Nothing was effective, though some drugs were astonishingly effective at making him almost completely nonverbal, along with other unacceptable side effects. I checked out of the Pharmaceutical Option Department and moved on to explore more natural means of treating the disorder.

My friend Amy had the same experience with her daughter Ava, who was six at the time. Ava's difficult behavior had been escalating for months, and although her parents knew that much of it stemmed from Ava's frustration over being nonverbal and unable to communicate well, they thought it was worth checking out with Ava's pediatrician. Together with the doctor, they went through the checklist for ADD/ADHD. She had 75 percent of the symptoms, a score high enough for concern. An EKG was required to go on stimulants; it was normal, so they went ahead with a Ritalin try.

Amy says, "We chucked it after three days. She was crazy. It scared us to death. Ava already had repetitive behaviors, but those became horrifically intensified. The worst times were when medication was wearing off. She became intensely upset, screaming and crying. She repeatedly signed "boo-boo" and pointed to her head during withdrawal. I said, 'I'm done. Forget it.' I confess that when you first told me you'd tried Ritalin with Jonathan for only three days, I thought you hadn't given it much of a try. Now I understand!"

A third child had a similar reaction. That tale and some solid advice comes from the mother, Kay. First, the tale: "When my son was seven years old we did try Ritalin on him, and instead of slowing him down and relaxing him, it had the reverse reaction. He was like a crazy nut.…I can remember him doing 50 somersaults in a row (his brothers found it amusing and were counting). When I found out what was going on, I stopped it. He would climb up on things and try to jump off. I ended up taking him to the ER, where they gave him some kind of medication to counteract it. As we were leaving, they told me to keep him away from stairs and windows!" And then Kay's solid advice: "I'm not saying this is going to happen to your child, but if you do try Ritalin, make sure he is with a parent the first day or two just to see how he reacts."

I second that advice. Monitor the effects of Ritalin or any drug carefully until you know for certain what side effects will manifest in your child. And make sure you find a doctor who values your input and observations, and who will work with you to find a pharmaceutical solution that works for your child.

What Then?

When I saw that Ritalin and its relatives weren't going to work (we tried several other drug types), I went to work. I researched various natural healing methods with a reputation for ameliorating ADHD. This book is not the appropriate tome for exploring those options in detail, but there is great value in knowing that there are indeed other options, and that many are well worth pursuing if you're not comfortable with a pharmaceutical approach.

I spent the next five years seeking out, getting training in, and applying various natural interventions to tame Jonathan's ADHD. The methods were helpful, and Jonathan did gradually heal. I used targeted nutritional supplementation bolstered by over-the-counter vitamins with DMAE (Dimethylaminoethanol, an organic compound), pure sound therapy (not music, but pure tones diagnosed just for him), and—most astonishing of all in effectiveness—pure castor oil hotpacks to the abdomen (Google it!). I used each method in turn for about two years, at which point Jonathan and I were both ready to move on to the next option. Those three therapies saw us through the next six years, and effectively brought him out of the ADHD tunnel into the light of day.

There are some claims that the arrival of puberty with its hormonal Mack truck actually helps ADHD somewhat (no kidding! puberty makes some problems *better*! who knew?). That seemed to be true for Jonathan, so another "natural" option may be to wait it out. *Riiiight.* That's an option I don't advise.

In the end, no matter what the additional diagnosis or treatment, I am convinced both through experience and observation that there are solutions to all situations, though some may resolve more brilliantly than others. Keep on turning over stones, networking with other parents, and clicking your way through the cyber highway. You'll get there.

You'll get there in especially good shape if you go back and reread "Nurturing the Parent!"

School Years

20

The Education Battleground

"The whole purpose of education is to turn mirrors into windows."
—Sydney J. Harris

Warning: The Surgeon General highly recommends that you down a double espresso before reading this chapter. It will be oh-so-much easier to absorb. Ready? On your mark, get set....

Camps can be divided when it comes to educational preferences and placement for students with Down syndrome. Public or private? Full inclusion or self-contained classrooms? Home schooling or not? And every other conceivable option or combination thereof.

My favorite position on this question is fence-sitting. That's right. I recommend that you sit on the fence and get your high-powered binoculars out. This is the wisest position with the broadest perspective. Don't concern yourself with labels and the perceived pressure to belong to a specific camp. There is no need.

The binoculars you look through have a singular focus: they show only the true *current needs* of your child. You have only to meet those needs; you don't have to choose a position in advance, nor do you have to stick to one philosophy or position. You only want to meet the true educational needs

---

What's That?

Inclusion: The educational practice of educating children with disabilities in a general education classroom along with children without disabilities.

In **full inclusion,** all needed instruction and supports (such as therapies) are provided within the regular classroom.

In **partial inclusion,** the child may periodically leave the regular classroom to receive supports or special instruction, or may be included for some, but not all subjects.

Practice varies from state to state and district to district.

---

of your child. Note that the operative word here is "true." Not "politically correct" or "educational trend du jour." You'll need to set aside other people's conceptions and perceptions and be clear about your own.

I have seen parents err in both directions: some parents have unrealistic expectations of educational systems that are already overburdened, and/or fanciful concepts of their child's needs and abilities. Other parents, with plates already overfull with other responsibilities, trust under-functioning school systems to meet needs without monitoring those systems to ensure that needs are being well met.

If you keep your expectations high but realistic, you will be well equipped to find the best solutions at each step of the process.

From that fence-sitting position, over the years I was able to place Jonathan in every educational variation mentioned in the first paragraph. Every one. Seeing through the binoculars of: "What is Jonathan's current need?" I made my choices, and changed his placement as his needs and age changed.

Here is a bullet-point guide from those of us who have walked through the various systems before you:

Binocular Check:

1. What are my child's current true needs?
2. What does my gut tell me about this teacher I am observing?

3. What does my intuition tell me about the principal of this school?
4. How do I feel about the way the school is run?

Let's take a closer look.

What Are My Child's Current True Needs?

When you assess your child's current needs, you're looking simultaneously at where he's been cognitively/socially/etc., where he is now, and where you'd like him to go. There will always be one area that pops, that corners your greatest concern for him.

Other issues will remind you that they also need attention, but not to worry; there will be a perfect time later for each of these issues to hog your attention. Later. Not now.

Look at the developmental timeline when you're deciding on the "true need" issue. Some issues need to be handled *now* while neurons are still making that critical plethora of connections; other issues can be deferred and grown into later. Reading, for example, is one of those connections that, the earlier made, the easier, and the greater the positive impact on all remaining school years. So that would be one time-sensitive issue you'd want to attend to.

Another critical issue is language/speech. If your child's language lags behind significantly, and especially if he has been given a diagnosis of Childhood Apraxia of Speech, that may be your primary concern.

Early training in sign language, establishing a productive working relationship with a speech-language pathologist, obtaining a recommended augmentative communication device, and training your child to use it, are all things you may want to be your child's primary focus in school.

What's That?

CAS: Childhood Apraxia of Speech: a speech disorder in which a child has trouble saying what he or she wants to say correctly and consistently. Not due to weakness or paralysis of speech muscles, the severity of CAS can range from mild to severe (National Institute on Deafness and Other Communication Disorders).

What's That?

SLP (Speech-Language Pathologist: a specialist who evaluates and treats communication disorders.

AAC (Augmentative and Alternative Communication): the use of equipment or a nonspeech communication method to supplement (augment) or replace (alternative) speech.

ACD (Augmentative Communication Device): equipment used by an AAC user to aid his or her communication.

AC devices range from low-tech (language boards with pictures that the user points to) to cutting edge equipment such as the iPad or electronic devices that "talk" for the child. I confess to an environmental bias, living as I do in the heart of Silicon Valley, but I lean toward the iPad when possible. I have seen parents successfully obtain school funding for the purchase of an iPad for their children with apraxia, and I think it's worth exploring.

Why? Number one, our kids are amazingly skilled at using electronic devices. They seem to be born hardwired into sync with software operation. It always amazes me. Secondly, the abundance of affordable apps (software applications) available now for special education, including

- **Apps for Augmentative Communication:** This link will get you started. The nonprofit organization Friendship Circle has done your homework for you. It lists seven Assistive Communication Apps for iPad: http://blog.friendshipcircle.org/2011/02/07/7-assistive-communication-apps-in-the-ipad-app-store

- **Special Needs Apps for Kids:** www.snaps4kids.com

- **Apps for Children with Special Needs:** www.a4cwsn.com

- Beyond that, a Google search will keep you busy for a while!

communication, is on a mushrooming binge. By the time you read this, you will have many more helpful apps to choose from than I do today. Using them can make life easier for your child and for you.

If your home is bilingual and you wish your child to be fluently bilingual, that might be another early concern to address. Depending on your location, you might find a bilingual school; one of my students attends one in my area. Or you may feel that home exposure is enough to meet your goal. Our children can indeed learn to understand two languages (or more), though they may choose to speak in only one.

Another of my students, Jacob, lives in a bilingual home where both Spanish and English are spoken. With an additional diagnosis of autism spectrum disorder, he often chooses to remain silent in our reading sessions (except when reading aloud for me). When he does speak, it is always in English. Recently, trying to draw him out, and knowing that his current school situation was problematic for him, I asked, "Do you like school?" Silence. No response. Then I asked him, "Te gusta la escuela? Si o no?" "*No!*" he shot out the answer instantly. (Note to self: *Use whatever Spanish you've got if you want to connect with Jacob.*)

If your child has moderate to severe behavioral issues, that might top your "Current No. 1 Need" list. Issues like behavior deserve immediate attention, before habits become iron-clad and patterns of social interaction become unworkable and disruptive in the school setting. You don't want your child getting a bad rep before he's out of the school starting gate.

Suggestion: don't get sidetracked by "later issues." This "later" category might include an inability to follow directions successfully, difficulty with making transitions from one activity to another, potty training, etc. These things take time and repetition. They will eventually get done.

Look also at whatever gap exists between where your child stands now on a certain issue—social skills, for example—and where you ideally want him to be. Don't be discouraged if the gap is wide: your child will be marvelously skilled at taking small but steady steps in the desired direction, as long as the needed training and environment are provided.

At the same time, be wary of overly idealistic goals that might reflect your own dreams but have little to do with your child's needs and abilities. Insisting on those goals can cause tremendous and unfair frustration on all sides. I'm not speaking about simple high goals here, of raising the bar higher and higher while assisting your child to meet each graduated level.

No. I'm referring to denial and all of its relatives. You don't want to get so far "up de Nile" that you need a paddle to get home.

Identifying your child's Number 1 Current Need will make selecting a placement a much more focused and effective process. You will of course have secondary needs in mind, so your total focus list may have several items on it; but keep No. 1 firmly in your binoculars and don't get distracted from that goal.

What Does My Intuition Tell Me about the Teacher?

Once you've clearly got the Number 1 Current Need in hand, you'll explore the venues where that need can most effectively be met. This search will bring you into as many situations as your local educational options can provide.

As you look at possible schools and classifications for your child, e.g., inclusion with support; Special Day Classes (SDC), what you want to be concerned about first is the teacher. Period.

What's That?

SDC (Special Day Class) or SCC (Self-Contained Class): School systems use different terminology to refer to these classes which consist only of children in special education; the class generally stays together for the day. Class size is always smaller than regular education classes, with more individualized attention for each child.

The teacher rules. If you'll indulge me, for simplicity's sake I'm going to refer to "teacher" as "she." She creates the classroom. Everything else, aides included, will fall into alignment with her.

So you want to observe intelligently, staying in your core, with your intuitive antennae up and working. Don't judge quickly; stay several hours to observe. Make arrangements to come back another day if you feel the need.

What kind of energy does she create in the classroom? Do you get the feeling she likes her students? This means everything, folks. Our kids can smell "I don't like you" from a thousand paces, and will completely shut down. Trust me on this. In the words of one mother, "It's as if they've been given an extra sense of 'who are the bad guys and who are the good guys.'"

Does this teacher pull her students up with higher standards and expectations, or does she aim low? How does she structure the flow of the day? Is the day balanced, or sluggish? Is time devoted daily to teaching what you consider most essential for your child?

Throughout Jonathan's academic years, I "teacher shopped." It was not openly acknowledged that this was permissible in the Cincinnati school system at the time, but it was then. When I realized that, I was on it. I observed whatever schools had an opening for a student until *Ker-ching!* I found the teacher I was looking for.

After you've checked out the teacher, look at the students in her class. A terrific teacher can override many classroom components that might be less than ideal, but if the class is an exclusive (special education only) classroom and demographics are heavily weighted toward behavioral disorders, emotional disturbances, or the more intense end of the autism spectrum, that influence on the class energy grid will overpower anything the teacher can do.

What happens if you like the teacher and the class demographics, but by the time Fall comes, the demographics have shifted and you now consider the situation unworkable? Pull out. Start a new search. Don't settle.

What Does My Intuition Tell Me about the School & Principal?

This question is telling. There is a distinct, formative energy which inspires each school, and it filters down from the top. Unless the current principal is newly arrived, the school will bear her/his mark. Look for the evidence of that mark.

An outstanding case in point was Jonathan's second elementary school. He was finishing first grade, and I was looking for a better option for second grade. Supported inclusion was a thing of the future, only in the formative stages at this time, and was not available in my immediate area. So I teacher shopped, looking for the best match for my child in a special education teacher. I found her at an inner city public school, in an undesirable—even sketchy—part of town.

After being sold on her, I then met the principal and took a good look at the "hall energy." Most of the children in this grade school were from challenged backgrounds, with poverty pervasive and too many parents on drugs, some even neglecting to feed their children sufficiently. Yet the school was calm and disciplined, the halls quiet and orderly. And, oh yes: healthy snack jars at the door of every classroom, essential for this student demographic. The principal ran a tight ship and met the needs of his students. It was immediately easy to respect him and the atmosphere he had created. His expectations were high, and students were expected to meet them. Period. And of course they did.

At the other end of the spectrum, let's look at the experience through which I earned the right to give you this "check out the principal" advice.

For kindergarten, without first checking out teachers, principal, or school, I enrolled Jonathan in a special education classroom in our local public school. I was a novice at this "placement" task, and not at all skilled. At that early point in 1991, I just enrolled him and crossed my fingers, an act unthinkable today.

Jonathan's body could not adjust to heat; he was incapable of perspiring, for some unknown reason. The hotter he got, the cloudier his thinking became. Though a school morning might start out cold, if the sun was intense by afternoon, he became somnolent on the bus home. There was no way he could think clearly to take off his jacket on the sweltering school bus, and rashes were the result of this situation.

The teachers and I used a notebook to keep in touch, and passed it back and forth if there was something we needed to communicate. They were aware of Jonathan's heat problem, but with their other duties often forgot to do anything about it, and the intense heat later in the day had his rashes raging. One day I wrote in the notebook, "Please take Jonathan's jacket off today before he gets on the afternoon school bus. Thanks."

I had no idea that the principal of this large grade school had been taking it upon herself to read my daily messages to the staff. Had she nothing else to do with her time? Amazing. She called me into her office. That was the day a new realization flew in my face: the truth that some humans are given positions of authority for which they are wholly unqualified.

She waved the apparently offending notebook in my face and yelled, "Why are you sending these ridiculous notes to my staff? What do you think my teachers are, *retarded?*"

Unbelievable.

Still a raw newbie at this assess-the-school game, I stumbled out of her office in a daze. And, of course, watched my notebook Ps and Qs, delivering the more delicate communications to my son's teachers in person until I could move him to another school.

Fortunately, this woman was only one exception in a long line of good principals, but I include this story to give you a broader perspective. And also to let you know that you will likely meet some unwitting "trainers" along your path that will help you gain knowledge, strength, and advocacy skills.

It's all good. "What doesn't kill you will make you stronger" is not a flabby aphorism. You can effectively use every situation you encounter to become more of what you want to become, whether for personal or child-centered reasons. You become equipped.

When Teacher-Shopping Is Against Your District's Policy

"Help! My school district does not permit me to shop for the best teacher. What do I do now?"

Such a good question. Here are some suggestions, gleaned from parents and educators currently on the school battleground.

First of all, how did this happen? Why are many districts now adopting this kind of policy? For several reasons. Visualize a district with 20 percent fantastic educators and 80 percent less so. There is, of course, a crush of requests for the outstanding teachers. This looks reeeeeally bad on a number of counts: reason number one.

There is also a legal reason, depending on your timing. Under the Individuals with Disabilities Education Act (IDEA), technically you cannot discuss appropriate settings for the next year until your Individualized Education Program (IEP) team has agreed on your child's goals and needed services. This typically happens in the spring, more or less, depending on your school district. So timing is important: IEP first, find appropriate settings second.

In many school districts, the number of settings that match up with the placement agreed upon in your child's IEP will be limited. For example, if the IEP team agreed that the appropriate placement for your child is full inclusion in his neighborhood school, then you can only look at teachers in the neighborhood school. If the team agreed that your child should be in a self-contained class for students with intellectual disabilities, and there are only two in your district for students your child's age, then you can only look at those two classes.

What's That?

IEP (Individualized Education Program): A written document for each child with a disability that is developed, reviewed, and revised in a meeting in accordance with legal requirements of the Individuals with Disabilities Education Act (IDEA).

IEP Meeting: A meeting at which a child's IEP is developed, discussed, or amended, attended by members of the Child Study Team, which usually includes a social worker, a psychologist, a learning specialist, and your child's teachers and therapists. Parents are *always* to be included in IEP meetings. IEP meetings are held at least annually, and often more frequently, at the parents' request.

LRE (Least Restrictive Environment): Part of IDEA, the LRE is identified as one of the six principles that govern the education of students with disabilities and other special needs. By law, schools are required to provide a free appropriate public education (FAPE) in the least restrictive environment that is appropriate to the individual student's needs. It means that a student who has a disability should have the opportunity to be educated with nondisabled peers, to the greatest extent appropriate.

Tip #1:

IEP Based on Individual Need, Not Diagnosis

At your child's IEP meeting, insist that his placement be made *on the basis of individual need*, and *not diagnosis*. If the school district is offering you only one option, and it's *not* the LRE for your child, then that goes against IDEA and should be disputed. Parents have the right to say no.

Often a school system not fluent in inclusion skills will promote the idea that the child's needs are so many and so specialized that an exclusive classroom (special day class, etc.) is the best option.

But those who've been there will argue that an exclusive classroom is often the "*most* restrictive environment." Yes, of course, your child may need supports: speech therapy, occupational therapy, an aide, etc. But in an inclusive setting, those supports must be brought to the child, regardless of whether it's convenient for the school system.

If you're told—as is often the case—"Our other programs are all full; this is all we can offer you," hold your ground. As long as the agreed-upon LRE is not being offered by the school system, the placement is up for dispute. Unfortunately, today many parents have to hire legal help to get the placement that they want for their child. But before you set sail on that legal ocean, make sure you have a case that's winnable. Your lawyer will tell you if it is.

- **IEP:** For more information on what an IEP should include, see: http://idea.ed.gov/explore/view/p/,root,regs,300,D,30 0%252E320, [comma at the end is essential]

- **IEP Meeting:** Who attends an IEP meeting? See: http://specialchildren.about.com/od/specialeducation/f/ iepfaq02.htm

Typically, options are more plentiful when your child is younger; choices may dwindle as your child moves up along the education ladder. Let's hope that if you have an infant in arms now, this will *not* be the case when you're ready to search for middle school, high school, and transition programs.

Martha Hogan, one of the founders of the Down Syndrome Connection of the Bay Area, encourages parents to write their own goals directly into the IEP. "Put in your goals, dreams, and objectives. Write it in the record. And never, never, never sign the IEP unless you're sure it's the right placement," Martha advises. "For instance, you can build a case that your child needs a certain therapy because of being duly diagnosed, but if it's not in the IEP, *it's not legally binding.* It all has to be recorded before it's signed. Otherwise, don't sign it."

State laws regarding signing IEPS vary, so it's wise for parents to learn about their own state's legal issues. For example, in some states a parent's signature is only required to initiate special education services, and on subsequent IEPs the signature only means that the parent attended the IEP meeting, not that she agrees with the IEP as written.

Find out what works in your state. Every state has support groups that assist parents in getting this information, and I encourage you to explore that route before you get into the mechanics of an IEP.

Tip #2:

Inclusion in Your Neighborhood School

One of your best options may be full inclusion in a general education classroom at your neighborhood school. While I'll cover the "how to make it work" details of inclusion in a later chapter, I want to stress at this point that only inclusion *with support* works. Tossing a child with special needs into a classroom with one teacher, a standard teacher's assistant, and 30 students is begging for failure, and when that is done, it is usually followed by the claim, "See? Inclusion just doesn't work."

What's That?

Inclusion: Inclusion of a child with disabilities in a general education classroom; inclusion values every student by setting up supports, services, plans, and activities that provide successful participation and genuine belonging in that classroom.

Your child will likely need support in the form of an additional adult (teacher, inclusion specialist, aide) to assist him, and to *modify materials* so that he can truly be a viable part of the class. If your child is in an inclusive classroom and brings home a huge stack of homework just like every other child in the class has, *that is not modification.* That is not making inclusion work. If your child's IEP specifies that he must be provided with modified work, then that is indeed what the school must provide. See the inclusion section in the chapter, "Inclusion and Testing," for more specific guidance on a modified curriculum.

If your child's IEP team (of which you are a vital, veto-empowered member) agrees that he needs a one-on-one aide, full or part-time, the district is responsible for funding this aide; generally, the principal of the school is responsible for hiring that aide.

Martha Hogan tells us, "You have every right to go to your neighborhood school, meet the principal, observe the classes, etc. Keep in mind that the principal is one of the key players in the inclusion game, and as such is very important. She is responsible for establishing your child's support system, and has the final say on who will be hired as an aide." She adds, "Our children need good peer models. Most children with Down syndrome are visual learners; throughout life, they learn by imitation. So we value the richness of the inclusive class environment, vs. a Special Day Class, where the peer models are not always the best."

Now let's look at two approaches to securing an inclusive placement in your neighborhood school.

Tip #3:

Inclusion When the Principal and School Are Receptive

The principal seems open to you? Fantastic. Meet directly with the principal to describe the kind of learning environment in which your child blossoms; describe the kind of classroom you believe will most benefit your child; and make sure you've already done your IEP homework. By that, I mean make sure that you've already included specific goals in the (now-approved) IEP that can best be met in that neighborhood school. Then follow up! Send the principal a positive letter re-stating those characteristics and thanking him/her for being so student-centered. Later, you will have another IEP meeting to get team agreement that the LRE for your child is indeed this neighborhood school.

Tip #4:

Inclusion When the Principal Is Not Receptive

At this point, if you're not getting receptive inclusion signals from the principal at your neighborhood school, it's time to go in softly through the side door.

Don't bully the principal. "I want *this* teacher!" To quote one seasoned advisor who will wisely remain unnamed, "You have to massage the principal." You take the softer approach, as in, "Gosh, the way that classroom is set up would just be awesome for my child!" or, "Gee, I'd like to see all of your programs. I'm still learning how elementary school (high school, etc.) works, and I want to see as much as I can so that I feel good about the team's placement decision."

Golly-gee-whiz. I may be overstressing the attitude, but you get the idea. This advice comes to me from the best of the best, so I'm passing it on. Martha Hogan adds, "Try to get the principal to feel that he's making the best decision by telling him how our children with Down syndrome learn best in any situation. You really need to get this person on board, and the way you do it is to frame it as 'how this would work for my child.'"

Ask to visit various classes, then follow up with a letter describing the qualities of the teacher you like the most—without naming the teacher—making it clear that these are the teacher qualities that your child most needs and will best succeed with. For instance, your child thrives with a teacher who has high expectations, gives consistent positive praise, etc. The more specific you are, the better. For instance, you might say, "Because my child has some language delays, she would *really* benefit from a teacher who has a background in speech-language pathology." Or, "Because my child has a mild hearing loss, she would really benefit from being in a class with a teacher with a lower, louder voice." You might want to find a special quality in the desired teacher that no other teacher has, and focus on it as a match for your child's needs.

In other words, if you find a teacher you really like, you can build your case around her/his qualities, giving the reasons why you want your child to be in one classroom rather than another.

Parting Advice

A few final thoughts about placement. If you can't manage to get the LRE of your dreams for your child, is that a disaster? No. Learning and growth in some measure will still take place. If in fact you determine that your child's needs will be better met in a less inclusive classroom, are you making the wisest decision in seeking that setting? Yes. As I mentioned at the beginning of this chapter, I utilized all options and variations on those options as my son moved through his academic years. I simply determined what his greatest needs were, and that guided his placement.

I know of two students whose ideal LRE was, in fact, in a *less* inclusive setting.

Ryan was assessed as being so high functioning that the school system placed him in full inclusion and refused him any services at all. His parents had to move heaven and earth to get him the help he needed. In their case, moving heaven and earth required the muscle power of lawyers (why are you not surprised?), and eventually the district was forced to support Ryan in a less inclusive setting.

Then there is Hannah, who at this writing has just received a regular high school diploma after passing the four "high stakes tests" required by her state. Her mother, Valerie, tells the story:

"Hannah spent all of elementary school fully included. This arrangement worked pretty well when she was in the early grades, but by fourth grade, it was clear to my husband and me that Hannah was not learning up to her abilities. There were many basic math concepts she hadn't mastered in earlier grades, but she couldn't get individualized help with her problems. The staff said she wasn't delayed enough to qualify for any extra assistance.

"Hannah was also having trouble keeping up with the writing demands and was often tuned out when instructions or assignments were given. However, because she mostly stayed in her seat and behaved herself and read aloud well when called upon, the school acted as if she was the poster child for inclusion.

"Hannah ended up her grade school years clinically depressed—feeling as if there was something seriously 'wrong' with her because she could almost, but not quite, keep up with the other kids. Adding to her misery, a handful of her classmates had taken to bullying her at lunch, recess, and other times when there was little adult supervision.

"To help Hannah salvage her self-esteem and get her the individualized attention we knew was key, my husband and I decided to find a *less* inclusive setting for her. We settled on a program for kids with learning disabilities who took all the regular classes, but were taught by special ed teachers at a slower pace and with a lower student-teacher ratio.

"We had to rattle a lot of cages to get Hannah into these classes—taping our IEP meetings, bringing in a psychologist to talk about how damaging the bullying was to Hannah, threatening to hire a lawyer—before the school system finally agreed to let Hannah out of full inclusion and into the program for kids with learning disabilities.

"Our efforts paid off. She excelled once she was in a setting where she was allowed to go at the right pace for her and where teachers were acutely aware of how each student in the class was doing and what they needed to do better. By the end of high school, her attention span, motivation, and work ethic had improved to the point that she once again felt comfortable taking many of her classes in an included setting.

"So, for Hannah, we had to prove that the LRE was *not* full inclusion; it was placement in classes where she could receive more specialized instruction that would allow her to reach her potential."

So there you have it. If you find yourself in a similar situation, you can move heaven and earth like Ryan's parents or rattle some cages like Hannah's did. Either option sounds empowering, not to mention athletic.

Now that you know what you're looking for in an academic setting and how you're going to look for it while sitting on the fence with your high-powered binoculars, let's examine the academic history of two men with Down syndrome. Between the two of them, the academic experiences were so diverse that you'll get an excellent overview of the possibilities and challenges.

21

Student One

"I not go to school today.
It's hot and sticky.
Makes me bonkers."
—Jonathan Hale, at 8

Jonathan, 26 at this writing, attended a typical preschool for two years. He was the only child with special needs in the school. Serendipitously, the school director had degrees in special education, and was happy to enroll Jonathan. In 1987, this open-armed welcome was about as common as a ten-carat diamond, and felt of equal value to me.

I would like to say that Jonathan took to the scene like a bird to air, but I can't. He didn't. For the first couple of months, he would go comatose shortly after his morning arrival, snoozing in any likely corner. He would resurrect when the morning was over and I came to get him.

Years would pass before I understood what was happening. This child with as-yet-undiagnosed severe ADHD couldn't handle the stimulation. It was overwhelming. All those frenetic little humans running around, yelling, crying…it was too much, and sleep seemed the wisest recourse. Which, frankly, it was.

Fast-forward to the school year's end, where Jonathan had progressed to sitting happily at a tot's table, being served "tea time" by equally happy small females. He had slowly adjusted and was now delighted with the situation.

Summertime saw our family regularly relocated to Northern Michigan, and Jonathan easily attended the typical preschool summer program there. He understood and accepted the social routine by this time, and there was no problem. Through high school and beyond, Jonathan attended the typical summer camp in that area, enjoying acceptance and friendships.

It was during one of those Michigan summers when Jonathan was five that I learned it was possible to teach him to read, and so homeschooling in reading and writing began then and continued through middle school.

Tally so far:
1. Full Inclusion
2. Home Schooling

For kindergarten and first grade, I enrolled Jonathan in the only option available locally, a self-contained special education classroom. This worked fairly well, though Jonathan was an anomaly because he was the only student in the class who could read.

Tally so far:
1. Full Inclusion
2. Home Schooling
3. Full Exclusion

As the first grade school year ended, I sat in to observe the second grade class at that school. I saw quickly that literacy in that classroom was so marginalized that it was virtually nonexistent, and I began a new search. I was not about to subject my little reader to a classroom flailing around in a literacy-crippled sea. Forget it.

A new teacher search led me to a remarkable covey of special education teachers that supported Jonathan so well, he was able to stay in one place for the next several years. No other students in his self-contained class were reading. Jonathan was a standout in this regard, and to my enormous delight, this fact was quickly noted by the school's special ed supervisor. An inclusionist at heart, she snapped him up and dropped him into an inclusive classroom for most of each day, herself acting as the aide support.

This was at an inner city public school, well-led and staffed by dedicated teachers. Jonathan flourished there.

Tally so far:

1. Full Inclusion
2. Home Schooling
3. Full Exclusion
4. ¾ Inclusion

Now it was time for middle school, and another set of needs presented itself. It was time to prepare for eventual transition to high school, and Jonathan's ongoing struggle with ADHD required a teacher with unique gifts. Because he needed the supervision that an 8-to-2 student-to-teacher ratio provided, we had to bypass the inclusion option, where the ratio could be as high as 30-to-1 (plus a classroom assistant). We had been enormously blessed in grade school, where the inclusion director herself acted as his aide; that was not an option in high school. Real, working inclusion was still in its infancy.

I was looking for a special ed teacher with powerful insight, an unbendable backbone, and absolute faith in the capability of her students. That might read like a fanciful wish list, but I found those qualities and more in Barbara Gamboa. A towering Amazonian-like woman, Barbara was capable of working near miracles with her students. I saw her turn nonverbal, out-of-control teens into verbally communicative students with budding self-control. Antisocial, withdrawn teens into smiling, dancing near-socialites.

She made Jonathan *work*. It was just the training he needed. Geography, spelling, literature…you name it. He labored over dictionary work and long spelling drills while classical music played subtly in the background. When the other eighth grade classes were working on a particular literacy project, Barbara took that book, read it aloud to her class, and designed developmentally appropriate unit activities to help them grasp the material.

A truly great teacher in this kind of small setting endeavors to draw out or discipline students according to their natures, and she sure nailed Jonathan's. If he lingered too long in making a transition from one activity to the other (transitions were never his forte), she would say to him, "Would the *Prince* please join us?" He understood the gentle sarcasm, knew she was fond of him anyway, and complied. She also let him know frequently, with absolute sincerity, "Jonathan, you are a fine young gentleman." She meant it and he believed it. It doesn't get any better than that.

She handled his "run-off-itis" problem expertly. With ADHD trumping Down syndrome for him, he had difficulty controlling his impulsivity. If his class was out on a field trip and the idea of leaving the group occurred to him, and it did frequently, he simply vanished. The "Where's Waldo?" concept has nothing on Jonathan. He would be gone, gone, gone.

After a few of these experiences, Barbara came up with a genius idea. On their next field trip, which was to the Cincinnati Zoo, a vast area where you would *not* want to search for a child, Barbara came equipped. As the group got ready to tour the zoo, she pulled a length of twine out of her purse. She tucked one end in her belt and the other end in Jonathan's pocket; neither end was secured. The ruse was only symbolic, but the result was immediately effective: utter humiliation. Jonathan was the only tethered cowboy in the posse.

You know any teenage boys who would knowingly incur this penalty more than once? Neither do I. It worked.

In that school district, funding was scarce for special ed class "extras" (extras that elsewhere would be considered minimal required equipment), so Barbara came up with a plan. Under her tutelage, the students learned the basics of operating a snack stand, including handling money and making change, keeping records, stocking supplies, and service with a smile. Soon the class was operating a snack stand which they would set up near a building exit just before dismissal every day.

Guess who raked in the bucks with *that* marketing plan? With the profits, Barbara bought electronic equipment for her class. Thievery was common in the large school, so she carved "Gamboa" into the metal of each piece of equipment. No way to erase *that* ownership. A brilliant solution, but I regret that she was up against such odds in teaching her students.

And let's take a moment to give kudos to that principal for backing such a plan. The students not only learned new skills, but enjoyed elevated esteem in the eyes of their peers. It was a win-win.

Jonathan was able to spend three years with this extraordinary teacher, and then it was time to search for a high school teacher and setting. At this point, age 15, Jonathan had experienced only female teachers and aides.

Plus, he was homeschooled by his mom. So when my search took me to a high school where the special education teacher was a man, where the aide was a man, and the entire class consisted of seven other male teens, I took a closer look. Having male authority figures and role models, along with having only guys for classmates, would give him another environmental experience entirely. And it did. This was the first time Jonathan actually developed a "hang-out-together" friendship with a classmate.

Jonathan spent two good years there, and we looked forward to a third. But on the first day of school that third year, Jonathan arrived to find that, with zero notification, both the teacher and the aide had jumped ship and swum to other schools. Jonathan had been assigned to another teacher, one that I was familiar with and felt was a poor match for Jonathan. Can you spell "scramble?" I knew that if all slots were filled at other high schools, we were in deep trouble.

By some miracle, Barabara Gamboa had meanwhile transitioned into teaching high school rather than middle school, and by a further blockbuster coincidence, she had exactly one opening in her class. Serious scramble now. I had to act fast and push the legalities through before the slot was gone. But it worked, and Jonathan finished his high school years in skilled hands.

If Jonathan were entering first grade today, at this writing, his entire school experience would be very, very different. I would expect him to be included meaningfully in a general education classroom and given all needed support, including (because of his triple diagnosis) an aide; and if he weren't included, I'd fight for it. I'd network. I'd consult with everyone I could think of to consult with. And I'd have my lawyer's phone number written on my palm in indelible ink.

That notwithstanding, I tried to craft each year to fit Jonathan's needs, using what was available at the time. I feel that each step in this academic progression added naturally to Jonathan's growth and to his life. It was varied, forming and flowing as his needs changed, and—along with indispensable homeschooling—has served him well.

All's well that ends well.

22

Student Two

"I can't stay for my reading lesson today.
I have to get going…I have a party to catch."
—Blair Hogan, age 33

Blair and I first met when he came to me for reading lessons at age 31. My overriding thought as our first session ended was, "This is a prince of a human being." I felt privileged to know him.

Blair today is 33 and is the son of Martha and Kevin Hogan. In 1998, Martha cofounded Silicon Valley's "Down Syndrome Connection of the Bay Area." Today, the DS Connection is a powerful, award-winning service organization attending to families throughout the San Francisco Bay area. It's been a long road to success for Blair and his family, and one marked by academic extremes.

In addition to the Down syndrome diagnosis, Blair is legally blind; he was born with cataracts in both eyes and later lost all sight in one eye. For those readers new to Down syndrome, I'll answer your question: that is not a frequent problem in Down syndrome. No more than Jonathan's complete inability to chew is common in Down syndrome.

In spite of this additional handicap, by the age of five, Blair was beginning to read. He had a sight word vocabulary of over 50 words, and loved the game of putting small word cards together to form sentences he could read. It was a joy for the whole family to watch, and as Martha says, "We had a ball reading."

For first grade, Martha placed Blair in the recommended special day class (SDC) for children with moderate to severe disabilities. But for second grade, she switched him to what was then called a "learning handicapped class." "I wanted him to have better peer models," she said. "I thought I was moving him *up*." It was a disaster. The teacher assigned to Blair didn't know how to teach him and settled on the solution of ignoring him. Martha continues, "He lost his confidence, his motivation, and just wouldn't try any more. He shut down. This happens to a lot of our kids when a teacher doesn't know how to teach them."

Folks, remember my advice to shop for a good teacher match? Amen, and I rest my case. Neither Martha nor I knew that guiding rule when we hopped on the edu-train, and we paid the price. You will be traveling in the right coach car, headed in the right direction, staying on the right track, by using that one indispensible ticket. It doesn't matter how good the school is. If the teacher doesn't have the knowledge or skill to teach your child and isn't interested in learning how, the rest is history, and it's not a history that's fun to read.

The staff in charge of placement convinced Martha to put Blair back in a SDC for third grade, so she did. Blair went to their neighborhood school through sixth grade, where his SDC class was heavily weighted toward children with severe disabilities.

Socially, this left Blair on his own, so he turned to the typical kids in the school, who befriended him and hung out with him. To understand how this happened so easily, you have to know Blair. Blair is all about people. When he first sees you and bellows his "How's it *goin'*?" you know that someone is really paying attention to you. He's there for you, is already enjoying your company, and intends to continue enjoying it.

A lifelong USC (University of Southern California) Trojan fan with a Trojan T-shirt/cap/shoe wardrobe that would go for top dollar on eBay, Blair's first meeting with then-coach Pete Carroll was one for the books. Blair walked up to coach Carroll and, in his most conspiratorial tone, said, "Hi, Pete. I'm Blair. If you lose, you should get fired." Coach Carroll grinned. "Blair, you're absolutely right." Martha comments, "It was a friendship made in heaven; Pete always pulled Blair aside when he saw him and they'd chat for a good ten minutes."

So, as difficult as close friendships were for Jonathan, for Blair it was as natural as breathing in and out. Socialization with his typical peers got him through sixth grade, but then his edu-train fell off the tracks.

Middle school saw him placed with a special education teacher who, once again, was a horrific fit for Blair. He spiraled downward and began to self-stimulate, flapping books in the air until they were in shreds. Officials stepped in and advised Martha to send Blair to the most severely handicapped class in existence.

Oh, right. Smashing idea.

At the risk of boring you, let me repeat that *a good teacher fit for our children is essential.* One of my reading students was placed at age seven with a teacher/class that was so mismatched he became completely withdrawn and depressed. The school psychiatrist recommended antidepressants. The mom recommended that she get her child the heck out of that school, which she did. The child flourished in a new environment, which was an excellent fit.

But back to Blair's edu-train, which was now lying off tracks on its side. Let's have Martha take it from here.

"I thought, 'I'm done.' I pulled him out and brought him home. I started looking around and found a model for inclusion in Canada, headed by Marsha Forest. I realized then that there was another option, and searched around for a few places that were doing inclusion in California. I found a tiny town in Northern California where they were doing full inclusion. I visited there and brought a program specialist with me, as well as a Down syndrome league staffer.

"Then I filed a civil rights lawsuit against the school district and decided to enroll Blair at our neighborhood middle school where my other sons had gone. But this was uncharted territory, and when I informed the principal that I was going to enroll Blair, the principal asked questions like, 'Can he talk?' and 'Does he know his brothers' names?' He had no idea what Blair's capabilities were.

"I held firm. I told him, 'We're going forward with this.' I made everyone involved—teachers, special educators, the principal—go to training sessions for inclusion. Because I had

filed a civil rights lawsuit, they went along with it. They had
to, and all of them attended several training sessions.

"After the trainings, we started him at the school with
the aide who had been acting as his home teacher while the
lawsuit was being settled. She became his middle school aide
as a transitional step from home to school. Then we replaced
her with a full-time aide. He also had the help of an inclusion
specialist from within the district system who oversaw his
whole program, who was there almost daily; she was his
manager. She designed peer support, academic support, staff
training, everything.

"Ever since this little guy was born, the educational
system as it existed then felt wrong to me. He was trapped
in an institutional like setting. He withdrew more and more
into himself, except at home. He lost the ability to read. Then
at age eleven, he completely lost the sight in his left eye.

"He was a seventh grader when he entered inclusion,
and the long story short is that he changed the lives of
teachers and of many, many students. For instance, he
influenced the computer teacher. Previously, she was hard-
nosed; no one wanted to take computer class. But she became
kind and patient, because she learned to be that way with
Blair. It was a transformation.

"I approached the band teacher because I wanted Blair
to be in the band.

'Can he play an instrument?' the director asked.

'No.'

'Can he read music?'

'No. But I bet he could play the drums.'

"The director responded, 'We might get this to work,
but I want you to know that I'm not going to treat him like a
student. I'm going to treat him like my son.' I cried.

"And so Blair learned to play the bass drum. He
continued with the band and went on to play with both the
regular band and the marching band in high school.

"He made such a difference in the lives of other
students. At the time of the first dance, the vice principal

called me on the phone. 'You have to come over and see this,' she said. Apparently a group of students had put out a flyer: *Blair Hogan, a new student here, is coming to the dance, and we want all of you to come out and support him.*

"I got to the dance and found the vice principal.

'Where's Blair?' I asked.

'Oh, you can't see him from here. See that crowd of students clustered over there on the dance floor? He's dancing in the middle of them. They're having a blast.'

"In class, Blair always got the content, no matter what; he got the richness of what was offered. He always had an aide with him to modify the material, and we always had good aides. We were blessed.

"He was always paired up with peers. Once his two older brothers were home from college when two gorgeous girls from high school showed up on the lawn, waiting to take Blair to a school practice. My sons were so busy staring out the window that they walked right into each other. 'What are we doing *wrong* here?' one asked out loud. No beautiful girls were showing up on the lawn for *them*. The guys raced out the door to talk to the girls, who weren't interested. They were just there for Blair.

"At graduation, knowing that Blair would have vision problems in navigating the black walk ramp, the staff slowed down the diploma line when Blair approached the ramp. When he got to the principal and accepted his diploma, many of the students and parents stood and applauded. Blair turned to the audience and pumped the air with both fists, and the crowd went wild.

"A man near me in the audience who did not know Blair, nor the fact that he has a disability, turned to his companion and said, 'Oh my God! This guy must be really special.'"

When Blair was eleven and first walked onto the middle school-high school campus, massive by elementary school standards, he muttered to Martha, "This place is too damn big." No, Blair, it was just big enough for you.

23

Inclusion and Testing

"If the Aborigine drafted an IQ test,
all of Western civilization would presumably flunk it."
—Stanley Garn, Anthropologist

Testing

At this point, I'd like to give you a leg up in two important areas: testing and inclusion. The more you know about both, the more you will increase the chances of your child thriving in the educational system, and the more skilled you will be at avoiding yawning manholes and the "If I Had Only Known" syndrome.

Caution! Standard IQ Testing

Often when the school does triennial assessments on your child, they will want to do standard IQ testing. See the yellow flag. See the red flag. Hear the sirens wail. Run, Dick, run!

Good. I've got your attention. The more informed you are about what you'll be dealing with, the better. So let's spend a moment on testing and the impact that will have on your child's records, on your emotional state, and on teachers' conceptual view of your child and your child's potential.

What's That?

Triennial Assessment: School districts are required under both federal and state special education laws to administer standardized assessments as part of a student's reevaluation every three years—provided the IEP team agrees that testing is needed to determine a child's continuing eligibility for services, if there are questions or concerns about the appropriate placement for the child, etc.

KABC-II (Kaufman Assessment Battery for Children, Second Edition): an IQ test used for children aged 3-18, designed to be culturally neutral.

CAS (Childhood Apraxia of Speech): Apraxia of speech, also known as verbal apraxia or dyspraxia, is a speech disorder in which a person has trouble saying what he or she wants to say correctly and consistently. It is not due to weakness or paralysis of the speech muscles. The severity of apraxia can range from mild to severe.

Typically, our children's intelligence—and certainly their abilities—cannot be accurately tested by using standard IQ tests. One example of the complications this can cause concerns a student I'll call Jimmy. Jimmy is an eight-year-old with Down syndrome who is nonverbal (CAS). As part of his triennial assessment, he was tested by his school district with the standard KABC-II IQ test.

The KABC-II, though designed to require more minimal verbal responses than some of the other commonly given IQ tests, is not designed to accurately test a child who is completely nonverbal. Because of this and other built-in response difficulties inherent in Down syndrome, Jimmy—a bright and highly social kid—received a profoundly low score not based on his actual capabilities, intelligence, or level of functioning.

Other Response Difficulties

"Other response difficulties? Like what?" Well, for starters, most young children with Down syndrome have difficulty computing "wh" questions: what, when, why, where. We can get them there eventually, but it's a process that takes years. Not a great setup for testing a first-grader.

Then there's our friendly neighborhood "In-Your-Dreams-I'll-Do-What-You-Want-Me-To-Do" response. Oppositional behavior complicates the IQ-testing conundrum. For example, right in front of Jimmy, the administering psychologist placed a toy on the table and covered it with a cloth. He then asked Jimmy to find the toy. Quite naturally, the child refused. I am qualified to say, "naturally," because I've taught Jimmy, and he was likely thinking, "You want me to do *what*? It's right in front of you, Dude. Not *my* job to find it for you. Besides, I don't feel like it."

Stamp! on his permanent record, which now includes the assessment that Jimmy is "partially functioning at an 8-to-12-month-old level." Do I need to tell you what Jimmy's parents thought of that assessment? I didn't think so.

What Are Your Options?

So, let's think positively here. What can you do to avoid a similar experience? For one thing, you can request that age range of performance not be part of the assessment. It is at the district's discretion whether or not to comply with that request, and some districts will honor that; some may not.

You can also request a specific test that you think might show your child's abilities better. For example, there are IQ tests that require little or no verbal response, which some parents prefer. The Leiter International Performance Scale and the Test of Nonverbal Intelligence (TONI) are examples.

Another option, if you can swing it financially, is for you to pay privately to have an IQ test done *before* the school does theirs. That gives you the chance to provide an optimum setup for your child's success in testing, because *you* choose the person who does the testing, and you can give that person up-front guidance on how to get the best response from your child. If you like the results, share them with the school. That's good ammunition.

If you have the time, you might want to do online research. You could start online with the legal article, "Standardized Testing Not Required For Triennial Assessments and Year-for-Year Progress Not Required to Receive a Free Appropriate Public Education."

Researching? You might start with this legal article on testing: http://tinyurl.com/44ry9px

Legal Counsel

If you want to get legal counsel, the first step before hiring an attorney would be to have a one-on-one chat with the principal and the teacher. Talk about the impact on your child of permanently including incomplete and erroneous results in his records; discuss the use of more desirable language within the IQ evaluation: For example, if your child is under eight, in some states you have the option to use the label DD ("developmental delay") instead of intellectual disability or MR ("mental retardation"). Many children with Down syndrome also receive special education services under the category of OHI ("other health impairment") or SLI ("speech or language impairment").

If they are approached privately before being alarmed into a legal mode, some educators and administrations are willing to work with parents on this, and willing to work with the school district attorney (or other requisite professionals) to get permission for a change in language.

If the IQ-testing deed has already been done and is damaging, you can do what Jimmy's parents did. They hired a lawyer and legally contested the assessment results. Their legal contention, along with the results of a previous conducted IQ assessment (done by a privately hired psychologist, with much higher results), is now a permanent part of Jimmy's legal record.

Most distressing for Jimmy's parents is the fact that his teacher, principal, speech therapist, and other staff who were initially opposed to the idea of inclusion (the practice is new to their district) had begun to really come around, pleased at how well the classroom situation was working for both Jimmy and his classmates. But after testing, when they saw the numbers lying flat on the page, their views reversed. Since these events took place shortly before this book was published, it remained to be seen if the teacher and the administration's attitudes and expectations continued to be skewed by the numbers, or if that turned around eventually. I'm voting for turn-around. Go, Jimmy!

So before you find yourself in the midst of a mishandled testing situation, get information. Talk to the teacher and the principal. Get legal counsel if necessary. And here's a tip from Linda, Jimmy's mom: "Although Special Education Advocates can provide invaluable help, in a situation where legal information is essential, a lawyer is better."

Linda explains, "A SEA is not a lawyer. For instance, a SEA might tell you, 'You need to demand x, y, and z from the school district.' But a lawyer might say, 'This is what the judge will tell you in response to *that* demand,' and that's essential information that can save you time and money and enable you to make a more effective plan."

What's That?

Special Education Advocate (SEA): "A representative that informs parents of their educational rights and assists families in negotiating and resolving disputes with the school district (www.ed-center.com)." A SEA assists parents going through the IEP process. In-depth definition: http://www.ed-center.com/special_education_advocate.

Inclusion

What You Need to Know about Inclusion Before You Get There

I'll step aside at this point and let you hear straight talk from Patti McVay. I'd describe Patti as an Inclusion Warrior. A Samurai, but Tai Chi-style: always the calmest one at the table. She is an educational leader who believes that "children and adults who are labeled disabled can change our world."

I asked Patti to define inclusion from her experienced insider's view, and she obliged.

"Inclusion is about valuing every person, every child, every student. Inclusive school communities value every child by respecting and welcoming them, not just to be present in the general education class, but by setting up the necessary supports, services, and activities. These inclusive communities set plans in place so that every child can be a successful participant and learner with a genuine sense of belonging.

"Inclusive education is still an area of great struggle, but in my career as a teacher, principal, and special education director, I've seen all kinds of placement and services for students with disabilities. I remain convinced that inclusion—done well with commitment, researched best practices, and heart—*makes all the difference in the lives of children with disabilities.*

An excellent place to start your search for information and understanding about inclusion is: http://specialed.about.com/od/integration/a/Inclusion-What-Is-Inclusion.htm

"Inclusion directly impacts academic achievement, future job opportunities, happiness, and life success. I've seen the difference!"

Patti hones in on her A-List of Inclusive Best Practices:

1. Build Your Relationship with the General Ed Teacher

"This is a critical step that encourages general education to take ownership for your child, and to model that ownership for all the students in the class. This takes away the assumption that special education or another adult (an aide, etc.) is responsible for your child; it creates the model that your child is truly a member of the class and the school."

2. Build a Relationship with the Principal

"Build a relationship with the principal by sharing successes; celebrate your child's growth, the general education teacher's efforts to value all children, and the team's steps to see your child's potential and progress. Occasionally, copy in the Superintendent and the Board of Education so everyone 'hears' how positive inclusion is for your child and all children."

3. Establish Relationships with Other Families in the Class

"Initiate having other students over to your house, to facilitate friendships and wider connections for your child and your family."

4. Use Visuals

"Be sure visual prompts are in place to support your child throughout the day—for schedules, organization, communication, friendship, success, and more."

I'll add to Patti's words that visuals are particularly effective for our children with Down syndrome, as they are typically strong visual learners. Years ago I read an article about the value of using visuals, cleverly titled, "I *See* What You Mean." I was still in the midst of challenging parenting years when I read the article, and its "This-feels-so-right!" wisdom influenced my parenting for years, and still impacts my teaching.

In the process of writing this book, when I realized who the coauthor of that article was, I was caught somewhere between laughing and thinking, "No *way!*" It was Patti McVay. Thanks, Patti…I knew your work before I knew you.

So, *make it visual*, and watch comprehension light up your child's ability to follow directions, learn more, and cooperate more easily!

Take a look at "I See What You Mean" by Patti McVay, Heidi Wilson, and Luci Chiotti; published in *Disability Solutions Newsletter*, Volume 5, Issue 4 (March/April 2003), www.disabilitysolutions.org.

5. Look at School Work

"Ask to see work samples—samples of daily lessons for *all* students; see how your child's curriculum is being accommodated or modified, if necessary. Ask how the team is making decisions to accommodate and modify that curriculum. Curriculum planning is a team effort that assures your child is learning at his or her own level, while still participating in the class. Participation equals respect and success. When teams talk about a totally separate curriculum or alternative curriculum, it may indicate separation rather than access. Access to grade-level, core curriculum is part of the law and best practice."

6. Ask Detail Questions

"Ask questions about details. If some of the answers aren't what you are looking for, it will be important to gather the team. Talk about communication skills; how are the school and teacher promoting friendship and connections for all students?"

This is Patti's list of questions for you to ask the team:
- How is my child participating in the lesson?

- How does my child play with friends at recess?
- How is my child communicating?
- Do other children initiate with my child?

7. Ask Yourself Questions

And here is Patti's list of questions you can ask yourself:

- Do your child's IEP goals reflect participation in the core curriculum?
- Do they reflect participation in grade-level curriculum?
- Do the goals reflect what we would want every other child to learn?
- Do the goals include interaction with peers, such as asking a peer for help before asking an adult?
- Do you meet regularly with the IEP team to problem solve?
- Do you meet regularly to *celebrate*?

8. Develop a Fade-Out Support Plan

"If additional adult support is part of the services for your child, do some research on that adult's role. Insist on a plan for fading that support and for teaching your child how to be as independent as possible. Be sure that you *do not* build a relationship with that person, but with the general education teacher. The general ed teacher's connection to your child models for all students and other adults that "This child is mine, just like every other student in my class." This model in turn prompts classmates *to believe the same.*

"When an aide is involved, insist that she or he help all children in the class; that auxiliary adult can then be viewed as a *classroom* assistant. This view will help prevent the adult support from becoming a barrier to your child's connection to the teacher, classmates, curriculum, instruction, and sense of belonging and value in the class. All adults should always ask, 'What would I do with any other child?' and 'Can a classmate do what I'm doing?'"

9. Celebrate!

"Celebrate often—the successes, highlights, and progress. Know that there will always be struggle, but that doesn't mean inclusion isn't working! It only means that this is life with people and kids, and that it's time to pull the team together. Focus on what's working and build from there. Let your focus be a child-centered solution."

Thanks to Navigators

Many thanks to Patti McVay and every educator like her, who makes promoting and facilitating Inclusion for our children their life's work. Take her advice and sail confidently into the sea of inclusion, knowing that you've got a navigator and compass on board with you.

24

Watch Your Language!

*"The finest language is mostly made up of
simple unimposing words."*
—George Eliot (a.k.a. Mary Anne Evans)

Economy: Key Word Speaking

In the "grammatical gospel according to Jon," prepositions, articles, and occasionally even verbs are a sheer waste of time and energy. Due economy must be observed in these instances. Heck, even undue economy.

I mean, why should one bother grappling with the grammatical gymnastics required for, "Mother, is Father still toiling at his desk at the University even now as we speak?" when one can simply inquire with eyebrows descriptively raised, "Dad?" and get the same information in response.

This is called "key word speaking," and the good news, according to Sue Buckley, the director of Down Syndrome Education International, is that often our key word speakers morph in their twenties. They often begin filling in those blank grammatical spaces in their sentences. I can vouch for this, because it eventually happened to Jonathan. Occasionally, the grammar is astonishing.

Recently, Jonathan called his dad Kelly to ask a question about his sister. Kelly told me later, "It was an astonishing call. His grammar was impeccable, his sentence structure mature, his thoughts beautifully expressed. If I didn't know better, I would have thought that someone was putting me on. But it *was* Jonathan. I was literally stunned, and thought about it afterward for hours."

Apraxia

A small percentage of our children with Down syndrome are challenged by apraxia (Childhood Apraxia of Speech) or a similar diagnosis, and have great difficulty making the speech connection; a small percentage of children with Down syndrome speak beautifully, almost like you or me. I've heard them speak, so I know this is true. But most of our kids will fall somewhere in the middle, a broad area where speaking with grammatical and articulate clarity is simply hard work. So, for almost all children with Down syndrome, therapy with a speech-language pathologist (SLP) is indispensable.

For children who struggle with apraxia or other speech difficulties, an SLP can help you identify an augmentative communication device (ACD) that will enable your child to communicate with pictures, etc., while therapy progresses.

Turn to the chapter "The Education Battleground" for a more in-depth look at ACDs and the use of apps and other electronic equipment. Here is a quick recap of just some of the information in that chapter:

What's That?

Childhood Apraxia of Speech (CAS): Apraxia of speech, also known as verbal apraxia or dyspraxia, is a speech disorder in which a person has trouble saying what he or she wants to say correctly and consistently. It is not due to weakness or paralysis of the speech muscles. The severity of apraxia can range from mild to severe.

Speech-language pathologist (SLP), or speech therapist: A specialist who evaluates and treats communication disorders.

Augmentative Communication Device (ACD): equipment used by an AAC user to aid his or her communication.

Can't or Won't?

Apraxia and related diagnoses aside, let me make this perfectly clear: it is not that some of our children *cannot* speak in full sentences, even eloquently or at least with great purpose and effect. No, it is that for some of our offspring with that extra chromosome, they *will not* speak in mellifluous grammatical complexities because it simply takes too much effort. It's a whole lot of trouble to harness tongues that are a little too big or a little too low in muscle tone.

Anybody remember watching "Corky" in the TV series *Life Goes On?* Chris Burke, the actor with Down syndrome, concentrated *very* hard to enunciate clearly, and you can see him working at it. Life is short and busy, and like any of us, our kids choose where to spend their energy. Keep this and the miracle of motivation in mind.

Motivation

A case in point: My friend Clarence is father to Mary, 19, who has Down syndrome. Mary has the parent-frustrating habit of mumbling under her breath as her primary communicative *modus operandi*. One evening, Clarence and Mary were sitting in the family den when Mary mumbled something incoherent to her dad.

"*What?*" said Clarence.

"Mutter-mutter."

"Mary, stop mumbling like that! I can't understand a word you say when you just mutter under your breath. Speak clearly so I can hear you! If you mumble like that *one more time*, I'm going to go outside and catch a bug and throw it on you."

Now, I'm not recommending this as a savvy parenting technique, but Clarence has his limits, and he'd already reached them. Capitalizing on his daughter's known bug-angst, he was going for motivation.

Mary mumbled again.

"That does it!" Clarence stormed outside and grabbed an imaginary bug from the air. He stalked back in and "threw" the imaginary creature at Mary.

Eeeeek! Mary was suddenly highly motivated. When her shrieking faded and she had a moment to mentally settle on what had just happened, she gave her dad a withering stare-down and declared with pristine clarity, "I am *soooo* disappointed in you!"

Motivation.

Number One Current Need?

Remember back to the chapter "The Education Battleground"? I talked about determining your child's Number 1 Current Need when you're planning school placement for the year, and encouraged you to focus your laser on it.

If speech/language is your top priority, go for it. *Now.* I say this urgently because of what I see in some of my teenage students who, though capable of far better, cannot be understood when they speak except by Dad, Mom, and Grandma. That just won't do. It's not enough to get them by.

I am not speaking about children who are struggling with apraxia. Their challenges run deep and the climb is steep.

No, I'm talking about kids whose speech either slipped through the cracks, or they've gotten away with murder. Or both. I know from teaching reading to these students (which always involves articulation) that these teens who can hardly be understood *are fully capable of articulating clearly.* I know that because they sit right across the table from me, and with enough prompting, *do it.* Perfectly clearly. But it's a bother and it takes effort, and *they do not have the clear articulation habit.* They never formed it. Habit makes permanent, and reversing that in teen years . . . ? Good luck.

There are some battles that you will wisely decide not to fight, in favor of putting your teaching and training energies elsewhere in raising your child; but the language and articulation battle is not optional. Speaking clearly is a skill that will be forever necessary to your child.

When Jonathan was five, he invented the unfortunate articulation habit of inhaling his final "s's," as in "toys, trains, drums." I personally find that amazingly difficult to do, but that was his habit; that was the way he figured out how to get that final "s" out of (or rather, into) his mouth. We didn't let up on him for years, training him to expire that last "s" rather than inspiring it.

It was a family effort. His sister Rebecca was three when this particular coaching began, and I can still see the dinner table scene, with little Rebecca sitting across from Jonathan. She could hardly pronounce some things herself—including his name—but she never tired of coaching him:

"Toy-*zuh*, Jon-tin! Toy-*zuh*. Train-*zuh*, Jon-tin, drum-*zuh*!"

If I could have seen into this three-year-old's future at that moment, I would have seen that she eventually chose the profession of teaching English as a second language (ESL). She started practicing early!

Speech on the Fringes

If you're fortunate, your child may pass through an era of verbal politeness whose source will mystify you: where did he hear this kind of talk? I assure you that this is temporary; pre-puberty will hit, and it will fly out the window. But for the moment, enjoy it. Jonathan went through this verbal chivalry in mid-elementary years, and it was delightful. Example: correcting his misbehavior toward his sister one day, I said, "Jonathan, please be nice to Becca." His angelic response: "Very well, Mama. Why, I surely will." *Surely?* Is this a throwback to the eighteenth century, or what?

At the opposite end of the scale, let's take a moment and look at the use of profanity by our adults with Down syndrome. Profanity is one of the great levelers of adults. The playing field is exquisitely even, with all players understanding the exact intent and meaning in the moment. Our adults with Down syndrome can use profanity meaningfully and appropriately, just as we do (who, *us?*) Oh, and did I mention that they need to hear a four-letter word just *once* and they've got it nailed? Of course. My personal view of our adults using profanity appropriately is one of respect. I think it's okay. It can also be hilarious.

My eldest reading student is Blair, 33. One day we were working on a spelling exercise. The picture-word card showed the picture of a fox and the word **f o** _. Blair's job was to provide the missing letter. Some days Blair has a tendency toward wild guessing, and this was one of those days. "K?" he suggested hopefully. "No, Blair; you're guessing!" I fairly yelled, "That would be *FOK!*" Total silence while he looked at me, eyes wide and hand clamped over his mouth. I looked at him, he looked at me, and we laughed helplessly for five minutes, neither of us ever saying a word about what that sounded like. I learned later from his mom, Martha, that this particular word is Blair's favorite word to drop, and the way he uses it usually fits the situation impeccably.

Therapeutically, profanity can help process emotions. Stephen, 28, experienced a devastating series of deaths from which he had great difficulty recovering. First his best friend Nick passed away; this was followed closely by the death of his grandfather. After that, he became even closer to his grandmother. His mother Vivian says, "He was very solicitous of her, very concerned about her. It made him sad that Granddad left and Grandma was so, so sad. He felt he had to make everything better, but he couldn't. That's when cussing started. He felt helpless, and the cussing helped him feel more in control."

As if this were not difficult enough, the situation spiraled downward dramatically when his grandmother *also* suddenly and unexpectedly died. This would be profoundly difficult for anyone to process. When Down syndrome is added to the mix, the task of recovery is overwhelming.

Stephen was helped in this process by therapy, but he had great difficulty controlling his anger, which usually manifested in a string of cussing that his mom likened to a "drunken sailor enduring a tattoo." An appropriate metaphor, because what Stephen was dealing with was intense pain. With therapy and parental guidance, Stephen learned to restrict his profanity to his room. It was his safe haven. He could get it all out of his system and say whatever he wanted, as loudly as he wanted to.

If it happened that company overheard him from downstairs, he would come down afterward and apologize to them, "I'm sorry; my heart feels sticky." Working through his grieving process, Stephen was helped by a homeopathic practitioner, who prescribed what he called "my sailor drops." When he felt the anger and cursing coming on, he'd go to Vivian and say, "Mom, I need my sailor drops!"

He had his good moments, too. When he saw a beautiful sunset, he'd say, "Mom! Look! Grandma's smiling at us." And there were times when he'd be in his room, "talking to Grandma." His mom says that after those times, he would come out of his room seeming peaceful, and his spirits would be lifted. "I saw Grandma," he'd say. "She's doing fine. She's happy. She's with Granddad; they're in Hawaii"—a place Grandma had always wanted to go.

The Many Faces of Language

Language, the healer. Language, the expresser. Language, the entertainer.

Jeremy is one of my students. At age nine, in spite of Down syndrome, this guy is no novice to the world of finance. At conferences, he stands by his mother Ellen's Discovery Toys booth and ropes in the customers. He says he wants to make lots of money when he grows up.

After Jeremy's tutoring session one day, Ellen neglected to write a check for our session. I didn't notice, and neither did she. As she and Jeremy drove away, Jeremy turned to her and said, "Jack Book! Jack Book!"

Not understanding, Ellen said, "Oh, did you read a book about Jack today with Natalie? A book about a boy named Jack?"

"No! Jack Book! Jack Book!" he yelled, more and more insistent.

Jack Book? Ellen finally got it. *"Checkbook?"*

"Yes! Jack Book!"

"I forgot to write a check to Natalie?"

"Yes!"

Thanks, Jeremy dude. You've got my back. His mom did offer to trade Jeremy's services as a get-Natalie-paid agent in lieu of a tutoring fee, and I'm considering it.

Then there's language, the heart-melter.

Around age six, Jonathan took to calling me Mama Bird. He'd say, especially at snuggle time after a bath, "I'm Baby Bird. You're Mama Bird." One day when I picked him up after school, ready to take him to speech therapy, he came running toward me, lunchbox swinging in one hand and backpack in the other.

"Oh, Mama Bird! You came *back!*"

Wahoo! Years

25

The Transition Process

> *"Life, it seems, is nothing if not a series of*
> *initiations, transitions, and incorporations. "*
> —Alan Dundes, Folklorist

After High School, What Next?

Transition programs come next. Each state is different, but most states legally require schools to provide special education services to students with IEPs from preschool to at least age 21. Starting when students are 16, schools are required to offer "transition services" to help them prepare for life in their community. These services should be individualized and based on each student's unique strengths, needs, and goals. Each school district is different, so, of course, services and programs vary. With luck, you'll get to choose between at least two transition programs, although many districts will offer only a single option.

Some families of high school students with Down syndrome choose for their child to remain immersed in academics until the age their peers graduate from high school—typically 18. Other families choose a second option, especially if they have held a child back earlier in the academic process: they might choose to let the student remain in school until age 21 and take advantage of the extra years in school, *if* they feel that placement is still contributing to the child's growth and development. If the first option is chosen and the student graduates with his/her peers, then, from ages 18 to 21, the student can either plunge full time into a transition program, or can continue to take some classes at the high school part of the day while participating in transition activities the rest of the day.

A good transition program is community-based rather than classroom-based. This is a vital time of getting out in the real world, learning job skills and independent living skills. In the transition process, you'll find out to what extent your child is competitively employable. This is a vital reality check—you need to know, because the answer to that question determines what programs or jobs you're going to look at for future placement.

Marianne Iversen, an educator now on the staff of the Down Syndrome Connection of the Bay Area, worked for many years in transition programs. "What I love best about this transition phase is the huge growth in self-confidence that comes with training in true independent living skills," she says. "I love to see that happen."

"This is real life learning; no more sitting in a classroom trying to solve math problems. Instead these young adults are going to the bank and learning to manage a checking account. They're learning to travel independently, to manage money, to plan meals and figure out a grocery budget. They're learning how to plan nutritious meals, to do their laundry and housework. In the end, whether they live independently or remain living at their parents' home, they are more responsible adults. And the self-confidence they gain from a good transition program opens doors for them to be more social, more confident in getting a job."

He's in Transition Now

When Jonathan was ready for a transition program, things looked bleak. The one program available was blocked to Cincinnati Public School (CPS) graduates. Seems there was some conflict between budgets, willingness to support, etc. But due to the embarrassing fact that CPS had absolutely zero programs to offer its graduates with special needs, a last-minute agreement was thankfully reached. Suddenly, twelve slots were open for Cincinnati Public School graduates, and Jonathan was in.

Several work training sites were available, and we chose Xavier University for Jonathan's. Specifically, the Fine Arts Department. This catapulted Jonathan into heaven: his dad was an opera professor, and I was a lifelong musician as well, so music was in his blood and in his environment since birth. He was used to being on a university campus and adored all things musical, so the Fine Arts Department couldn't have been a more perfect venue for his training. The staff was outstanding: caring, disciplined, and running a well-planned program broad enough to include training in everything from office work to gardening and ground maintenance, and we were all thrilled.

But once again, Jonathan's triple diagnosis of Down syndrome, ADHD, and Oppositional Defiant Disorder threw its wrench into the smooth workings of the program. By the end of the year of training, he was the *only* one of twelve students assessed as not being competitively employable. Though he had worked hard and endeared himself to the equally hard-working staff, he just couldn't keep either the ADHD or the ODD in check.

This was not the first time we had run into this problem. While he was still in high school, I had worked hard to get him a job-in-training at our local grocery chain. He successfully completed the computer test (with mom's coaching), got his uniform, and began training; his job coach was an excellent aide from his high school, so things were looking good. Until the day that "impulsivity component" of ADHD kicked in. While doing shelf duty in the megastore one afternoon, he decided it would be a great joke to play hide-and-seek with his job coach. She turned away for a split second; that's all it took to give Jonathan time to vanish.

But where to hide so she wouldn't find him? Under the general manager's computer desk, of course, two minutes before the manager was to hold a staff meeting in his office. And, yes, he was indeed fired, but not because he'd been disobedient. It was a runaway safety concern that the manager—understandably—did not want to shoulder.

In spite of that experience, I still held out great hope that Jonathan could become competitively employable. But near the end of the transition program, I had my moment of truth and realized that "a triple diagnosis doth not a single diagnosis equal." I had to do the math: one plus one plus one does not equal one. It equals three. It was a sobering moment for me, one I had not had to face squarely until that point. There were a number of young adults with Down syndrome in the transition program, and they were *all* competitively employable by the end of the program. They were all "one-sies"; Jonathan's profile was cast in triplicate.

Regardless, that transitional experience was stellar. Jonathan loved it, especially the social interaction and the chance to move independently around a university campus, and we all eventually adjusted to the idea of searching for a different occupational placement for Jonathan. We found it in an unusual Goodwill program that is thankfully available in Cincinnati: Goodwill's Center for Advocacy, Recreation, and Education (CARE).

On to the Next Step: Post-Transition

While Jonathan was still enrolled in the transition program, I took him to observe his adult options, since competitive employment wasn't going to work for him. I wanted him to choose the program that most appealed to him, and he did, decisively. Fortunately, the parental vote was for the same program, so it was unanimous. This should, in fact, be part of a good transition program: the young adult should be able to observe the job training sites or post-transition programs available and have his or her vote count.

We felt lucky to find the CARE program. Well staffed and run, it provides ongoing training and activities for adults with a variety of disabilities. Depending on the skill level of those in the program, different jobs typical of Goodwill are done in the afternoons, and small paychecks are garnered. Cooking skills and community activities are a regular part of the day, and I am relieved to say that the group is allowed exactly one DVD per week total, and the choice is decided by community vote (to Jonathan's chagrin). This is not babysitting. During the one free period of the day, Jonathan (a.k.a. "Google Hound") can always be found online in the computer lab. He likes the friends he's made there and continues to be stretched. In short, he enjoys his days.

Transition for a "One-sie"

Some graduates with Down syndrome are interested in continuing their education, getting job training, associate degrees, or similar certification. Happily, educational institutions across the country are now catching on to this growing need, and more and more institutions are offering postsecondary programs for individuals with special needs.

If a graduate has her heart set on a particular job or interest, whether volunteer or salaried, you can give her a leg up to get her started.

I know of many parents who initiate contacts in the business community and get the ball rolling, with training and support provided, and with a successful outcome.

Postsecondary Education

- For great information on educational institutions and programs that cater to people with disabilities, as well for information on federal financial aid such as Perkins and Stafford loans, try this site: www.thinkcollege.net

- For general information about transition, try the book *The Down Syndrome Transition Handbook: Charting Your Child's Course to Adulthood* by Jo Ann Simons (Woodbine House, 2010).

My student Blair's postsecondary experience gives us a good example of how transition *should* work when done correctly. His mother, Martha, tells me:

"Blair's transition was community-based; he and the other young adults were always out and about, learning life skills. Blair went to community college and took courses he really wanted to take: music, swimming, and horticulture. He loved it! Then he said, 'I'm done. I want to go to work.'

"He now works at a country club in golf services, and has been there for four years. He maintains golf carts, greets people, stacks balls, and more. He's busy the entire time and gets minimum wage. His employers expect a lot of him, including courtesy and knowing everyone's name—they've raised the bar for him, and he's stepped up to it.

"Our challenge now is achieving balance for him as an adult who still lives at his parents' home by choice: we're always striving for that balance between his independence and the reality that he still needs a lot of support in many ways."

He Covers Our Mortgage

Many adults with Down syndrome need to limit the amount of money they earn at jobs in order to keep their eligibility for government benefits such as SSI or Medicaid. It can be challenging to find a full-time job, but some adults with Down syndrome do it.

My friend Rachel has a grateful story to tell about her son, Paul, who works full-time. "My husband had to retire on a pension, and I can only work part-time. Paul still lives with us, but he has a full-time job. It's Paul's paycheck that pays our mortgage every month! We are proud of him, and grateful." I should add that Paul and his family live in an area of the country where mortgages can still come in under 1K a month! Nevertheless, Rachel is very proud of Paul, and financially he's a huge assist to his parents.

There are as many transition and employment stories as there are adults with Down syndrome. One way or another, this way or that way, our children come into their own by adulthood. It's an amazing and satisfying process to watch.

Plateau or No Plateau?

This is an important question, and the answer is a myth-buster. Do our offspring with Down syndrome plateau in their learning process? Will there ever come a time when we must say, "Yep, that's it. He's finished. He can't learn any more; he can't make any more progress?"

No and no. There is no plateauing with Down syndrome, any more than *you* are going to plateau in your mental, emotional, or spiritual development after tomorrow. What if someone told you, "You're cooked, Dude. End of the road for you." How would you respond to that? *Excuse* me?

What sometimes appears to be plateauing is raw failure of an individual's environment to support continued learning and development. It's that simple. And that true. It happens much too often in educational settings: a child stops learning and the ball gets dropped. It is assumed that "they can't learn."

Reading is a perfect example: I have students with Down syndrome who came to me as teenagers who never learned to read. They weren't able to learn the way they were being taught, so the system dropped them and they fell right through the cracks in the educational floor, and stayed there for years. The problem *wasn't* that they couldn't learn; the problem was that the system didn't understand how they could learn best and most easily. These teens who came to me illiterate are now reading. Of course they can continue to learn!

With very little effort, you can enlighten yourself and others by doing online research and discovering a mountain of continuing success stories. I know of individuals with Down syndrome who continue learning, no matter what the age. Beginning to study piano at age 26, and succeeding in playing Mozart; learning to read at 35 years of age; learning to dance the Fox Trot, Waltz, Cha Cha, and Tango at age 39; the list goes on.

As it should.

What if someone had told Karen Gaffney that because she has Down syndrome and a crippled left leg that she couldn't swim across Lake Tahoe and many other lakes? That she couldn't organize a relay swim team to join her in successfully swimming the English Channel?

What if?

A plateau might be a nice spot to sit for a bit and catch one's breath, but it's not a destination for our children. Let's hope our children will always be "transitioning" in their lives.

26

Traveling Alone

"My parents moved a lot when I was young,
but I always found them."
—Rodney Dangerfield

Independent Travel

When our children grow up, will they be able to travel alone? Yes, no, and maybe so. It all depends on the innate ability of the child, the training he's been given, and how he's responded to that training.

I know of many adults with Down syndrome who travel independently—whether it's by bus, train, or plane. They're experienced and confident in doing this, and of course they value and love their independence.

Jonathan can't travel independently on the bus because he falls asleep within minutes and would forever miss getting off at his stop. But this sleep habit works great for air travel: on a plane he can handle himself just fine, entertains himself for hours with no problem with his earbuds and electronic equipment, and catches up on his zzzs. Parents or caretakers get gate passes and walk him to the airport gate on one end and pick him up at the gate on the other end, so he can't get lost. He has flown back and forth between Los Angeles and Cincinnati many times.

The first time he flew alone from Cincinnati to Los Angeles (nonstop, you betcha), he arrived in L.A. with his lunch bag untouched: he'd had nothing to eat or drink for five hours. My "fretful mother" internal file clicked open, and I said, "Jonathan! You didn't eat or drink *anything* on the plane?" I was astonished.

"Nope." He smiled and explained, "I just relaxed."

I suddenly realized that, perhaps for the first time in his twenty years, he had spent five hours without anybody telling him what to do. No supervision. He was independent. He clearly relished the experience, was happy, and was in no need of anything. But what if something went wrong?

Let me tell you a story.

Jake

Jake Snyder was a typical kid with a bigger-than-typical dream. He wanted to be a pilot. He didn't just want to pilot a Cessna; he wanted to fly the big ones, the commercial jets. As he grew up, Jake nurtured that dream as he watched his mom nurture his siblings, including his youngest sister. His sister was born with severe cognitive delays and profound disabilities, and died when she was just six. By that time, Jake had already acquired understanding and compassion far beyond his peers'.

Jake did eventually reach his goal: he became a pilot for Delta Airlines. He was now Captain Jake Snyder, and he loved his work.

On October 19, 2010, Captain Snyder had just gone off duty in Los Angeles and had hopped on Flight 1814 to Cincinnati as a passenger in first class. In pilot lingo, he was "dead-heading" on the flight, going home, and he was weary. His seat in first class promised some valuable snooze time.

But there was a glitch. After the plane pushed away from the gate, it was discovered that its computer wasn't functioning normally, and the plane had to return to the gate. It could take hours to repair the problem. Pandemonium ensued, with passengers grabbing their luggage and jumping ship.

A flight attendant pushed her way through the confusion to Captain Snyder. "Jake," she said, "there's a young man with Down syndrome in coach who's upset and doesn't know what to do."

The captain jumped up and made his way to the young man. He sat next to him and smiled reassuringly. "Hi, Jonathan," he said. "My name's Jake."

And that is how my son was rescued on his eighth "solo" excursion on a flight gone haywire.

Way Above and Beyond the Call

I was totally unaware of the plane's difficulty, of course. I had waited only until the plane pushed away from the gate, and I was already an hour away from the airport. My cell rang.

"Hello, Natalie? This is Captain Jake Snyder with Delta Airlines." Not the kind of call a mother wants to get! But he immediately reassured me. "Don't worry, everything is fine. I have Jonathan here with me in first class. The plane's computer has run into difficulty and we had to return to the gate to wait for a repair. Jonathan's pretty upset, and I thought you might like to talk to him." He handed Jonathan his cell. Jake later told me that the moment Jonathan heard my voice, he calmed down.

"We don't know if the plane can be repaired in time," Jake continued when he got back on the phone. "Everyone is de-boarding at this point. I want you to know that I will take responsibility for Jonathan. I'll keep him with me and get him to Cincinnati. If the plane can't be repaired in time, and if you and Jonathan's father give me permission, I'll take him with me on whatever connecting flight we need to take in order to get him to Cincinnati. I'll get him home."

I was astonished at this captain's compassion and intervention, and "grateful" doesn't begin to describe how I felt. For the next couple of hours until the plane took off, Jake kept close contact with me via cell phone, regularly updating me and reassuring both Jonathan and me that everything would be fine. We talked about Jonathan's need for another meal (the one I'd packed in his bag wouldn't be enough for the additional hours), and about the fact that he couldn't chew. In the end, the crew had to settle for giving him juice, and his dad met him at the Cincinnati gate with supper in hand.

The flight did eventually take off three hours late and arrived safely in Cincinnati.

Days later I phoned Captain Snyder to thank him again for his compassion. He explained his family background and his little sister's disabilities, and said, "It's amazing to me that people who don't have any experience will just walk by a person with special needs and not understand what's needed. I see it all the time in airports: people who are blind, mentally disabled, ill....It doesn't take much to give these individuals help, but people just walk by."

Jake did not "just walk by," and I will be forever grateful!

Hats off to Jonathan as well, for adjusting to the scene of scores of upset passengers yelling, grabbing luggage, and trying to hop off the plane onto other flights. For him, a guy whose M.O. is "thou-shalt-not-change-any-previously-set-plans-*ever*," this was the equivalent of throwing an alligator into his swimming pool. But as the captain told me later, "Jon was a well-behaved young man, and became calm and relaxed after the initial upset."

Right after the plane landed in Cincinnati, I texted Captain Jake my thanks. He texted back: "You are so welcome. Jonathan was a joy to be with. He is also blessed to have you."

Angels come in many forms; this one was easy to recognize. So, while we encourage our young adults to travel independently and train them as well as we can, let's also hope that if plans go awry, an angel appears to smooth the way.

And in the meantime, cell phones are a great idea if your child is willing and able to use one responsibly, and many young people are. It's not an option for Jonathan, who is still hypersensitive to anything besides loose clothing touching his skin (no cap, no watch, no cell phone, etc.). If we gave him a cell phone to carry on his person, within seconds it would find a home in the nearest trashcan. Trust me on this. (I'm only talking about *carrying* a phone; because of his sensory issues, he never wears a belt. That would mean the cell would have to go into his pocket—against his body, and that would be intolerable for him. He has no concept of the cost of such a thing, and would simply get rid of it. I've talked to other parents who say the same thing.)

But working with this situation, we make sure that all of his flights are direct, and now practice the wisdom of waiting until the plane has not only pushed away from the gate, but is *in the air* before leaving the airport. Now why didn't I think of that before?

My pilot friend Rick pointed me to nifty apps that will let me know when Jonathan's plane *is in the air*! Here's one that I downloaded; I anticipate that it will be a significant mind-easer!

- Flight Track—Live Flight Status Tracker by Mobiata ($4.99)

27

Dance Rocks

*"Stifling an urge to dance is bad for your health—
it rusts your spirit and your hips."*
—Terri Guillemets

There is a refreshing new breeze blowing through this country, and it has caught up our young people with Down syndrome right along with it.

It's ballroom dancing. The whole nine yards: tango, swing, foxtrot, salsa, merengue…shall we dance? There are more than a dozen different dances in this sport, and our adults with Down syndrome rock at it. My son, I'm sure, is not the only one to watch *Dancing with the Stars*; and he checks to make sure I'm tuned in.

One of the regular dance professionals on the show, Kym Johnson, has long led dance classes for individuals with special needs, both in Los Angeles and in her native Australia. In 2009, the Down Syndrome Association of Los Angeles gave Kym their Vision Award for her work supporting individuals with special needs.

Company d

To my knowledge, the first folks to get serious about dancing and Down syndrome were the founders of *Company d*, based in Memphis,

Tennessee. Founded by artistic director and choreographer Darlene Winters in 2001, this group of fourteen teenagers with Down syndrome first blew me away when they performed in Atlanta for the National Down Syndrome Congress in 2006.

Thoroughly trained in the discipline, these young people were onstage in their snappy black costumes, waiting for their musical cue. No one in the audience knew what to expect from this performing group, but everyone was excitedly anticipating the start. Well, no start. The tech personnel were having trouble finding the right track for the group's first dance. They tried, oh how they tried. In the end, the conference staff chose what they thought was the right track and the music started.

It was the wrong music.

So what did these kids in *Company d* do? Without a second of hesitation, with coordinated eye communication, they began their modern/jazz dance routine as if this were planned, and no one in the audience knew any different. They finished that routine and began another (with the correct track playing).

I was mesmerized. I felt transported by the dance these young people were doing. It is not too much to say that I felt the energy of the room was angelically transformed by what the dancers—*with Down syndrome*—were creating for us. They were totally into their own expression, dancing for and from their own hearts. We, the audience, were blessed just to be watching.

At that time, I had been involved in ballroom dancing for a year. Though I didn't know it at first introduction, Mary Cook, the dance teacher I'd chosen in Cincinnati, was herself the mom of a son with Down syndrome, then-five-year-old Matthew. So when I saw *Company d* perform, I longed to see a similar dance group form in Cincinnati, and I knew Mary was the key.

I spoke by phone with Darlene Winters to get a better understanding of the organization behind *Company d*, and then met with Mary to plant the idea in what I knew would be "miracle gro" soil.

Inspired by *Company d* and the dance enthusiasm of her own son, Mary started a free dance class for individuals with Down syndrome 16 and older. "When Matthew is at the studio, all he does is dance. Selfishly, I wondered if he could grow into a dancer, and so part of my motivation for starting a class was to allay my own fears. I didn't know if it was possible for young adults with Down syndrome to be dancers. As a parent, sometime the future is scary; now I'm not afraid of the future. These young adults function well. They're very capable."

A-Marika Dancing Stars

The class opened with six students and three volunteers. Two and a half years later, it's still free and now well funded, with thirty-six dancers (ages sixteen to forty-nine) and fifteen volunteers from Mary's dance studio. The numbers on both sides are growing all the time. One of the dads is a lawyer and is in the process of setting up *A-Marika Dancing Stars* as a nonprofit. They have held many fundraisers, and are now nicely bankrolled; costumes are on the way!

So how did they raise funds prior to becoming a 501c3? They threw their own "A-Marika Dancing with the Stars" gala and enlisted the dance presence of local celebrities, including the now-merengue-proficient chief of police and a local TV news anchor. The only judging paddle provided was a "10," and *everyone* got a trophy. Sheer genius. The class performs regularly at various venues, including the annual Buddy Walk held by the Down Syndrome Association of Greater Cincinnati, and Mary somehow manages to get discounts for everything, including the brand-new costumes. She persuaded a local grocery to donate bottled water for the classes. I don't know how she does this discount thing so consistently, though being cute and four-foot-something doesn't hurt her cause a bit.

What's That?

501c3: U.S. Internal Revenue code for a tax-exempt, nonprofit corporation or association.

Buddy Walk: An annual event founded by the National Down Syndrome Society; local groups sponsor one-mile walks to raise funds and to promote acceptance and inclusion of people with Down syndrome. For more information: www.buddywalk.org

I put Mary's *A-Marika Dancing Stars* model forth because it's simple and is working for everyone. For instance, a family member or caregiver for each dancer is required to stay for the weekly class; this eliminates the need for a special license or trained aides.

Richard Chappell is one of the original volunteers, and has been with Mary from the beginning of this venture. A long-time ballroom dancer and one of the kindest men on the planet, he says, "The enthusiasm of these young people is enormous. They will come in the worst winter weather: 'We've got to go dance at Mary's tonight!' In the beginning, we volunteers came for Mary's sake; but once we came, we were hooked. It's fun and it's rewarding: these young people are so polite and appreciative. If you give them some encouragement, they just beam. That makes us volunteers feel good about ourselves, and we love the fact that we are enlarging the dance population to include a group of people that would not be able to do it without our help."

Richard adds, "Because it's gotten so popular with the young adults, they come running in, hugging the volunteers. It's a good, happy atmosphere for an hour. We love it."

The Parents' View

If the volunteers love it, you should hear what the parents are saying.

Theresa, the mother of teenaged Brennan, says, "It's encouraged her to explore movement, socialization, and social skills, especially with members of the opposite sex. She's learned appropriate boundaries. She looks forward to it because it's a place where she can be herself. She's so happy here.

"It's been heartwarming for me to see these kids have an opportunity to express themselves in dance form. Brennan's happy here. I mean *really* happy.

"And on a selfish note, it's so great to be with other parents. We're reconnecting from when our children were very young. After age five, we didn't see other parents much at all. This is a reminder that we're not alone. This is *so* not isolating. It's inclusive."

Another mom, Marcia, said, "This is the *only* leverage I have to get my high school daughter to comply!" I hear you, Marcia.

John is 33; he took ballet and tap as a child and was one of the original dancers when *A-Marika Dancing Stars* formed. His mother, Peggy, says, "This class has given him more socialization and mixing. He's making friends and more friends, and has a favorite volunteer partner here. He's learned the cha cha, salsa, fox trot, swing, waltz, tango, and merengue. When he goes to social events at church, he asks people to dance, even elderly widows. Women say, 'He knows how to dance better than my husband!'"

Of course he does. Does your husband know the cha cha, salsa, fox trot, swing, waltz, tango, and merengue? I rest my case. Or if you're a guy reading this and you're like most husbands, you *wish*.

Then there's Daniel, 13, who is a special case. When Mary first met him, he always had his head down and clung to his mother, Jill. Jill explains, "Daniel is nonverbal. When we first started coming, he didn't even want to come in the door and refused to dance. But Mary came over to him and took his hand; then he was all smiles. Now, every Wednesday, he's so excited that he signs "dance" all day. He smiles the whole time he's here. This is the first activity he's had that's *about Daniel*. Now he has something wonderful to sign about."

The night I visited the class, I would never have know that the grinning thirteen-year-old boy dancing the salsa with Mary was ever anything but enthusiastic!

Another mother, Susan, has three teens with Down syndrome. A few years after giving birth to April, she adopted Jacob and Sam. April and Jacob are old enough to be in the dance class. Susan says, "They love to dance. They've learned all these dances, so when they're in social situations, people are surprised at what they can do. They're amazed that they know these dances, including line dances like the Electric Slide and the Cuban Shuffle. And Mary's doing this for free, so it's accessible for everyone. They can't wait to come every Wednesday night."

Over the Rainbow

Mary starts each class with their signature line dance to "Somewhere Over the Rainbow," followed by another favorite line dance. Then the group breaks apart into couples and learns two or three steps in each of the seven ballroom dances I've mentioned. Mary repeats the whole sequence in that hour, and repeats their signature Rainbow Line Dance. Mary laughs, "We end every time with the Electric Slide, and they go crazy, like they've never heard it before!"

Dance is more than it seems at casual glance. It's obviously fun, social, and helps us lose weight (one teen in Mary's class is there mostly to shed some pounds and "look good," as she says). But there's more.

Let's have the medical community weigh in on this. Dr. Emmet Oz, long associated with the Oprah Winfrey Show, enthusiastically endorses dance. He says that dancing lowers dementia levels and stimulates many different parts of the brain. Specifically, dance stimulates these parts of the brain: the amygdala, the emotional center of the brain; the hippocampus, which is responsible for memorizing the dance steps; the frontal cortex, which helps process the whole deal; and the cerebellum, which is responsible for your coordination.

So there you go. Dance rocks.

The Last Word

28

Dance and Drum

"If you want to be happy, be."
—Leo Tolstoy

Dance and Drum

Say that phrase quickly, again and again.

Now you can see why Jonathan was so easily confused as a child: he thought he had "Dance and Drum."

Well, yes, he does.

And we would do well to go with the program and realize that our children do indeed have Dance and Drum. Have you ever seen a child, teen, or adult with Down syndrome dance? I rest my case.

Years before A-Marika Dancing Stars formed, when Jonathan was twenty, I took up ballroom and Latin dancing for fun and exercise. I sometimes took him along, equipped with his mini-DVD player and earbuds for entertainment. He professed not to be interested, but of course he was. This coincided with the release of the first *High School Musical* movie, a pre-teen dance elixir, bar none.

Jonathan possessed the *High School Musical* DVD the moment it was available. Some time later, I came upon him watching the DVD's special choreographing feature and dancing along to "Bop to the Top." Unseen, I watched him do the whole dance. Over and over. Exactly the same each time. He had memorized every movement, every sequence.

Later, we talked about it and I casually suggested that he could perform the dance routine for my ballroom friends one evening after our class. Would he like to do that?

"Sure!" He grinned.

The night came. My video camera in hand, boom box poised to play, I waited for Jon to be ready to show his stuff to the ballroom class. He looked stiff from nerves, and for a minute I wondered if he would freeze up.

But as the music started, he began his dance moves, warming to the act with each phrase. Soon he was traveling the length of the dance floor, whooping it up and pumping the air with a yelled, "Bop to the Top!"

The small audience went crazy with applause, and the last footage I have on that video is of Jonathan grinning with joy and running toward me for a congratulatory hug.

The Drum Set

And what about the drum?

Like most three-year-old boys, Jonathan had a toy drum with small drumsticks. Unlike most three-year-olds, he got serious about it very quickly. He drummed with those drumsticks on every possible surface, including kitchen counters (which he could reach only with great difficulty). But I had my kitchen rules.

"No drumming on counters, Jonathan." I was stern. "No drumming on counters!"

His response to this was my first inkling that my child was brilliant, absolutely brilliant. He looked at me sideways, and without missing a beat, moved to beating his drumsticks on the precise edge at which the counter surface met the vertical cabinet surface. Technically safe, yet satisfyingly disobedient in spirit. Genius.

One evening after bath time, before I could get clothes on him, he began drumming with his hands on different surfaces: the side of the tub, the top of the hamper, the closed toilet lid. Anything he could find to make great sounds, different sounds.

The "Aha!" moment finally kicked in. "This kid needs a drum set," I decided. "A real drum set." So I set about looking for a used drum set.

I don't know how I found the source, as those were the days before Internet searches, but a short time later, I found myself in an underground bar talking to a young man wearing a four-inch blue Mohawk for hair. Yes, he had an old set, easily repaired, and the price was a steal.

And that's how Jonathan got his very own drum set, which he banged on for years. I hesitate to say "played for years," as he never quite got the hang of exact rhythm, but he loved those drums dearly and they were a constant part of his life for a long time.

Dance and Learn

So what can we learn from our Dance and Drum children? I think Adam Beck, a young man with Down syndrome, said it best, years ago. Martha Beck tells the story of her son Adam when he was twelve. It was the day after 9/11, when the world was stunned into stillness and grief.

Martha was at her computer, working under a writing deadline for her regular article in *O, The Oprah Magazine*. Urgently trying to distill her own thoughts and insights about an event that was incomprehensible, she sat at the keyboard.

At that moment, Adam came up to her with a request that was at once typical of any teenager, but wildly out of place in the world scene at that moment. "Mom, I found new dance videos. Get them for me? I want to learn some cool new moves."

Martha looked at Adam with a mixture of intimate concern and disbelief. "Adam, do you understand what's happened? Do you know what happened yesterday at the World Trade Centers?"

"Yes."

"Well, what do you think about that?" She wanted more of his thoughts, more of his vision. This is the young man Martha calls her "portable Zen master," so his thoughts count. She waited.

When he knew, he said quietly, "We have to keep dancing."

Well said, Adam.

Whether it's Dance and Drum or Down syndrome or any other challenge, grief, or joy, we just have to keep on dancing. And if you dance holding the hand of a child with Down syndrome, I can guarantee that you'll be led through more unexpected moves and laughter than you ever thought possible.

Just keep dancing.

29

Epilogue

"Life consists not in holding good cards,
but in playing those you hold well."
—Josh Billings

Jonathan Today

At this writing, Jonathan is 26 and he's got a life in Cincinnati, the city in which he was born and raised. He likes his life, is always busy, and loves living in his own apartment.

He lives in that apartment with a housemate and a set of rotating caregivers. When he talks about "home" now, he is careful to stress, "*my* apartment." He shares his apartment with a compatible housemate who is similarly challenged, and they get along just fine.

Those of you who have read through this book (versus picking and choosing chapters) know that, even though Jonathan had a wonderful transition program, his DS/ADHD/ODD combination KO'ed his chances for competitive employment. (And if you can swallow four acronyms in one sentence without blinking, you must text your kids a lot.)

So instead of going to work Monday through Friday, Jonathan goes to Goodwill, where he's incredibly fortunate to be in a program called CARE, the Center for Advocacy, Recreation, and Education, and that's exactly what it is. Lots of activities, structure, an excellent staff, friends, an hour or two of work a day, and a computer lab, where for a limited time each day, Jonathan can indulge his Google Hound habit (target: anything Disney).

He also has a social network called Starfire, for adults with various disabilities, and he enjoys outings with those friends as well, whether they go to the theater, bowling, dances, or whatever he's chosen from the schedule for the month.

Everything Changes

For reasons completely unrelated to Down syndrome, his dad, Kelly, and I divorced when Jonathan was 21. At first, the topic of a group home or apartment subsidized by the county seemed too overwhelmingly foreign to discuss, so we didn't. But Jonathan adjusted easily to the divorce and for a year alternated weeks living in two locations, his dad's house and my home.

As the year progressed, I was increasingly struck by Jonathan's lack of need for me. Those weeks he stayed with me, he'd get home from Goodwill, get some juice, and head to his room. "See you later!" In the evening, I'd be in his company again for a few minutes of having dinner together, and then he was off again to his self-entertainment empire (his room). I wouldn't see him again until bath time. In fact, I hardly saw him.

I was fleetingly tempted to feel neglected, but I've learned to listen to Jonathan's unspoken messages over the years, and this one said, "I love you, Mom, but your job's over. I'm moving on."

I had strong family and spiritual ties to California, and for many years traveled there often. Jonathan was used to me flying to California, and always wanted to hear about my visits there (especially if I went to Disneyland). A year after the divorce I considered moving there, even though I knew Jonathan's setup in Cincinnati was ideal, and that he would stay in Cincinnati. Of course, this was not a decision I would make without the pure insight and permission of my son.

Having learned long ago how to ask Jonathan questions in a way that was clear to him, I asked, "Jonathan, do you think it's a good idea or a bad idea for Mom to move to California?" He always prefers cutting to the chase.

He considered for about a second and announced, "It's a good idea." Permission granted. And he hasn't changed his mind since.

A New Life

Having only one parent instate freed up county funds to help subsidize Jonathan in an apartment, so the way was now clear. When we asked Jonathan if he'd like to live in an apartment with staff and probably a housemate, he jumped on it. "Yes!" He had sometimes visited his sister's college apartment across town, and totally got the scene: his own place, no parents. What twenty-something male wouldn't jump at that?

That inner knowledge, that ability to size up people and situations intuitively and almost instantaneously which I've talked about in this book, came through for Jonathan. He "got it," knew what he wanted, and was ready for it. He wanted to be as independent as he could and live in an apartment.

Kelly and I weren't so sure. We had no idea how he would actually take to an independent, though assisted, life. Jonathan and his dad have always been close, so I thought that in the beginning he'd want to spend weekends at Kelly's house. That would be a nice way to transition to an apartment away from parents, wouldn't it? In your dreams, Mom. That never happened. In his view, his apartment is now his home.

Now if his dad visits but lingers too long for Jonathan's plans, he sometimes says, "Isn't it time for you to go home now?" If I call him on the phone and it's not a good time, he lets me know clearly. "I'm too busy now." My cue to call back another time.

This is, of course, somewhat bruising to a parent's ego, but it's also the fulfillment of a parent's dream. When my children were very small, I learned two bits of sage advice and took them deeply to heart: "A parent's job is to work themselves out of a job," and "Give your children roots and wings." I felt the truth of those adages, and kept them always somewhere in the back of my mind.

In retrospect, I see that Jonathan's move to an apartment with a caregiver freed him from limitations that I had imposed on him because my nose was too close to the picture. I was still "hovering." I didn't know he could now do things for himself that he formerly couldn't do.

With a transition to independence, Jonathan stepped up to the plate. Eager to pay the price of independence, he learned to zip zippers and button buttons instead of forever wearing pull-up gym pants; those were skills I had given up trying to teach because they were so difficult for him.

He learned to be more patient. He learned to be more adult, and more social. He leaned more heavily into valuing and developing friendships at Goodwill and Starfire.

It seems that every few weeks, I am blown away by new things that Jonathan has now incorporated into his life.

Mary, one of his primary caregivers, recently told me about the TV station Jonathan likes to watch during breakfast each day before he leaves for Goodwill. "It's *his* apartment, so I give him the remote control when he sits for breakfast," she said. So what's his cable choice, this child of mine with narrow interests who loves music more than life itself and lives for Disney?

"CNN. Every morning."

"CNN?" I yelled.

"Yep," said Mary. "He likes to keep up with the news."

The Last Laugh

Having a mom who now lives in the Land Of All Things Disney is totally in line with Jonathan's life ambitions. He gets to go to Disneyland every fall. That's when the Haunted Mansion attraction, his favorite, gets its annual makeover as "The Nightmare before Christmas," or as Jonathan calls it, "Haunted Mansion, Nightmare Style."

The last time we were at Disneyland, we had just walked into the park and the piped music speakers were playing a jazzy tune. As a ballroom dancer, I recognized it as a great Swing piece and danced a few little triple-step moves on the sidewalk.

Jonathan was horrified. He almost hissed, "You're freaking me out! You're freaking me *out!*"

When I realized what he meant, I laughed with pure delight. My son is now capable of being totally embarrassed by his *mother's* behavior. How absolutely gorgeous is that?

My, my, how sweetly times have changed.

About the Author

Natalie Hale is the mother of an adult son with Down syndrome. A national speaker on the topic of teaching reading to learners with Down syndrome for the last 20 years, she founded Special Reads for Special Needs in 2000 to provide reading materials designed for her favorite audience of readers. She lives in the San Francisco Bay area and continues to travel, speak, and teach. Natalie is the author of five books; visit her online at specialreads.com. Her most recent book, *Managing My Money*, was published by Woodbine House in 2010.